NEWSPAPER EDITING

NEWSPAPER EDITING

GRANT MILNOR HYDE M.A

Instructor in Journalism in the University of Wisconsin;
Author of "Newspaper Reporting and Correspondence"

MAVEN BOOKS

Chennai Trichy New Delhi

This edition has been published in india by arrangement with Carson Books, UK

ISBN 978-93-90877-99-7

MAVEN BOOKS

No. 44, Nallathambi Street,
Triplicane, Chennai 600 005

MJP 1036

Publisher : C. Janarthanan

Publisher's Note

The legacy of a country is in its varied cultural heritage, historical literature, developments in the field of economy and science. The top nations in the world are competing in the field of science, economy and literature. This vast legacy has to be conserved and documented so that it can be bestowed to the future generation. The knowledge of this legacy is slowly getting perished in the present generation due to lack of documentation.

Keeping this in mind, the concern with retrospective acquiring of rare books has been accented recently by the burgeoning reprint industry. Maven Books is gratified to retrieve the rare collections with a view to bring back those books that were landmarks in their time.

In this effort, a series of rare books would be republished under the banner, "Maven Books". The books in the reprint series have been carefully selected for their contemporary usefulness as well as their historical importance within the intellectual. We reconstruct the book with slight enhancements made for better presentation, without affecting the contents of the original edition.

Most of the works selected for republishing covers a huge range of subjects, from history to anthropology. We believe this reprint edition will be a service to the numerous researchers and practitioners active in this fascinating field. We allow readers to experience the wonder of peering into a scholarly work of the highest order and seminal significance.

MAVEN BOOKS

TO

THE MEMORY OF

MY FATHER

PREFACE

THIS book has been prepared as a manual for newspaper desk men and a textbook for editing classes in the schools of journalism. Although a number of good handbooks on journalism have appeared in the past few years, the writers of such books have been so interested in the needs of the reporter that they have rather generally neglected the copyreader—a man of even greater responsibilities. It is to fill this need—a need that has been impressed upon the author by five years' experience as teacher of journalism—that this book was written. And, just as in his "Newspaper Reporting and Correspondence," published three years ago, the author has not tried to cover the entire field of newspaper work, but has confined himself to the particular branch.

The intent of the book is not only to present the tools and methods of the copy editor but to show, as well, the interesting possibilities in his work. Too many newspaper men, especially reporters, regard desk work as unimaginative drudgery and feel that to be placed "on the desk" is to be pushed back out of the firing line. To counteract such a feeling is sufficient reason for the writing of a book. Desk work, when done in the proper spirit, is as interesting and constructive as any other branch of newspaper work; in fact, from many points of view, it is the most fascinating. But to realize its full possibilities, the desk man must look beyond mere "copyreading" and "heading up." To this end, many subjects have been introduced into this book which may seem, at first glance, somewhat "outside the copy editor's line."

The discussion of type and printing processes, for instance, may seem irrelevant to some copyreaders, since there is always a composing room foreman to consult. But for a newspaper editor to say that he "is not strong on type" is a confession of incompetence. It means that he lacks the foundation for ideas and initiative in developing the make-up of his paper. He is, in other words, only half a desk man and could not competently fill a more responsible position on the staff. He is like the reporter who can ferret out difficult news but cannot write a readable story. Such men can never hope to grow larger than their jobs—nor as large.

For the same reason, the detailed discussion of the physical side of the newspaper is included in the chapter on "Newspaper Make-up." It is safe to say that typography and physical make-up are of greater interest to-day than ever before. The managing editor is rare who does not welcome ideas in this regard. It would be impossible and impracticable, of course, to attempt an exhaustive study of the subject in such a book, but the author has tried to open up the subject and interest young newspaper men in this direction.

It is for the small newspaper editor and the student of journalism that the study of "Small Publication Work" is introduced, since its relation to the work of the city desk man is less direct. The subject cannot be treated adequately in so small a space, but it makes possible a discussion of many publication and printing methods that the newspaper man should know. It offers, furthermore, an opportunity to suggest some systematic ways in which the handler of copy, whether in the newspaper or magazine office, may improve and facilitate his work.

In response to many requests for style books for classroom use, a condensed style sheet has been bound into this volume. It is one that was compiled from the style books of many newspapers and tested for several years. The use of such a style sheet in the study of copy editing provides one of the few tangible ways of enforcing accuracy in details. Insistence upon accuracy in typographical style, as well as in spelling, punctuation, and grammar, sharpens the copyreader's eyesight and emphasizes the importance of accuracy itself.

The list of significant dates in the history of printing and the development of the newspaper is not offered as a history of journalism. It is intended merely to emphasize in graphic form the time relation of various elements in the newspaper's evolution. Doubtless some of the dates are merely approximate, since reliable data in this field is difficult to obtain, as every teacher of journalism knows.

The greatest problem involved in such a book is obviously the selection of average, uniform methods from the practices of American newspaper offices. Desk work in various parts of the country involves not only different terms and symbols but diverse divisions of duties. In his work on the staff of a New York City daily, the author learned methods rarely seen in the desk work in Middle Western offices; ways of handling proof and copy learned in one office may seem strange to men trained in another. Out of these, the author has tried to select the average and most common and in the selection, he has discarded the more slipshod methods of smaller offices in favor of the systematic practices of large newspapers—

in fact, in many cases he has incorporated the highly systematized methods of magazine offices in which he has worked.

The method throughout the book, it may be added, is one that has grown out of classroom work. Little attempt is made to lay down rules. Rather, the effort has been to present the fundamentals of each kind of work and answer the questions that arise in the student's mind. In many cases, the answer is one that, it is hoped, will tend to open up broader aspects of the case. Editing, like other newspaper work, cannot be bounded by iron-clad rules and regulations. Its very nature demands initiative and originality. When these desirable attributes are lacking in the newspaper man or journalism student, the cause is most often too narrow an outlook upon his work. A broader horizon is his chief need, and it is hoped that he will derive this, at least to some degree, from the reading of this volume.

Madison, Wisconsin, June 20, 1915.

CONTENTS

PART I

PART II

NEWSPAPER EDITING

PART I

CHAPTER I

THE COPYREADER'S PART IN NEWSPAPER MAKING

THE copy desk in a city newspaper office is merely one workbench in a great manufacturing plant, and a copyreader is but one of a large group of workmen engaged in the manufacture of a finished product—a newspaper. The copy editor is, from one point of view, the most important workman in the entire plant, since he puts the finishing touches upon practically all the raw material that goes into the product. From another point of view, he is only one of many skilled workers, many of whom are responsible for work as important, if not more important, than the copyreader's. That paradox is one of the things that differentiates the organization of a newspaper plant from that of almost all other manufacturing businesses—and one of the things that makes newspaper work as fascinating as it is.

The copyreader, while occupying a comparatively subordinate position among the newspaper's other workers, bears part of the responsibility of making the newspaper good. Carelessness or inexperience on his part may ruin all the good work done by others; excellence in his work may cause the newspaper to win the coveted reputation of being "well edited." Every stroke of work he does shows in the finished product. There is no one between his desk and the purchaser to gloss over the good or bad quality of his work. The same is true of almost every worker in the newspaper plant; his work shows in the finished product with all the good or bad workmanship that he puts into it. There is little chance for the inspection and grading employed in other manufacturing enterprises. Criticism must come after the work has gone into the product. Criticism of bad work done today may improve tomorrow's output in the newspaper plant, but it cannot help the fact that today's bad paper has already gone to the buyer.

The copyreader, when he takes his desk in a newspaper office, must know the relation of his work to the work of others in the office and at the same time must realize thoroughly the responsibility of his work and its effect upon the finished newspaper.

I. NEWSPAPER ORGANIZATION

The average American citizen thinks of a newspaper office as a hive of peculiarly unbusinesslike men assisted by some printers and machinery engaged in the somewhat doubtful occupation of disseminating more or less reliable information and opinions. That they should want real money for their work, or for its by-product, advertising space, is often to him a humorous thing. Some newspaper men have the same conception of their work.

The modern newspaper plant, however, should be thought of as a highly businesslike manufacturing enterprise engaged in producing a salable product—and endeavoring to make a legitimate profit out of its manufacture, like any other business concern. The product is a few or many thousand printed newspapers each day to be sold at a specified price per copy. The raw material that goes into their manufacture is paper, ink, and current events. The only difference between their product and any other is that considerably more than half of the raw material is composed of an illusive substance called "news," whose production is a mental rather than a physical process. If the newspaper is bad, its owner and proprietor should be classed with any other manufacturer of bad wares. The ethical conception of the dishonest newspaper publisher is the same as that of any other dishonest manufacturer. If he does not put pure raw material into his product, he is selling mislabeled goods. If he colors the news that makes up considerably more than half of his product, he is an adulterator. It is easy enough to apply this conception to the quality of paper, ink, and typographical impression, but it is hard to apply it to the rest of the raw material. Every newspaper worker, including copyreaders, should, however, have this idea of his work. He should feel that he is a manufacturer who must deliver honest and pure wares to his customers.

To carry on the manufacture of newspapers, a publishing plant has a mechanical department, a business office, and a sales department, like any other manufacturing concern. It also has another staff of men engaged in the production of the raw material—news. Ordinarily the plant is organized on exactly these lines. All sales and other business relations are managed by a business office; the physical production is carried on in a mechanical department; and the raw material, news and opinions, is handled by an editorial staff. All newspapers, large or small, contain the three separate departments, whether they employ a thousand men or one man, like the country editor who embodies the three departments in his own person.

1. The Business Office.—The business office of the average newspaper is in charge of a business manager, who is primarily a financial expert responsible only to the owner or owners of the newspaper. His duty is to make the enterprise financially successful. He is independent of the other departments and has no authority over them except through the mediation of the proprietor. A few newspapers, to be sure, have a general manager who guides the work and policy of all three departments and welds them together into a working whole. but he is really a newspaper expert whom the owner employs to exercise general supervision in his stead.

Besides a staff of clerks and bookkeepers, the business manager has in his office several other men to take care of the various branches of the financial work. One is a circulation manager who has charge of the sale of finished newspapers. Under him are subscription clerks, mailing room men, newsboys, wagon drivers, and other agents of distribution. Another is an advertising manager, who has charge of the sale of advertising space—both want-ad and display. He usually has a number of advertising solicitors to assist him in his work. Another is a cashier who has charge of all the newspaper's money, paying all salaries and other expenditures and receiving all money paid to the newspaper for advertising, sales, or other purposes.

2. The Mechanical Plant.—The mechanical branch of the newspaper plant is in the same way in charge of a single man responsible only to the owner or his representative. There are ordinarily four or five separate departments in his branch. One department is the composing room, in which typesetters, printers, linotype operators, copy cutters, bank men, proof-readers, etc., convert manuscript into type and make it up into the form of the finished pages. Another department is the stereotyping room, in which the flat page forms, composed of type and cuts put together by the printers, are reproduced in curved metal plates for the rotary presses. The third department is the press room, which contains one or more huge presses for printing newspapers at a high rate of speed. Each of these departments has its specialized workmen who are hired to do various mechanical work. Sometimes the newspaper has an engraving department whose work is to make plates for the newspaper's illustrations—cuts, as they are called. When the newspaper has automatic mailing machines for wrapping and addressing subscribers' copies, the mechanics in charge of them are a part of the plant's mechanical force.

3. The Editorial Department.—The third and most important division of the newspaper's plant is the editorial department which prepares all the reading matter, except advertisements, that goes into the printed paper. Whether the paper be large or small, the work of this department is divided into a variety of separate and distinct branches of work. Perhaps all the branches may be taken care of by a few men, or, if the staff is large enough, each branch may be in the hands of a specialist. But, however great or small the extent of the staff, the various kinds of work are entirely separate and specialized.

Since the reading matter of every newspaper is distinctly separated into two classes—news and comment—the main division of the editorial department is along the same lines. One staff of men, commonly known as the news staff, is employed for the special work of gathering and writing news. Another staff, usually designated as the editorial staff, is engaged in the work of interpreting the news. The one staff prepares the news pages; the other prepares the editorial columns. So distinct are the two staffs, that each requires of its men a different kind of ability and experience, and seldom is it that a man steps from one department to the other. Whereas one group is engaged in the specific task of drawing conclusions from facts and writing comments on the facts, the other group is usually forbidden to show the slightest evidence of an opinion on anything.

The Editorial Writers.—The news interpreting, or editorial staff, is made up of a group of men called editorial writers, working under an editor-in-chief. This editor, usually the only person whom the outside world recognizes as editor of the paper, guides the paper's editorial policy and dictates the paper's point of view on passing events reported in other pages. He deals out editorial topics to his small staff of writers and passes upon the acceptability of their editorials. He bears entire responsibility for the character and content of the paper's editorial columns and sends all his copy directly to the printers without any corrective editing by any other member of the staff. His group of editorial writers may consist of one or two men, or it may include as many as a dozen, some of whom spend a large part of their time at the state or national capital and have an extensive library to use in their work of molding public opinion.

The News Staff.—The news staff, which prepares the news columns for the paper, is ordinarily larger and composed of many branches. Its head is called the managing editor. Under him is one group of men designated as the local staff, another as the telegraph room, and others known as department editors. Perhaps there is also an art department and a library.

The Local Staff.—The local room, or staff, is concerned with the gathering and writing of all news of the city in which the paper is published. It is entirely in charge of a city editor—or day and night city editors, if the men work in two shifts—who hires and directs all the men in the department. The staff usually consists of a number of reporters and a few desk men. The reporters, all working under the city editor, gather the news and write the stories that make up the news columns. Some of them are department men, making regular daily rounds on a run or beat of news sources; others are assignment men, employed to work up special assignments under the city editor's direction. The desk men, on the other hand, are not writers or newsgatherers but correctors of the reporter's work. They are usually called copyreaders and, if there are several of them, they are organized into a small staff under a head copyreader. Their work is to take the stories which the reporters have written, correct them according to the paper's style and practice, write headlines for them, and prepare them for the printers. Since the telephone has come into common use in newsgathering, certain of the desk men are employed as rewrite men to prepare stories from facts telephoned in by reporters. All of these desk men are assistants of the city editor and work under his direction. The table at which they work is the "copy desk." Another of his assistants is the news editor whose work it is to make up the newspaper just before press time.

The Telegraph Room.—All news from outside the city, distinguished in the printed paper by date-lines, is handled by the telegraph editor and his assistants. This staff usually comprises one or more telegraph operators, besides the editor and his assistants, and in many cases one or more copyreaders to edit and write headlines for telegraph copy. Some papers, however, have one force of copy editors to handle both local and telegraph news. But, however the staff may be organized, it handles all news that comes to the office by telegraph, mail, cable, or long distance telephone. It has its staff of reporters, also, working under the direction of the telegraph editor, but they are located in distant towns and cities and are known as correspondents.

Department Editors.—These two departments, the local and telegraph rooms, comprise the greater portion of the newspaper's news staff. Others are mainly specialists in charge of small departments of the paper. One is the sporting editor, who, working alone or with assistants, prepares the contents of the sporting page. Another is the society editor who gathers and writes social items. Other special editors, varying in number and importance, are the financial and market editor, the railroad editor, the dramatic and musical critics, the real estate editors, and the exchange editor. Each one has his own small section of the paper to fill but whenever he secures any news too significant to be buried in his corner he must turn it over to the local staff to be played up in the more prominent news pages. Each of these various department writers is called an editor because his copy goes to the printer without passing through the hands of a copyreader or another editor.

Other Branches.—If the newspaper has a Sunday supplement or a special Saturday edition, it has a Sunday or supplement editor who devotes his time to preparing the content of the special pages that are folded in with the regular news pages. Many city papers also have an art department, composed of artists, cartoonists, and photographers who prepare illustrations. Another very important member of the editorial staff is the librarian who keeps up files of information in such shape to be easily accessible on a moment's notice. One part of his files, called the "morgue," consists of a collection of biographical facts and photographs of prominent men that may be put together into an obituary sketch whenever the prominent man is in any way connected with the day's news.

II. A STORY'S COURSE THROUGH THE OFFICE

Perhaps the copy editor's part in newspaper making will be more clear if we follow the career of a story through the various parts of the office of an afternoon newspaper. The story was suggested to the city editor, let us say, by a morning paper's report to the effect that the state legislature was considering a bill for the authorization of paid "civic secretaries" to look after "social centers." He entered the idea in his day book and gave the assignment to Jack Robbins, one of his reporters: "Robbins, go and ask the mayor what he thinks of the appointment of civic secretaries. Ask him if he thinks it will aid the social centers. You've been out to the Webster School at every meeting and know all about it." That was the way the story began. It might have originated in some other way; some reporter might have picked it up on his run or some social center worker might have telephoned it to the office. Robbins went to the mayor's office, at any rate, and after a while returned with the tidings that the mayor thought it a fine idea. "Did he have much to say?" asked the city editor. "A barrel full," answered Robbins and he briefly outlined the mayor's ideas. "Write half a column on it, playing up the mayor's point that it will increase fifty per cent. the public's use of public property."

Robbins wrote the story and placed it on the city editor's desk. Other stories were coming in with it from other writers, some from other reporters, some from rewrite men sitting at the telephone, some from the telegraph desk, and even some from outsiders seeking needed publicity. The city editor glanced at Robbins' story and handed it to his head copyreader with the instructions, "Cut it to five hundred words; put a little more punch in the lead; give it a No. 8 head." The head copyreader, whose desk was piled high, passed the story and the instructions to one of his assistants. But first he made a record: "Civic Sect. Mayor—500—Robbins—No. 8—10:15."

The copyreader read through the story, correcting a misspelled word here, straightening out a grammatical construction there, consulting the telephone directory for the initials of a social center worker mentioned, toning down an overenthusiastic paragraph, brightening up a bit of summary with some new verbs, and changing the typographical style to suit the style sheet over his desk. The editing finished, he turned back to the first page and put more punch into the lead by incorporating a striking expression that he found buried in the last paragraph. Then skimming through he crossed out sentences here, paragraphs there, useless words and phrases in other places, until he estimated that what was left was about five hundred words long. On page 3 he sliced out a long paragraph by cutting through the manuscript above and below the paragraph with his shears, pasted a blank sheet of copy paper in its place, and wrote a summary of the paragraph's contents in one-third as many words. When he had finished the editing, he took the first page again and wrote in the blank half above the lead the content of a three-deck headline of the style known in the office as No. 8. Beside the head he wrote "No. 8" with a circle around it. At the top of the sheet he wrote "Civic Sect. Mayor," and folded the sheets together ready to hand to the copy boy. Just then the city editor called, "Who's got that interview with the mayor? Here's one with the president of the school board to add to it." The copyreader turned to the last page of the manuscript, crossed out the mark—"# # #"—that indicated the end of the story, and wrote in its place, "More." After the copy boy had taken the manuscript to the composing room, the second interview reached his desk via the head copyreader and his first move was to write at its head "Follow Civic Sect. Mayor."

When the copy reached the composing room, it was placed on the desk of the copy cutter. After glancing at its length, he swiftly pasted the five sheets together end to end in a long string and cut the story up into three pieces, or "takes," more or less equal in length, taking care in each case to cut at the end of the paragraph. The headline constituted the fourth take. At the head of the first sheet he wrote "C. 1," on the next he wrote "C. 2," on the next "C. 3." As the boy took it from his hands, he wrote in his record "Civic Sect. Mayor—10:33—C. 1—4." The boy took the three takes to three linotype operators designated by the copy cutter and in a few moments each of the three was setting up his part of the story. In this way, the entire story was in type in the time it took one operator to set one-third of it—one-third of the time it would have taken one man to set the entire story. Take No. 2 was finished first and the operator sent it to the "bank" man who makes up the stories. While the bank man was placing take No. 2 in the center of a galley, labeled "C" according to the copy cutter's schedule, take No. 3 came to him and he placed it below take No. 2; then take No. 1 and the headline came for the head of the galley. At the bottom of the galley he turned over the rule to indicate "More to come." The bank man therefore held the galley until the interview with the president of the school board came along known as "Follow Civic Sect. Mayor" and labeled C. 5—7. As this was marked "End," he turned the galley over to another printer and cleared his bank. The galley was then taken to a proof press and a printer "pulled a proof" of it. In a small glass-inclosed office in the corner of the composing room a proofreader read the proof aloud to an assistant who followed the reading with the original copy. With the corrections marked on the margin, the proof went back to the original operators for revision. They set up the new lines to be inserted in the galley in place of the faulty lines. The galley was then "revised" and revise proofs were pulled. One copy of it went to the proofreader for a second reading, another went to the news editor, and a third to the managing editor.

Meantime many other stories had followed the same course and were in type and proof form. By one o'clock several of the back pages of the paper had been "made up" and "put to bed" on the stereotyper's stone. About two o'clock the news editor gathered up a bundle of proofs marked "Front Page" and started for the composing room to "close up." Just before he left his desk, the managing editor stepped out of his office and said to the city editor, "Kill that interview with the president of the school board; he just telephoned me that he'd give us some better stuff tomorrow." The word was passed on and the news editor drew a line through the "Civic Sect. Mayor Follow" on his proof. Then he went on to the composing room and with the guidance of a "dummy" diagram he had made up beforehand he started taking the first-page stories from their galleys and directed the placing of them in the front-page "chase." He was nearly through when a copy boy came down with the instructions from the editorial room, "Hold front page for fire story." A reporter had just telephoned in that a leading hotel was on fire. It was fifteen minutes before press time but that was time enough for a rewrite man to dash off two hundred words about the fire while a copyreader wrote a headline for it. Ten minutes later the story was in type, revised, and on the make-up stone. But this was more copy than the news editor had counted on and he had too much type for the page—about three stickfuls. As the other pages were closed and there was no time to open them up for a "break-over" of any front-page story, the news editor quickly threw away the last paragraphs of three of his stories. One of them was the interview with the mayor. It was now down to four hundred words. He locked up the form, leaving the upper six inches of the two right-hand columns empty, and sent the page to the stereotypers.

A stereotyper quickly laid a wet papier-mâché matrix over the first page form, passed it under a roller and pushed it into a steam table. In four minutes he released the press, drew the form out, pasted a few strips of cardboard in the hollow places in the back of the hard-baked papier-maché matrix, and sent the type form back to the news editor. The matrix was then slipped in the circular casting box of an automatic platemaking machine and in a few minutes it had served as a mold for the casting of half a dozen curved stereotype plates. Shaved and trimmed and cooled as they passed out of the plate machine, the plates were carried to the press room and bolted upon the proper rolls of several rotary presses. The plates for the other pages were already in place and a pressman was setting the latest news into the "fudge" roll. The news consisted of a handful of linotype slugs which read, "World Series Score 2 to 0 at End of Sixth Inning," and carried the score by innings up to the last moment. When the last fudge bolt was twisted tight, the signal was given and the rotaries started grinding out copies of the "Afternoon Edition"' at the rate of many thousands per minute. On the front page of each was the interview with the mayor. Inside of a short time, final score of the game had come in over the telegraph wire in the press room, a linotype machine standing beside one of the presses had incorporated it in new slugs, the presses were then stopped long enough for a pressman to change the slugs in the fudge roll so as to include the final score of the game. When the wheels began to turn again they were printing the "Evening Edition" with the final score. The mayor's interview occupied the same place as before.

In the meanwhile, more complete news of the hotel fire had come to the office and a two-column story was in type. The news editor remade the front-page form so as to include it. The fudge space was omitted, but even then there was not enough space and he was forced to cut down some of the other stories. Among others, the mayor's interview was cut to three hundred words and by the time the presses were printing the next edition it was a very much less prominent story than when the reporter wrote it.

By the time the presses had printed enough copies to make up the "Home Edition" for the newsboys, the news editor had remade the paper for the "Mail Edition." Page by page, he had opened up the forms of the four or five news pages and inserted national news for local news and changed their content. When he reached the front page he decided that the mayor's interview was not of interest to people outside the city. Rather than throw it out entirely, he picked its lead out from the first-page form and slipped it into the miscellany column headed "City Items" on the fifth page. In the papers that reached the out-of-town subscribers the reporter's original eight-hundred-word interview had dwindled to seventy-five words, but not a line of it had been reset.

Into this finished newspaper, every employee in the plant had added his share. The business department had secured and incorporated into copy many columns of advertising, both classified and display. The circulation department had prepared for the marketing of the edition, through paid subscriptions and street sales. The mechanical force had set up and paged many thousands of linotype slugs and individual pieces of type, besides stereotyping and printing thousands of copies. The editorial department had supplied from 60,000 to 100,000 words of new reading matter, all duly classified. The editorial writers had contributed two or three columns of editorials; the department editors and special writers had turned out a column or more each. The reporters and correspondents had prepared two or three times as much reading matter as was needed, and the copyreaders had boiled this down, composed headlines for it, and reduced it to the uniform style of the newspaper. The work done by the newspaper plant for this one edition was greater than that required to write and print several books—

and the plant had accomplished it in less than twenty-four hours. By the time the presses were at work on the last edition, every desk and bench throughout the plant was cleared for action and work had begun on the issue to follow less than twenty-four hours later.

III. THE DESK MAN'S PART

The copy editor's part in the work is now clear. It is an important part, even though it is a modest one and without much fame. A reader comes to know the newspaper's writers from their signed articles, their visits as newsgatherers, and their opinions on the editorial page. But he is seldom aware that such a person as the copy editor exists. He does not know that it is the copyreader who reduces all this written matter, coming from the pens and the typewriters of many scribes, to the uniform style and policy which characterizes the newspaper itself. He does not know that it is the copy editor who is the watch dog that wards off errors and libelous statements, besides writing the headlines that catch the reader's eye and sum up the news so that he can read the entire paper in a few moments.

The work done by the copy editor requires a broader training and a larger store of knowledge than almost any other post in the newspaper office. Certainly it requires much more than that demanded of the reporter or correspondent. To edit copy swiftly and accurately, the desk man must have a thorough understanding of English grammar and diction, must know news value more thoroughly than the average reporter does, and must be acquainted with the intricacies of the libel law. He must know his own city inside and out, must know the affairs of the nation, and must be on more than speaking terms with all the great questions and thoughts of the day. He must know type and printing processes as thoroughly as his printers. Headline writing in itself is an art that can be developed only by much training and knowledge of typography. The mere summarizing of an idea whose expression has taken several hundred words is task enough, but to make that summary fit a typographical scheme mapped out in unit letters and spaces is trebly difficult.

The young desk man should remember that the duties of his position require above all that he be a critic of the first water and also that he be enough of a writer to recast instantly the feeble attempts of other writers. But half the difficulties of his work will be met by a proper knowledge of its requirements. Only study will point out these requirements, for no city editor has time to put his assistants through a course of instruction. In this study he will find that his best textbook is the work of other copy editors, as shown in the newspapers they edit. This book is merely a summary of observations of the methods of work of many copy editors.

CHAPTER II

COPYREADING

In all publication work, be it newspaper, magazine, or book, there is always an intermediate step between the written manuscript and the composed type, known as copyreading, or editing. Since man first began to multiply his written ideas, there has always been a third person between the writer and the printer to "edit" the manuscript. His office is that of corrector, auditor, or checker. In the magazine or book publishing office he is known as an editor. In the newspaper office he goes by the more commonplace title of copyreader, since the newspaper editor is more ordinarily occupied with other things beside the editing of copy. To avoid confusion in our discussion of his duties, we shall call this intermediate person simply the copyreader and his work copyreading.

The work of the copyreader consists in preparing manuscript for the printer. He works with other men's penned or typewritten manuscript and his only tool is a large soft lead pencil. He rarely does any writing himself but he often develops sufficient individuality in his alteration of manuscript to be cordially disliked by the writers whose manuscript he edits. However true may be the accusations made against him, he is a very necessary member of every newspaper staff, and the tone of our publications would be decidedly lower were it not for his work. To rectify errors of fact, spelling, grammar, punctuation, typographical style, and sentence structure, to tone down the bubbling exuberance of some reporters, to brighten up the dead matter-of-factness of others, and to write the necessary interpretation in others, constitute his task, and the extent to which he brings his own individuality into the task is entirely a matter of his personality. If an error or a libelous statement "gets past" him to appear on the printed page of many thousands of copies of the paper, it is not usually the original writer of the article who receives the blame, but the copyreader, who should have "caught" the error when he edited the copy.

In the large American newspaper office, the copyreader works directly under the charge of the city editor who directs the newspaper's staff of reporters. He is the "desk man" who is always in the office and far away from the glamour usually attached to the thought of newspaper work. He is nothing more or less than the assistant of the city editor and his office grew out of the overcrowding of that dignitary's duties. In smaller, poorer offices, where the income of the paper puts narrow limits on the size of the staff, this assistant of the city editor is lacking and his work is done by the city editor. When a copyreader is added to the staff, he simply takes over a portion of the city editor's work—that of editing copy and writing headlines. The city editor still has charge of the reporters and directs the writing of all stories.

When a reporter comes in from his run or assignment with the facts of a news story, he reports to the city editor and receives directions as to the length of the story he is to write, its character and the feature that is to be emphasized in it. As soon as he has completed the story, he takes the copy directly to the city editor. If he has no copyreaders, the city editor must himself prepare the story for the printer. But if he has one or more desk men to assist him, he glances through the story to note its content and then passes it over to one of his copyreaders for editing and headline. He usually accompanies the copy with a few brief verbal directions, to guide the copyreader and to indicate the kind of headline desired.

The copyreader then prepares the story for the printer. He reads it through carefully to correct all the errors in it and makes all the alterations between the lines of the manuscript or in the margins. He may perhaps rewrite the lead or he may cut off several paragraphs. Here and there he inserts a word or two to clarify the meaning or crosses out half a sentence to eliminate repetition and wordiness. When he has finished editing it, the story is in final form, with guide lines and type directions, ready for the printer. Then in the blank half-page which the reporter has left above the beginning of the story, he writes a suitable headline of the size designated by the city editor—but the writing of the headline is another story which will be considered in a separate chapter. Before he calls the copy boy or slips the manuscript into the tube leading to the composing room, he makes a record of the subject of the story, its length, the name of the reporter who wrote it, a designation of the size of the headline written on the story, and the exact time it was sent to the composing room. The record may look something like this: "Smith—Council Meeting—800—No. 8—10:45." His task would be an easy one if he had only one or two stories to edit and plenty of time in which to edit them, but usually the stories are coming to him in a continuous stream, as fast as he can handle them, and along toward press time he is so crowded that he is forced to edit several stories at once, page by page, as they come from the reporters' typewriters. One moment he is editing page 3 of a fire story, the next he is dashing through page 5 of the account of a political convention, a minute later he is writing a new lead for an interview with one of the candidates nominated, and then as the last page of the fire reaches his hands he writes the headline to be carried above it. He has no opportunity to hold all the pages of one story long enough to handle all of it at once, but must pass the pages on as rapidly as possible so as to keep all of the linotype machines working at full capacity. He must therefore hold the content of several stories in his mind at once, keep them separate, and edit each one as accurately and painstakingly as if he were a schoolmaster leisurely marking a bundle of student themes.

Although the copyreader's work combines the writing of headlines with the editing of copy and not infrequently a bit of proofreading in his leisure moments, we are concerned at present only with his work of editing or copyreading.

I. REVISION—NOT REWRITING

The first thing about his work that the young copyreader must understand thoroughly is that he has been employed, not as a writer, but as a corrector of other men's writing. His job is to revise and reconstruct, not to rewrite. And before he has held his desk position long he will come to realize that the ability to revise is quite different from the ability to write and that it requires the cultivation of very different methods of thinking. The young copyreader's first impulse, when he is given a badly written story to edit, is to throw the reporter's copy into the waste basket and rewrite the story. Very often, of course, that is the easiest and quickest way to make the story printable. But as a general practice such copyreading methods involve too much duplication of work for a busy newspaper office. If the reporter who was employed to write the story in the first place is not able to do so, he has no place in the office and should be reported to the city editor for discharge. More often, however, the fault lies with the copyreader, for only a small amount of the copy that comes to him is so bad that it must be rewritten. The feeling that the story must be rewritten is usually the result of the copyreader's unconscious inability to subordinate his own manner of expression to that of another—to see good in the writing of others although its qualities may not at all accord with his own ideals of writing.

A young copyreader must first of all remember that his office is merely that of corrector and reviser. If he does not have it at the outset, he must develop the ability to correct and revise another's writing, without destroying in it evidences of the original writer's personality. As he grows older in the work he will learn that there are few stories that he cannot whip into shape without rewriting, and that the impulse to rewrite is merely an evidence of inexperience in the work.

II. THE COPYREADING SIGNS

The established copyreading signs—the tools of the desk man's trade—are few and simple and should be thought of as time-saving signals which he may use to indicate changes to be made in the copy. Their development has been a gradual evolution and is not yet complete. Their usefulness depends upon the printer's understanding of them, and therefore some offices in which the copyreaders and printers have worked together for a long time have a more fully developed system of copyreading signs than offices in which the employees are more transient. In general, the group of signs listed below will be understood by all printers, except in the smallest country offices, and the copyreader may use them with perfect confidence in any office. The one thing to remember about them is that they were developed by necessity and their use is still governed by necessity.

Unlike the signs used in proofreading, these symbols used by the editor of copy are not placed in the margin, but in the body of the written matter. The reason for this difference is simple. When a printer is revising proof, he does not read the content of the proof but glances down through it to note the corrections; it is therefore necessary to indicate corrections in the margin so that he will surely see them. In setting up material that has been edited, however, the printer must read each word and line and needs no signal in the margin to draw his attention to a correction. In fact, the placing of copyreading corrections in the margin is a decided fault since it is impossible to carry the corrections into the margin without muddling the copy and leading to confusion. Usually also all corrections and marks are placed above the line to which they refer so that the compositor will see them before he reaches the words involved. Inserted material should be written between the lines or on a separate sheet, marked "insert," never in vertical lines along the margin; since the margin insertions make it difficult for the copy cutter to divide the copy into takes. In editing copy, furthermore, the copyreader should use a soft black pencil and should make heavy black signs that will show distinctly in the feeble light that illuminates the copyholder of a linotype machine.

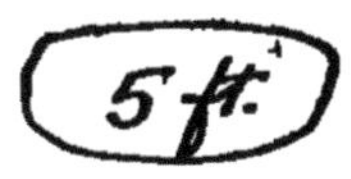

Circles around figures or abbreviations indicate that they are to be spelled out.

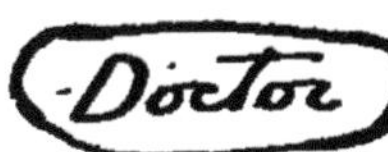

Circles around words or numbers spelled out indicate that they are to be abbreviated or expressed in figures.

One line under a letter or word indicates that it is to be set in Italics. (In some offices single underscoring, or a wavy line below, indicates bold-face type.)

Two lines under a letter or word indicate that it is to be set in small capital letters.

Three lines under a letter or a word indicate that it is to be set in capital letters.

An oblique line, from right to left, through a capital letter, indicates that it should be a small letter.

Letters are brought together by a half circle below.

Letters are separated by oblique lines from left to right.

A cross, or a period in a circle, is used for a period.

Quotation marks, either double or single, are often set off with half circles to indicate whether they are beginning or end marks.

The beginning of each paragraph is indicated by a paragraph mark or an angle. The paragraph mark is always used to mark a new paragraph, not intended by the author.

Elements to be transposed are encircled in a long figure 8.

A caret indicates the spot where material is to be inserted.

The end of a story is indicated by the end mark (#) or the number 30 in circle.

The "run-in" or "bridge" line is used to connect two consecutive elements separated by material that has been crossed out.

The use of these signs may be illustrated by the following piece of newspaper copy edited and marked for the printer:

Pitts field, Ill., June 25th —Seven men were probably fatally burned to day in the works of the Atlas Experiment Co by an explosion of gasolene. All of the 14 people on the second floor leapt from the windows blazing like torches in the air.

The explosion came with frightful suddenness at three-twenty o'clock. Most of the workmen were gathered in the labratory on the secnd floor. Without warning a twenty-gallon retort burts in to flames, and blazing petrol flew about the room. THE cause of the exp losion is not definitely known, although many surmises are being made. Experiments on a new process of manufacturing gasoline were being made at the time, and it is thought that the retort became too hot and exploded. "the first hiss of flame was folloewd by a blast of blazing gasolene," said Chas R Samuels, foreman of the labratoy, this afternoon. "We had no time for fireescapes,—we jumped.

#

III. WHAT ERRORS TO LOOK FOR

Although armed with all the copyreading signs and the ability to use them, the copyreader will find his efficiency greatly increases if he analyzes and studies the errors to look for and to correct in the copy that passes through his hands. There are certain errors that are likely to appear in any copy and a classification of them may assist him in catching them all. Knowing what errors to look for is easily half his work.

Reporters' mistakes in general may be classified in the following six general groups:

A. Errors of expression
1. Grammatical errors
2. Errors in spelling
3. Errors in punctuation

B. Typographical style
1. Capitals
2. Figures
3. Punctuation
4. Quotation marks
5. Addresses and titles

C. Inaccuracies
1. Misstatement of fact
2. Misrepresentation of fact through omission of qualifying facts
3. Inaccuracy in the use of names (in spelling, initials, or identification)
4. Carelessness in the handling and copying of figures
5. Mistakes in dates

D. News Values
1. Inadequate lead
2. Failure to begin with the feature of the story

Inadequate summary of long story in the lead
3. Failure to follow up and explain the feature
4. Failure to prepare for cutting in make-up
6. Lack of paragraph unity
7. Comment and opinion

E. Diction and Style
1. Use of long sentences and complicated grammar
2. Use of unemphatic sentence beginnings
3. Failure to use short, compact paragraphs
4. Use of unemphatic paragraph beginnings
5. Wordiness
6. Use of general rather than concrete, definite words
7. Failure to use bright, vivid expression, especially in verbs
8. Lack of dignity of expression, especially in the use of nicknames, undignified reference, and slang

F. Libelous statements

A. Errors of Expression.—1. *Grammatical Errors.* Among the grammatical errors that occur in reporters' copy there are certain ones that appear with sufficient frequency to be watched for constantly. They are:

(a) The lack of agreement between subject and verb, especially when the two are widely separated, when the subject consists of one or more singular nouns, or when the predicate noun is of a different number:

A different outlay of funds and assets were ordered.
None of the employees were on duty.
The man with the gun and his accomplice was convicted.
The backbone of a newspaper are the news stories.

(b) The use of dangling participles which have no definite grammatical relation to the remainder of the sentence and therefore are indefinite and lacking in emphasis:

The policeman stood his ground, the robbers fleeing.
The train having gone, the reporter hired a taxicab.
They were married in secret, Justice Smith officiating.

(c) The separation of relative clauses from antecedents so that the reference is not clear:

He saw the ladder against the wall that the robber had used.
It was the pleasant secretary of the chief that I met.

(d) The use of a sentence (unquoted) as the subject of *is* or *was:*

The bank is on firm footing is the statement made by——

(e) The use of a conjunction between a relative clause and the principal clause or between two relative clauses having the same antecedent:

He bought the red auto, but which had no self-starter.
He saw the man from the station and whom the sheriff wanted.

(f) The use of a subordinate when or where clause at the end of a sentence to express later action—usually the most important action in the sentence:

We were walking down Main street when suddenly a man fell.
He moved to Dakota where he later became wealthy.

(g) The relation of pronouns to their antecedents:

A crowd of we boys went fishing.
When we met him, he said that he had not seen him.

(h) The position of adverbs in relation to the words they modify:

To indefinitely postpone the action is his proposal.

2. *Errors in Spelling.*—There is, of course, an infinite number of misspellings that may creep into reporters' copy and there are few rules to help the copy-reader in catching them; his only resource is a dictionary, a good memory, and a vigilant eye. But there are some varieties of misspellings that are more common than others; for instance:

(a) The misuse of doubled letters, especially before a suffix. In most cases a knowledge of the derivation of the words will assist here: *repeated, omitted, referred, occurring.*

(b) The failure to drop the final silent *e* before a suffix: *judgment, statement.*

(c) The forming of plurals of nouns ending in *y* or *ey: chimneys, families.*

(d) The combination in one word of certain pairs of words: *all right* (*alright*), *percent.*

(e) The splitting of certain words into two words: *something, sometime, anybody.*

(f) The misuse of *ance* for *ence: occurrence, countenance.*

(g) Misuse of digraph *ei* and *ie: receive* and *believe.* A good way to remember these is to note that if *l* precedes the digraph, *i* follows *l;* if *c* precedes, *e* follows the *c*, as in *Alice.*

(h) The confusion of two words of different spelling and meaning, but same pronunciation: *correspondent, corespondent.*

3. *Errors in Punctuation.*—To many young writers, punctuation is a serious problem because to

them it is a mere matter of arbitrary rules. But if they will consider punctuation marks as tools that have been developed by the necessity of employing some means to indicate the breaks in thought in written speech, as pauses and inflection mark them in spoken speech, they will find that they can formulate very logical rules for their guidance. The chief fault that the copyreader will discover in reporters' copy is excessive punctuation and he can put down as his first maxim the iron-clad rule of eliminating every punctuation mark for which there is not some definite, logical reason. Even if he carries this to an extreme degree, he will do less damage than the writer who uses too much punctuation—too few points cause less confusion and easier reading than too many. Every point, furthermore, takes up almost an em of space.

The following rules of punctuation will, in general, cover most cases that arise in newspaper writing, since the simple sentence structure demanded in the newspaper office makes unnecessary many of the rules followed in literary writing.

Use the comma:

1. To separate the clauses of a compound sentence only when the subject changes.
2. To separate the clauses of a complex sentence only when the dependent clause precedes the principal clause.
3. To separate the succeeding members of a list—whether the members be nouns, coördinate adjectives or adverbs, parallel clauses, parallel phrases, or any other parts of speech. The comma is needed between the last two members of the list, whether or not there is a conjunction, because the purpose of the comma is to indicate

the extent of each member rather than the omission of a possible conjunction.

4. In pairs—in the places where our forefathers might have used parenthesis marks—to set off explanatory material which has no grammatical place in the sentence. This includes substantives in direct address, appositives, absolute phrases, geographical names explaining preceding names, non-restrictive phrases and clauses, and all other parenthetical matter.
5. (N. B. There is no need of commas in newspaper writing to indicate pauses or to avoid misunderstanding—outside the above cases. The fact that a comma seems necessary is sufficient proof that there is something wrong with the sentence. Good newspaper grammar is so simple, direct, and straightforward that no artificial explanation, in the way of commas sown broadcast, is needed.)

Use the semicolon:

1. To separate groups of individual members and modifications in a list following a colon.
2. To separate the clauses of a compound sentence when they are not separated by a conjunction. It is understood that only "and," "but," and "or" can qualify as conjunctions in such a case.
3. (N. B. There is no reason in newspaper writing to add to the above rule that the semicolon is often needed when there is a conjunction simply because the several clauses are so complicated or so bespattered with commas that the line of division is not clear. This defense is sufficient evidence that the grammar is bad. Such a sentence should be broken into two or simplified. More punctuation marks add complication.)

Use the colon:

1. To precede a list or a quotation which begins with a new paragraph.

Use the dash:

1. To mark an intentional break in grammar.
2. To emphasize the element which follows it.

The commonest punctuation errors of which reporters are found guilty are the following :

(a) The omission of the second in a pair of commas (see Rule 4).

(b) The omission of the comma before the conjunction in a list (see Rule 3).

(c) The use of unnecessary commas.

(d) The use of a comma instead of a semicolon when a conjunctive adverb separates two independent clauses (see Rule 2).

(e) The use of semicolons in places where commas will do the work.

(f) The use of colons in place of commas and semicolons.

(g) Excessive use of the dash to remedy loose construction.

With reference to other punctuation marks not discussed above, the copyreader will find it necessary to keep watch for the following errors:

(h) The omission of apostrophes in the possessive case and in contractions.

(i) The omission of periods after abbreviations.

(j) The confusion of single and double quotation marks.

(k) The misuse of quotation marks in continuous quotations of several paragraphs.

(l) The omission of the quotation mark at the end.

To aid himself in eliminating these many and varied errors of expression that so often mark the printed page of newspapers and magazines, the copyreader will find that he can use to advantage a large dictionary and a good handbook on English grammar, punctuation, and spelling. When these references are not at hand, he must think of grammar and punctuation as a logical thing developed for practical use. He will often find, moreover, that the quickest and easiest way to settle a mooted point of grammar or punctuation is to recast the sentence into some unquestionable form. There are so many possibilities and varieties of expression in the English language that there is little reason to allow a questionable expression to pass or even to approach the borderline of argument. If the sentence in one form strains grammatical rules, he need not stop to puzzle over the intricacies of it, but may quickly recast it into some simpler, easier form.

B. Typographical Style. — Inasmuch as there are many mooted questions of capitalization, punctuation, use of figures, etc., that scholars and writers of English have never been able to decide, every reputable newspaper office has its own office rules to cover many of these matters. Sometimes the office rules are unwritten and rather intangible, but more often they are embodied in compact form in a pocket booklet, or on a card, called a "Style Sheet" or "Style Book." The mandates of the style sheet are often arbitrary and sometimes rather queer, but they have one defense that makes them necessary and desirable— "uniformity in typographical style is more to be desired than strict deference to rhetorical rules." For the sake of uniformity throughout its columns, then, every newspaper demands that its writers and editors follow its rules of typographical style. However arbitrary and ridiculous some of them may seem to the copyreader he must follow them to the letter. Unfortunately, although the copyreader often has little to do with making the rules, he is the one who must enforce them. With a constantly changing staff of reporters and a shifting group of journeyman printers in the linotype room, uniformity of typographical style would soon go by the board were it not for the man who edits the copy. While everyone else in the office is trying his best to violate them all, it devolves upon him to check up every capital letter and every figure to see that it conforms to the office style—simply to insure uniformity. He must come to think of an error in style as a matter as serious as an error in grammar, spelling, or punctuation, and must look for them as carefully. The result will be a "clean" uniform sheet that critics will call "well-edited"—and they will condone other faults accordingly. However trivial a capital letter or a misspelled word may seem to the young copyreader, he must remember that it is difficult for the reading public to credit the accuracy of large statements in a newspaper that is bespattered with minor inaccuracies. The presence of trivial errors and the lack of uniformity spells to the newspaper reader lax office methods and he questions its general truth-telling accordingly.

Common Errors in Style.—It is impossible to classify errors in style that occur in reporters' copy beyond the extent that they are classified in the average style sheet. They are usually concerned with (1) the use of misuses of capital letters; (2) the use of figures; (3) the overuse of abbreviations; (4) the form of street address; (5) the .handling of titles; (6) the mooted questions of punctuation; (7) the use of quotation marks. Although the rules of grammar and punctuation are often questionable, the copyreader has in the matter of typographical style a set of hard and fast regulations that he can enforce absolutely and he should know his newspaper's style sheet from beginning to end, besides understanding its general intent and being able to read between the lines of printed rules. If the general intent of the style sheet is "down" (that is, it advocates the use of small letters instead of capitals when there is any question) he should follow out the intent by adopting the maxim: When in doubt, use a small letter. Styles in newspaper make-up are changing constantly and no two newspapers have exactly the same ideas of beauty in the printed page, but the copyreader must be as ready to change his style as his coat and feel as much at home in the new one. (A typical newspaper style sheet is included in this volume, Appendix II, for classroom use in the development of accuracy in details.)

C. Inaccuracies.—Inaccuracy, intentional or otherwise, is the chief fault of most newspaper reporters and the copyreader is practically the only check upon the evil. It is his most significant duty to wage continual war on inaccuracy, big and little, careless and intentional, if his newspaper is to escape the blanket accusation of criminal inaccuracy that many critics make against American newspapers in general. But the task is a difficult one. Inaccuracy in newspaper writing crops out in so many and devious ways that it is practically impossible to classify all the possibilities and absolutely impossible to catch all the evidences. To eliminate all the inaccuracies that appear in the copy on his desk, the copyreader would need to be practically omniscient. The material which he is called upon to edit includes in its scope every phase of human activity and every branch of human knowledge. To accomplish his task, he would need to be a specialist in every art and science. Even so, his memory would fail him occasionally, or his watchfulness, and some few glaring misstatements would pass him.

But since absolute perfection is not demanded in any man's work, there are some humanly possible approaches to the task within reach of any copyreader of average intelligence, if he makes a conscious effort to equip himself for the work and is determined to uproot as many inaccuracies as possible. Although newspaper copy puts no limits on its range of subject matter, nine-tenths of it is concerned with material that any alert man can keep in hand if he makes the effort. To do his work with fair efficiency, the copyreader should be thoroughly acquainted, in the first place, with the city in which his paper is published. He should know its geography, its industries, its history, its politics, its people, and its interests, as thoroughly as the clergyman knows his flock. Fifty per cent. of the copy he edits will be taken care of by this knowledge. The affairs of the nation must be within his range—its history, its present and past politics, its finance and economics, its prominent people. So far as possible, the history, politics, business, people, and geography of other countries should be at his finger tips. He should have a general knowledge of every subject of general information at the present time, whether art or science, material or spiritual. Familiarity with the technical language and special words of these subjects increases his efficiency. All of this means that he must devote much of his time to reading—he must read newspapers, magazines, books, pamphlets, everything that comes to hand, for the purpose of extending his acquaintance with the world's affairs. And he cannot rely on past reading—the interests of the newspaper change not by years or decades, but by days and minutes, and he must keep up with the changes. But better than all the knowledge that he can crowd into his brain is a systematic acquaintance with all sources of information. If the copyreader is not acquainted with the subject in hand, he should at least know where to find the information he needs.

The inaccuracies that appear in reporters' copy may be classified loosely in the following groups:

1. *Misstatement of Fact.*—This includes both the basic facts of his story and the minor facts that make up its background. Nothing but a broad fund of knowledge and common-sense will enable the copy-

reader to check up all the facts that appear on his desk. But he can do much by putting them all to the test of reasonableness. A fact or a statement that seems to him unreasonable or absurd should never pass unchallenged, even if the challenge involves a confession of his own ignorance. No statement at all is better than a misstatement. Whatever appears absurd to him will appear absurd to the paper's readers, and his challenge may result in an inserted explanation that will make evident the fact's reliability.

2. *Misrepresentation of Facts Through Omission of Qualifying Facts.*—The omission of necessary qualifications will often make a true statement appear as inaccurate as a false one. This appears most frequently in the quotation or explanation of men's statements and opinions. The reporter gives the public their broad general statements and neglects to add the modifications, limitations, and reservations, or he reports their negations without the affirmations that accompanied them. Very often the careless omission of a qualifying phrase or even an adjective will make the major statement ridiculous, and it is this very fact that enables the copyreader to catch the inaccuracy. The only test that he can apply is that every fact must meet the demands of his own intelligence and common-sense.

3. *Inaccuracy in the Use of Names.*—Not only in attaching the right names to the right actors in a story are reporters careless, but also in presenting a name when it is the right one. The copyreader must

check the spelling of the name itself, the initials or first names that precede it, the address or other identification that accompanies it. The fault of "getting names wrong" is the commonest in newspaper work and brings more ridicule than any of the other inaccuracies of which the newspaper is guilty. It is impossible for the copyreader to prevent all the inaccuracies in names, because the compositor and proofreader may add a few after the copy leaves his hands, but he should be sure that every name is correct when he reads the copy. In many cases, especially in local stories, he can trust to his own knowledge and memory. But he must not depend too much upon them. He must have at hand a city directory, a telephone directory, a copy of "Who's Who," and many other directories of names to use as his authority. He will find that it will take him but a moment to run through the pages of the directory and verify every name that appears in the copy he reads—and the moment will be well spent. Errors in the use of names are not limited to names of persons. The copyreader must verify all geographical names, all names of clubs, societies, and organizations, all names of business firms and commercial or political bodies. Many a libel suit has resulted from confusing the name of a bankrupt house with its more prosperous neighbor whose designation is different only in an "&" sign—as many as have resulted from reporting before the bar of justice the reputable citizen whose initials are only slightly different from those of the vagabond who was arrested. Many of the principal persons involved and many an honest citizen has been enraged by the appearance of his identical name and initials in connection with an activity which he does not countenance. Since newspaper reporters cannot be trusted to "get names straight," the duty of verifying them and correcting them falls upon the copyreader—and he must consider it a solemn duty, since a man's name is a sacred thing.

4. *Carelessness in the Handling and Copying of Figures.*—How often the public has been amazed by a variation of four deaths in two reports of an accident, and how often newspaper critics have scoffed at the fact that in three reports of a fire loss the figures may vary by $50,000. The newspapers answer that the mistake is due to the difficulty in securing the facts. As often, however, it is due to a reporter's failure to grasp the significance of the figures and a copyreader's failure to check them. Working at his desk in a noisy office, the copyreader often has difficulty in verifying the figures that a reporter has brought in, but he can be sure at least that there are no conflicts or contradictions in the figures contained in the story and that the figures stand the test of his common-sense.

5. *Mistakes in Dates.*—Dates cause less trouble than other exact facts, but they are often wrong in spite of this. It is the duty therefore of the copyreader to check every date that he reads and be sure that it is right.

The books of reference that the copyreader may use in checking up reporters' inaccuracies are numerous and varied—and sometimes expensive. There are some, however, that he must have: the latest city directory; the latest local telephone directory; telephone and city directories of all nearby towns and cities; "Who's Who in America"; "Who's Who in England"; "Wer Ist's" in Germany; "Qui Etes-vous" in France; the World Almanac; the Times Digest of the year; a standard encyclopedia; latest copy of State laws and statutes, etc. The copyreader should also make a habit of treasuring up all lists of names and printed directories that come to his hand. Even then he will often find that he must fall back on the newspaper's "morgue" and general library.

D. News Values.—Because the basis of newspaper writing is news value, the copyreader must make himself an arbiter of the form of the news stories that pass through his hands. In the large, rich office he will find that the reporters know news values and the news-story form as well as he and he will seldom have to revise a story except to change its emphasis. In smaller offices where the staff is largely composed of "cubs," he will find that he must bear a large share of the brunt of teaching the new reporters the form in which to write their stories. For, with the exception of the feature story and the occasional narrative story that is appearing in many of the best newspapers, the writing of news stories follows rather generally a conventional form—a form which consists of a summary lead and a story whose news and interest are crowded toward the beginning. If he has not learned this form through experience as a reporter, he must learn it through a study of newspaper stories. For the news-story form is as much an inherent part of American newspaper making as the bulletin headline.

Without going into a discussion of the conventional news-story form, it is possible to point out some of the common faults that appear in "cub" reporters' stories. The copyreader must remember, however, that they are all to be subordinated to the general idea of presenting the story's most interesting content at the very outset and summarizing the entire story in the lead, or first paragraph. The common faults are:

1. *Inadequate Lead.*—The lead fails to give the gist of the story and to summarize all the elements that follow. Perhaps it fails to answer all the reader's questions about this summary, viz., *when, where, who, how,* and *why.* The summary may be inadequate in that it does not give both sides of the question or mentions only one phase of a story that contains many phases. For instance, the lead may give the impression that the story is a report of one man's speech although the story is really a report of an open meeting including a number of speeches. It is quite evident that such a lead gives undue prominence to the one speaker and may lose readers who do not happen to be interested in this man or his words. The lead, in other words, should include or suggest every phase of the story—the story in its entirety—for the sake of giving a rounded impression and of attracting as many readers as possible. This summary may require one paragraph or half a column, but it must

be complete before the running narrative begins.

2. *Failure to Begin with the Feature of the Story.*—The lead, furthermore, should always begin with the most interesting fact in the story—the *feature* as it is called. Never should it begin with general explanation, the time, the place, or any subordinate element, unless that element is more interesting than everything else in the story. The copyreader must learn the advertising value of the first printed line. He should remember that the white space above the first line causes it to stand out with sufficient prominence to emphasize the first six or seven words as if they were heavier, blacker type. Realizing this, he should be sure that this important position is devoted to six or seven words that are significant and interesting enough to hold the eye that is drawn to them by their prominent position and to carry the reader down into the story. Partly because they do not realize the importance of the beginning of the news story and partly because it is psychologically difficult for the human mind to begin its narrative with the climax, young reporters are inclined to waste the beginning in useless words. Or, understanding the significance of the beginning, they may strain too hard and make the beginning unnatural. Their inclination in such a case is to go outside the story for a beginning—to drag in a witticism or a parallelism or an unwarranted superlative. Such a beginning is just as much a waste of space as the other, for after all it is the facts of the story that the reader wants and not a feeble attempt at cleverness. It is well to remember that if

a story is worth printing at all, there is some fact *in it* that deserves the first line, and it is much more effective to seek out this significant *part* of the story instead of rambling around the world in search of a clever saying that will *lead up to* the story. In general, the ideal lead is simply a summary of the story beginning with the most significant element in that summary.

In editing leads, the copyreader is safe in refusing to allow any story to pass which contains any fact in the body of the story that is more interesting than the facts in the lead or any story which has phases in its subsequent narrative which are not summarized or suggested in the lead. If all the facts are there, the rest of the problem is a mere matter of grammar. Practice will enable him to see the quickest and most effective way to put these facts together grammatically, by rearrangement or breaking up of sentences.

3. *Inadequate Summary of Long Story in the Lead.* —This fault is a part of the preceding fault. Many reporters stubbornly refuse to recognize that the lead is sometimes more than the first paragraph. Their stories begin with an interesting feature and contain a summary of the facts related to that feature but fail to include the rest of the story. The fault appears most often in a long story—the report of a series of speeches, for instance. The writer neglects to list the speakers in the lead and hence in the make-up one or more speakers, who are mentioned only at the end of the story, are cut out of the report entirely. The copyreader must insert a summary paragraph

ahead of the running narrative, to gather up the loose ends that the lead has neglected.

4. *Failure to Follow Up and Explain the Feature.*—This occurs most often in stories that begin with some striking attendant circumstance. The reporter uses this fact, the most interesting in the story, for his beginning, and then forgets to mention it again. The effect upon the reader is that he has been cheated out of something that he should have, since the feature played up in the first line is more or less an advertisement of what he is to find in the story. Very often this feature, which is so utterly neglected in the narrative, is the only thing in the story that has news value, that makes it worth printing. For instance, a reporter writes a three-hundred-word story on a fire whose only reason for mention is a strikingly unusual cause—say, a cat and a candle. The reporter begins with the cause to attract attention to the story and then forgets to explain how the cat and the candle accomplished their costly work. The reader whose only idea in reading the story is to find out about the unusual thing the cat and the candle did, is decidedly disappointed. The story has advertised something that it doesn't have in stock. The writer should, of course, have devoted the major part of the story to the feature, or at least one paragraph, and since he has failed to do so, the copyreader must write in the missing narrative as best he can.

5. *Failure to Prepare for "Cutting" in Make-up.*—The exigencies of make-up in a newspaper office require that every story be written in such a way as to

allow for cutting without leaving the feeling that the story is incomplete. Some offices require this because it makes possible the gradual cutting down of stories through successive editions, without rewriting or re-setting. But many young reporters do not grasp the idea at once and their stories cannot possibly be cut without rewriting. Usually the fault lies in an in-adequate summary in the lead and the failure to crowd the interesting facts toward the beginning of the story. The copyreader must remedy it by adding to the lead and by rearranging the rest of the story.

6. *Lack of Paragraph Unity.*—The exigencies of newspaper make-up also require that each paragraph, except the first, be a separate unit by itself that may be omitted without seriously injuring the story or breaking up the coherence. Each paragraph must be perfect in unity—that is, it must deal with one phase of the story and be absolutely complete in itself. Then an alteration of the story to match later news is possible without resetting. But many reporters fail to outline their stories carefully and build them up of mutually independent paragraphs, or blocks. The copyreader must do it for them.

7. *Comment and Opinion.*—There are few news-papers which permit their reporters to pass judgment on the facts discussed. The editors prefer to gather all the judgment and comment into the editorial columns. But the young reporter has an almost ir-resistible impulse to give his readers an inkling of his opinion on the facts. He fills his stories full of in-conspicuous comments that color the story and the

copyreader must edit them out. Sometimes the comments are so subtle that it is very difficult to find them—only the general tone is noticeable. They usually creep in through qualifying and comparative adjectives and adverbs; sometimes a verb is responsible; again the use or omission of a title will give the tone. Superlative expressions are probably the most common offenders, for reporters seldom realize that a superlative is in itself a comment. If he is to do his work well, the copyreader must watch closely for "feeling" in the stories he edits and must eliminate *the particular words* that give the feeling.

E. Style and Diction.—Many of the other faults that the copyreader must look for in the copy he edits may be grouped under this general head. They are not so conspicuous as the errors listed above but they are nevertheless flaws and must be corrected. Some of them are:

1. *Use of Long Sentences and Complicated Grammar.*—Since an essential requirement of the modern newspaper is that it be easy to read, its diction must be clear and swift. The rapid reader of today in glancing through the news will not take time to decipher long, involved sentences, dig through complicated grammar, or wade into a sentence so complicated that its writer must needs go back and pick up his subject again on the second breath. The grammar must be clear and straightforward; there must be no turning back or reversal of idea; even a change from active to passive voice is often confusing. The only style that will satisfy this is one made of

comparatively short, simple sentences. The length is not so important as the simplicity; a sixty-word sentence is often easier to grasp than a four-word sentence. But the average young reporter, trained as he has been in the flowery, oratorical style taught in the average school composition class, delights in tangling his ideas into an impenetrable mass of complicated grammar. Until he learns that, however valuable the oratorical style may be in other writing, it has no place in the newspaper, the copyreader must untangle his grammar and make it readable. Usually the easiest way to simplify it is to break the sentences into several shorter, more unified sentences.

2. *Use of Unemphatic Sentence Beginnings.*—Since the emphatic sentence beginning which rapid reading demands is directly contradictory to the sentence emphasis which the young reporter is taught in school composition, the copyreader finds that a large part of his editing consists in breaking down climatic periods and overturning oratorical efforts. Before he has been "on the desk" long he will find himself unconsciously throwing explanatory material back into the sentence and dragging emphatic phrases to the beginning. He may think that he is doing it to put "punch" into the story, but more than that he is making it easy to read. The reporter, before he took a place on the staff, was taught to write the kind of style that is most effective when read aloud, and it takes him some time to learn that the same thing is not effective when read silently and rapidly. While he is learning that the demands of journalistic writ-

ing require him to put his best foot forward in each sentence, as well as in paragraph and story, his copyreader will find the earmarks of the oratorical style throughout his story. The most evident of them are the many sentences beginning with "He said—" and "They are of the opinion that—"; the sentences that are halted by "however" and "nevertheless" on the front doorstep. One sweep of the pencil carries these obstructions back into the sentence out of the way and when the trained copyreader has finished, the sentence begins with its most interesting content in the first few words. Periodic sentences, generally speaking, are out of place in newspaper writing; the looser the sentence is, the more effective it is for rapid reading. Under no circumstances should a newspaper sentence begin with explanatory matter.

3. *Failure to Use Short, Compact Paragraphs.*—Coming to the office with a thorough training in the writing of two-hundred-word literary themes, the young reporter forgets that he is now writing for a column two and one-sixth inches wide—for lines of only six or seven words. He forgets that the narrowness of the columns makes his paragraphs look twice as long and that there is nothing so uninviting to a newspaper reader as a long, heavy paragraph. The copyreader must therefore become very adept in the art of scattering paragraph marks through the reporter's copy. An easy guide that the copyreader may follow is the fact that one typewritten line makes almost exactly two lines of type; since twelve lines is a heavy paragraph in a news-

paper, six lines of typewritten copy should be almost the limit of length. Gradually he will learn how to estimate longhand copy to produce printed paragraphs of the proper length. In the same connection, he will notice the reporter's tendency toward burying his quotation marks in the midst of his paragraphs and combining summary and indirect quotation in the same paragraph. Realizing the value of a quotation mark to catch the reader's eye, the copyreader will learn to put paragraph signs in front of most of the quotation marks he finds thus buried.

4. *Use of Unemphatic Paragraph Beginnings.*—The question of paragraph emphasis must also be considered in the same connection. Just as the first line of the story is emphasized by the white space above it, the first line of every paragraph is set off by the white space of the indention and the short line above it. Each paragraph beginning is therefore a spot which the reader's eye is likely to strike and the copyreader must see to it that the first line says something of interest. In other words, the emphasis of each paragraph, just as in the entire story, must be thrown toward the beginning so that the content may be grasped in the shortest possible time.

5. *Wordiness.*—Conciseness is one of the most important characteristics of newspaper writing, because every day the paper gathers more news than it has space to print. Conciseness, almost to the point of baldness, is absolutely demanded of its writers. No word should appear in a story unless it has a definite reason for existence. But conciseness is a very hard

thing to learn because it is built of close, compact thinking. It is necessary for the copyreader to wage continual war on wordiness. He must question the value of every word, phrase, and clause; he must constantly try to substitute one word for several words; he must continually tighten up the loose sentences his reporters write. Sometimes the wordiness results from needless repetition; again it can be blamed on a small vocabulary. One of its chief evidences is in the splitting of an idea into two sentences—half the space can be saved, without sacrificing content, by condensing the two into one. This condensing process is called "boiling." It consists in pruning the language down to the skeleton of thought. It is not necessary to eliminate any thoughts or facts in condensing; the mode of expression may simply be boiled down, so that two ideas may be expressed in the space of one. The process is justifiable in the newspaper office because to the newspaper writer English is a means rather than an end—he cares more for the thought than its expression. And the meaty, close-packed style that results from the copyreader's boiling is characteristically journalistic. It has a greater specific gravity.

6. *Use of General Rather than Concrete, Definite Words.*—This is a subject that is worth a volume in itself because it involves the life of newspaper writing. The question of vocabulary would seem to be more a concern of the reporter than of the copyreader, but the copyreader must make up for the reporter's shortcomings. He must accept the excellencies which

the reporter possesses and add to them his own. He must coöperate with the reporter in keeping newspaper writing from becoming a dead, dry rehearsal of facts, and there are certain things that he may well bear in mind as he scans for actual mistakes. Brightness and interest in writing depend upon exact, definite words. Whenever he sees a broad, generally meaningless word he must cast about for a concrete expression of it. If the reporter says, "many persons rushed to his aid," the copyreader can make the sentence more interesting by substituting the exact number. He will also make the sentence more creditable, for we are more prone to believe definite statements than hazy ones. The more he sets forth the exact details of the story, the more likely we will be to see the picture in its entirety and be interested in it.

7. *Failure to Use Bright, Vivid Expression, Especially Verbs.*—Interest demands more vivid expression. How many verbs there are in English to express a man's manner of walking, and yet how many reporters are satisfied with "he crossed the street"! How many ways there are of recording vocal expression, and yet how much "he said" is overworked! For almost every action in the world, English has a verb and the more of them a story contains the more interesting it will be. The copyreader must not be satisfied with the old stand-bys; he must usher out some of the little-used nouns and verbs. He will then find less occasion for the use of slang.

The question of active and passive voice is directly

related to this. Action expressed entirely in passive verbs gives the feeling of walking backward—the receiver is continually preceding the giver; the result is ahead of action. To right about face and proceed face forward gives the style swiftness, directness, and interest. Sometimes the active voice takes more space, but it is worth it. A careful study of reporter's copy will disclose the fact that more than half his verbs are passive and hence the copyreader, to eliminate this fault, must question the presence of every passive verb he sees.

Trite expression should be avoided. Not all the old stand-bys of newspaper writing are trite. Some of them are simply good words worn threadbare. But many of the tiresome words to which the newspaper reader objects are simply trite, one-time supposedly clever expressions worn to the bone. No good English word in its proper usage is trite or tiresome; you say "noon" every day of your life without tiring of it or realizing its presence. The trite word is the word that is taken out of its proper place and given a new meaning. It tickles the reader the first time it is used, but the third time it is stale. The first reporter who said, "They staged a good fight," had invented a clever expression, but we are tired of it now because "staged" is out of its proper meaning and no longer clever. The same applies to many of the tiresome newspaper expressions that the reporter dashes into his copy. He uses them because he does not take time to think and the copyreader can brighten his story by crossing out the trite words and substituting the good English words whose meaning the reporter desired.

8. *Lack of Dignity of Expression.*—The accusation that the newspaper is having a bad influence upon American speech is partly due to the lack of dignity in the columns of many papers. Through haste and carelessness, rather than through viciousness, many newspaper workers forget the great educational influence that their words spread broadcast and shirk their duty as educators of a large share of the population. If they but remember that one coarse expression which they pass to the composing room may be picked up and gleefully repeated by thousands of readers, young and old, they will hesitate before they take the responsibility of lowering American life by so much as this one coarse expression. The bustle and rush of their work makes them unmindful of its influence. Sometimes they feel that they must "get down" to the level of their readers. But some of the most successful American newspapers are successful because they have stood steadfast in their high place and brought their readers up to their own level. The educational influence of the newspaper makes it imperative that a newspaper, while gauging the level of its readers, should strike slightly above their heads in its expression and so educate them up slowly to a higher plane. Every copyreader, therefore, should think twice before he allows to pass any of the undignified expressions that his reporters pick up on the street. For in every case he will find words just as bright and vivid in the dictionary. This applies

especially to the use of slang and other perversions of the mother tongue. It also applies to the numerous nicknames and undignified references that reporters delight in sprinkling through their copy. To refer to a man by other than his proper name, is to be rude and familiar, and the action reflects not upon the man but upon the newspaper.

F. Libelous Statements. — The copyreader is the watch dog who must keep libelous statements out of the news columns; at any rate, he usually receives the blame when his newspaper suffers libel action because of statements he allowed to pass. The position is an uncomfortable one, for the exact nature of libel is an indefinite thing, depending as much upon circumstances and the verdict of the jury as upon law, and no newspaper can fulfill its office as a dispenser of news without now and then laying itself open to libel action. It is practically impossible to print all the news, at the time when it should be printed, without running into danger of hurting someone's good name to a damageable extent; but for one libelous statement that results in legal action and recovery, ten as serious go by unnoticed. Hence the desk man learns to judge individual cases by instinct, balancing the news value of stories against their libel content and deciding each case on its own merits.

A libelous statement is an untruth that hurts someone's private, professional, or business reputation. The old basis, "the greater the truth, the greater the libel," no longer holds good; now only an untrue statement is libelous. But all untrue statements are not libelous; they must hurt someone to be libelous. Just what constitutes damage to one's character is the question concerned. In general, any statement that holds an individual up to public contempt, ridicule, scorn, or shame, if untrue, is libelous—to accuse him of a loathsome disease or suggest lack of morality or integrity in his business or private life. In the case of a professional man, anything that suggests lack of skill or knowledge or charges incompetency is libelous, but the statement must "touch him" in his professional capacity. The same applies to business concerns and enterprises. Public officials, while open to criticism in their public capacity, cannot be attacked as private citizens or accused of moral or mental unfitness for office. Criticism must be concerned with their official acts. But any of these accusations or implications is harmless of libel if the newspaper can prove it true. When it is untrue, and the victim wishes to retaliate, he can do so only by bringing suit and recovering such damages as the jury thinks are equivalent to the injury he has suffered. The case is not decided on the basis of the newspaper's intent or innocence of malice, but on the basis of the injury suffered by the victim. This is true except when the statements may be such as to lead to a "breach of the peace" and the evident motive results in criminal proceedings against the publisher.

Besides truth, however, the newspaper has another defense in its injurious statements about individuals—privilege. Certain statements, even though untrue, are protected from libel action because they are privileged—because the information came from a privileged source. This privilege covers all information secured from the proceedings of judicial, legislative, and other public or semi-public bodies whose doings are of public interest. If the newspaper publishes damaging facts derived from such proceedings and publishes them fairly and accurately, it is protected from libel action even though the facts are untrue. But there are dangers even in this. In the report of sessions of Congress, the State Legislature, the city council and other public bodies, to be privileged the damaging statements must have been made during and as a part of the public session and must be reported with great accuracy and fairness. In the case of reports of court action, damaging statements are privileged only when taken from the proceedings of a court of record and must be confined to the proceedings themselves. What constitutes a court of record and at what point in the proceedings privilege begins are matters determined by State law and differing in the several States. In general, the proceedings of a magistrate's court or police station hearing are not open to protected report and ordinarily the proceedings are not privileged in a court of record until the trial actually begins—preliminary pleadings and short affidavits are seldom privileged. Whether the records of other semi-public bodies, such as clubs, lodges, church boards, etc., are privileged depends upon the amount of public interest in them. All public statements of various officers and official bodies and petitions made to them are privileged after the statements or petitions have been received by the proper officers. Criticism of public officers and of writers or other artists is privileged so long as it is confined to the public doings, acts, or works, of these persons.

Out of this maze of rule and precedent, the desk man finds that his only recourse is to investigate the State laws and rulings which govern his newspaper and to weigh each dangerous accusation, implication, or suggestion with regard to the chance that it may be untrue, that it may be of sufficient public interest to be privileged, and, more than that, to what extent it will injure the person concerned and how likely he is to bring action to recover damages. It is to be noted that the newspaper writer's good intentions or haste are no defense, that the use of "it is rumored," etc., or even the source of information, is no protection ("alleged" is used to show that the material came from a privileged source), that failing to express a name when identification is possible makes no difference, that innocent mistakes are actionable, and that a retraction will do little more than prejudice the jury in the newspaper's favor.

IV. THE REQUISITES OF GOOD COPYREADING

1. The Ability to See Errors.—The ability to see errors is one of the first things that a young copyreader must cultivate. And it is a difficult thing to acquire. The ordinary reader does not see half the mistakes in the things he reads. Even a second reading will not bring all the errors to his attention. It is because he has an unconscious tendency to seize the thought without noticing the means of expression; he is so used to English expression that he reads by sentences and clauses rather than by words, grasping a line at a time and skimming through the elements that make up the expression. The copyreader must, however, concentrate on the means of expression and take into his mind, not only the thought, but the individual words. This ability to see errors comes only with practice and can be developed to the point of being an unconscious habit. The beginner can cultivate it best by going back to the elemental actions that constitute the process. He must first break himself of the habit of scanning what he reads; he must train himself to read word by word, developing the faculty of seeing and noting every letter and every punctuation point. At first, it may be necessary for him to read line by line with a card, as the proofreader does, to force his mind to concentrate on the details. Not only while he is actually reading copy should he watch for errors, but he should force himself to watch the details in everything he reads, until the process becomes a habit. Not until he has become so observing that a misspelled word and a misplaced comma stand out like a blot, is he a good copyreader.

2. Neatness.—Neatness is another characteristic of the good copyreader. He takes pride in leaving the copy he has edited as presentable as it was before. His office is to prepare it for the printer, as well as to correct it, and he should increase rather than impair its legibility. To secure legibility and neatness, he uses a large, soft pencil whose mark may be readily seen in the dim light over the linotype's copyholder. When he puts in a run-in line to guide the printer's eye, he makes it definite and straight. When he crosses out words, he eradicates them thoroughly and draws a bridge around the gap to emphasize the fact that the word is gone. Whenever there is any doubt about consecutive positions, he connects the doubtful words with run-in lines. He is especially careful to do this when his cutting has left a word stranded at the beginning or end of a line. With his firm, black lines he blazes a trail through the corrections, for he knows that the printer is trained to follow the connecting lines. He also uses as few marks as possible and takes pains to write legibly whenever he is forced to insert words. Inserted material he writes above the line—in fact, all marks are placed above the line, so that the compositor will see them in time, and no additions are written vertically in the margin because this complicates the task of cutting the copy into takes. Where the revision requires so many corrections that the corrections become confused, he rewrites the sentence or paragraph on a separate sheet of paper and pastes it into place. He prepares each piece of copy as if it were to be handled by the most stupid printer on earth and as if it were to be a record of his neatness in editing.

3. Swiftness.—Swiftness is as necessary as accuracy in his work. There is no place in the busy newspaper office for the man who must putter and ponder. But at the same time the good copyreader realizes that haste makes waste on the copy desk as elsewhere. Instead of plunging into the copy and deluging it with corrections, he stops long enough to decide the easiest and quickest way to make the desired change. The fewer the marks, the better the editing. When he sees a fault, he analyzes it clearly and chooses the simplest remedy before he touches his pencil to the paper. He is sure then that his correction has accomplished its work and has not added confusion. In the end, he gets through the work faster than the man who blunders blindly ahead, altering the beginning of a sentence before he has read the end, and "butchering" the first line of a paragraph before he has found out how essential it is to the thought of the rest of the paragraph, or crossing out an adverb before he notices that the next sentence requires its presence. Every correction that the copyreader makes must have a reason and the blunderer is never as efficient as the man who works rapidly but keeps his head at the same time.

4. Mere Cutting.—Mere cutting is not good copyreading. Some copyreaders seem to have a feeling that their work is not complete unless they have crossed out so many sentences and slashed off so many paragraphs. Such copyreaders are rightly dubbed "copy-butchers" by their reporters. Indiscriminate copy cutting is bad because it deprives the story of its coherence and continuity. If condensation is necessary it should be accomplished by boiling—by eliminating useless words without throwing out facts and ideas. A story that is ruthlessly cut is usually worse than it was before, because it has lost many of the facts that make it worth while, and what remains is just as wordy and scatter-brained as before.

5. Boiling.—Intelligent boiling is a matter that must be practiced. It is concerned with words and phrases rather than with sentences and paragraphs. Condensing, skillfully done, leaves the story better because it has stripped much of the useless fat from the meat of the thought. It consists in substituting one word for several, in putting related sentences together, in compressing the original thought into smaller space without allowing any of the thought to escape. Boiling is an art that the copyreader should strive to acquire. Nine out of ten of the stories that come to his hands will be improved by careful condensation. Good writers practice it on their own work to counteract their tendency toward wordiness. They find it a better way to reduce the length of their works than to slash out entire paragraphs of ideas and facts.

6. Expanding.—Expanding stories is just as much a part of the copyreader's work as condensing them and should be done as intelligently. Some writers expand their stories by reiterating and repeating ideas they have already covered. This kind of expansion has no place in the newspaper office. No story should fill more space than is required to present its facts clearly and concisely. There is only one way to expand intelligently and that is to add additional facts. The copyreader, working at his desk far away from the source of a story, is often at a loss for additional facts.

He will find, however, that most stories suggest far more facts than they express and fail to elaborate sufficiently to insure clearness. He may expand stories by the simple process of writing in the facts that are suggested. But he must expand systematically so as not to destroy the story's balance. If he expands one phase of the story he must expand other phases accordingly. The easiest way to decide what phases are in need of elaboration is, he will find, to look at the story from the point of view of the reader and determine what parts of the story are the most interesting or most in accord with the interest built up by the lead. Usually he will find that the facts he has left in the lead are the most significant and the best ones to elaborate. But this elaboration does not mean the invention of imaginary facts to fit the case; it means the writing in of real facts that the reporter has suggested but has failed to make clear.

V. PRACTICE THAT WILL ASSIST THE COPYREADER

The beginner may develop his proficiency at copyreading by undertaking the task as systematically as the pianist learns the technic of his art. There are finger exercises in copyreading as well as in instrumentation. (1) The first is to watch for errors, grammatical, typographical, and logical, in everything he reads—to edit mentally everything that comes to his hands. In this way he will sharpen his copyreading eyesight. (2) Another is to begin reading copy word for word, perhaps moving the lips to assist the mind in concentrating. If necessary, he may force concentration by following the copy line by line with a card. (3) As there are so many things to look for in copyreading (listed A, B, C, D, E, and F under III above), it is often good practice to begin the study by looking for one kind of error at a time. The first reading may be devoted to catching errors of expression; the second, typographical style; the third, accuracy, and so on. This method will insure good thorough work until the copyreader has learned to watch for all of them at once. (4) Since it is impossible to do much with the news value of a story until one has grasped its entire content and a complete reading is necessary to learn the content, a young copyreader can often improve his work by consciously breaking the task into two readings. During the first, while he is grasping the story's content, he will correct all the small errors that come to his attention, e.g., A, B, and C. He is then ready to go over it again to change the arrangement, e.g., D, E, and F. Careful preliminary practice, like the pianist's finger exercises, will in time enable him to gather in the story at a glance and correct it page by page as it comes to him.

VI. PREPARING COPY FOR THE PRINTER

In addition to correcting the manuscript and numbering the pages, the copyreader must also mark it with printer's directions and label it for reference. All of these marks must be placed directly on the manuscript, in the margin, at the head of the first page, or at the end. The usual custom is to inclose them in circles so that the printer will understand that he is not to set them up.

1. Type Directions.—Type directions are always placed at the head of the first page, usually at the left. They indicate the type, length of line, and character of display. Ordinarily it is not necessary to specify the type for the headline further than to indicate the style of head—No. 5 for instance—since the printer knows from his schedule what type is desired. In newspaper work, the copyreader is not greatly concerned with the style of type since only a slight variation is possible. He may mark it 8-point or 7-point, as the case may be, although the office practice will usually make that unnecessary. If he desires display, he may mark it "bold face" or "leaded," or "indent 1 em," or "1 em hanging indention." In some cases he may mark it "double measure," meaning lines stretching across two columns. More exact type specification is necessary in other kinds of work and this will be discussed in another chapter.

2. Guide-lines.—Guide-lines are signs or labels by which the copyreader indicates to the printer the content of a piece of copy and the position it should have in the final make-up of the paper. Their purpose is to facilitate make-up and to keep track of the many pieces of copy that he sends to the composing room. The term guide-line, or catch-line, includes a number of different kinds of labels with different purposes. One kind of guide-line is used to indicate the position of the story as a whole; another designates the position of various parts of the story. But whatever its purpose, the guide-line is usually set up by the printer and placed at its head, so that the same label appears in all the proofs until the paper has been made up in final form. The make-up man removes the guide slugs when he places the stories in the form.

Every story in the first place is given a name or short designation as soon as it reaches the copyreader's hands. The name may be "Smith murder," or "Council Meeting," or "Wreck No. 1," or "Wreck No. 2"—some short name that indicates its content. If the story is sent in one piece with headline attached, the name serves as a handy designation. If the story is sent to the composing room in sections the name becomes an identification of the various parts.

For example, if the city council is holding a prolonged session and the staff of the morning paper is receiving the story in sections and rushing it to the linotype machines, it may be labeled thus: The first piece sent down carries the catch-line "Council Meeting" at the head and "More to come" at the end. A turned rule at the end of a galley is the printer's indication of "More to come." As the various parts are written and edited, they are labeled "First Add Council," "Second Add Council," and so on. If other items are to follow the story under the same headline, they are designated "First Follow Council," "Second Follow Council," and so on. When the lead is ready it is marked "Lead Council." The head that goes down a few moments later is marked, "Head Council." If after all is ready, the reporter brings word that the council had at the last moment delayed adjournment long enough to transact a piece of business more important than all the rest, the copyreader must prepare corrections. First he sends down a piece of copy marked "Insert Council After Lead." Perhaps there are inserts "A" and "B" or more. Then "New Lead Council." After that "New Head Council." Perhaps then he is forced to send instructions to "Kill Fourth Follow Council"—meaning to throw away part of the original story. With a series of guide-lines such as these a copyreader is able to label each piece of copy with brief and exact instructions to the printer. It will be noted that each one invariably contains the original name of the story. In some offices these catch-lines that designate the various parts of a single story are not set in type and do not go beyond the man who puts the story together in a galley. Very small stories are not ordinarily "slugged," as the small headline is set on the same machine and serves as sufficient identification.

Another use of guide-lines is to indicate the department of the paper to which a piece of copy, item, or story, belongs. One story is labeled, "Society," another "Sports," another "Market." The catch-lines are always set up in type and placed at the head of the story; in some cases, in fact, the office has a series of department slugs already cast in larger type for this use. When a story appears in the proof with such a designation at the lead it is said to be "slugged."

The one guide-line that the copyreader never omits on any story is some mark at the end to tell whether or not the story is complete. If it is complete, as it stands, he always places an "end mark" in the space below the last line. The mark may be a double cross, "#," or the telegrapher's end mark, "30," or simply "End." If the story is not complete, he writes "More to come," "More," or some other definite information like "List to Follow." Unless these is some such designation at the end of the copy, the printer cannot be sure whether to close up and set aside the story or hold it open for additions.

CHAPTER III

HEADLINE WRITING

Few newspaper readers realize that the modern American headline, in the form in which it appears throughout the pages of every daily, semi-weekly, and weekly newspaper in the land, is a native American invention and almost an exclusive possession of American newspapers—that it is barely fifty years old —that it is one of the most difficult and exacting kinds of writing that fall to the lot of the newspaper worker. It is one of the things that make the American newspaper typically American—up to the minute, interesting, and easy to read. Like the summary lead of the news-story, the verbatim interview, and many other inventions of the American newspaper man, it was developed to meet the needs of our busy, wide-awake life and, for all the faults of which unskilled hands make it guilty, it is one of the things that make our newspapers what they are—"newspapers" rather than "journals." That it is typically American is shown by the fact that it was adopted throughout the United

States almost on the very morning after its invention, and even today, fifty years later, is very slightly used in other countries outside the western hemisphere.

When the American citizen gleans the morning news out of twelve or sixteen newspaper pages of fine print and acquaints himself with all the world has done overnight, in the short space of time given to his morning coffee or his ride to the office, he is doing something that only an American citizen can do: He is extracting the gist of 60,000 to 80,000 words of reading matter in the space of time required to read half a column. To be sure, he is getting only the gist of the news, but the elaboration is there also and is in such shape as to be found without much hunting or wading through material that does not interest him. That is because his newspaper was written especially for him by men who realized how short a time he can devote to learning the world's events. It is because, before the paper was left on his doorstep, a newspaper desk man had painstakingly extracted the gist of all this news and put it in the most readily available shape.

When the statement is made that the American headline is a new thing and an American thing, the statement refers, not to the form of the headline, but to its content. The idea of placing a title or heading in larger, blacker type over every separate article is as old as printing. The practice, also, of dividing this heading into a series of decks, or layers, is not new. But the idea of saying something—of making a definite, concrete statement in the heading—is the new thing.

Early Headings.—Back in American colonial days, when newspapers were weekly budgets of opinion-molding editorials rather than recorders of events, editors were wont to place at the tops of their columns such headings as "Local Intelligence," "European Events," "Marine News." But the heading was a mere label of the kind of news contained in the column and the same label might be, and was, used day after day regardless of the significance of the facts that it announced. Even in the early days of the nineteenth century, when editors of daily newspapers tried to make their publications more interesting by expanding the single title into a series of display lines extending halfway down the column—limited in number only by the variety of type afforded by the office cases—the impressive headline was merely an elaboration of the first title or a series of subtitles appropriate to the variety of news reported below. To the American newspaper man of today it seems incredible that these trade ancestors of his could use so much type and at the same time say so little. It was as if they had purposely tried to put as many different labels on their bottle as possible, without revealing the secret of its contents.

The New Idea in Headings.—Not until the days of the American Civil War did newspaper editors conceive of the idea of substituting for this meaningless label a headline with something to say. They discovered it then because the war was their first big news story and, in handling it, they were forced to develop the means that are inherited by us of the present day. It was only within the previous twenty or thirty years that newspaper men had come to understand that news, rather than editorials, was what the American people wanted, and until their first big story came in the 60's they had been entirely concerned with learning what a vast number of things constituted the news and how to gather it accurately and speedily. Before the war they were so interested in securing facts that they cared little about the form in which they presented them, and their readers were glad enough to get the news without questioning the amount of time required to extract its kernel from the verbose, roundabout, boastful articles of the news-gatherers. But when day by day the news of the great war came into the cities, the editors began to realize that their readers were not satisfied if they had to plow through lengthy dissertations on the difficulties encountered by the brave correspondent to find at length his glowing account of the battle and its result. They wanted the result first and the explanation afterward. As the editors began to realize this, they turned the correspondents' stories around and put the result first—developing thereby what we now call the news-story summary lead. And to the same end, they threw out the label head which announced day by day "The Great War," or "News from the Front," and used its space to present the answer to the readers' great question—"Vicksburg is Taken"—"20,000 Killed on the Potomac." The first editor who substituted such a war bulletin for the standing label was the inventor of the American headline.

One Effect of War on Newspapers.—What the Civil War taught American newspaper men in headline writing was to make of the headline a bulletin of the news contained in the story below. More recent wars have taught them other things. The Spanish-American War added to this idea of using the same headlines as advertisements of the contents of their papers. It was during and just before this war that headlines grew in size and blackness and spread beyond the column rules until sometimes they stretched entirely across the front page. The sensational newspapers, to be sure, had been developing the advertising possibilities of their headlines, but it was the war that brought the "spread" and the "streamer" into common use. The present European war is bringing still other ideas into headline writing—the necessity and advantage of variety and originality. Perhaps it is leading to an overuse of display that will bring a reaction.

I. WHAT THE MODERN HEADLINE TRIES TO DO

The modern American headline has at present two distinct purposes: to bulletin the news and to advertise the news.

A News Bulletin.—The modern headline bulletins the news by presenting in summary form the content of the story printed below it. It selects the gist and the most salient facts in the story and displays them in concise, readable form for the benefit of the rapid reader who has not time to read the story. It is a complete thought that would be clear in itself without the explanations that follow. Its many-deck form makes possible the emphasizing of the most interesting phase of the story in the first deck and the presentation, deck by deck, of the subordinate facts that qualify it. If the headline is well written, the rapid reader need not read the story to know its content.

A News Advertisement.—The advertising value of the modern headline is a corollary of its bulletin nature. If the news bulletin is sufficiently interesting in wording and prominent in form, it catches the reader's eye and interests him in reading the story. This applies both when the reader is browsing through his paper and when he is looking over the news-stand's wares with the idea of buying a paper. The banner head, which is merely a news bulletin in large type across the top of the page, serves the same purpose in America as the news contents bills which the London newsboys display in selling their papers. It catches the eye and interests a possible buyer in what the paper has to tell. The sales value of this headline is evidenced by the fact that evening papers, which depend largely on street sales for their circulation, now use the banner head quite generally on every edition.

Is It Sensational?—In considering the advertising value of the large, black headline, it is necessary to point out the fact that large headlines are not in themselves an indication of sensationalism. The quality of sensationalism in American newspapers is not at all dependent upon make-up. The paper that is most conservative in its make-up may be extremely sensational in its appeal and "yellow" in its treatment of the news. The paper with the screaming front age may, on the other hand, be decidedly conservative .nd fair in its news. It is merely trying to sell its ditions. "Yellowness" is a matter of content and ppeal, rather than display and make-up.

[. HOW THE HEADLINE FULFILLS ITS PURPOSE

To constitute a bulletin and an advertisement of he news, the modern headline must possess several istinct characteristics:

1. **A Summary.**—It must, as a whole, summarize ıe story which it heads and present the gist of its ontent. It should display the facts of the story in keleton form.

2. **The Newsy Feature.**—It must present in the first eck the feature of the story—the thing that gives ıe story its news value. As all the emphasis is in the ɔp deck, this should be the most interesting. Since ıe news value of the story often hinges upon certain leas already in every reader's mind, the first deck hould make a direct appeal to these ideas. Whenever ıe story's entire interest is embodied in one word or ne phrase, as is often the case, that word or phrase hould be in the first deck.

3. **A Verb in Each Deck.**—The first deck, and as ar as possible every other deck, should contain a erb. As a bulletin of events, the headline must conain action, and only a verb or some part of a verb an express action. The tense of the verb also indiates the time of the story and avoids the use of dverbs of time.

4. **Definite Statements.**—The headline should con-

tain definite concrete information. General statements have no place in it. It is a bulletin of a specific event and as such it should be specific.

5. Easy to Grasp.—Each part of the headline should be easy to read. Unless the reader can grasp it and understand it clearly at a glance, it is of little value as a bulletin.

6. Complete in Itself.—The headline should be perfectly complete and clear in itself. It should contain the necessary qualification and explanation so that it is not necessary to read the story to understand it. The puzzling, mysterious title to be explained by its story has its place in other kinds of writing, but not in newspaper writing. No newspaper reader can be expected to go back and solve the meaning of the headline after he has read the story.

III. THE FORM OF THE HEADLINE

The form of the headline has become more or less established in American newspapers. Much latitude is permitted in the size and character of type and the combination of parts, but the character of the parts offers little possibility of novelty. Every headline is made up of a series of layers, or "decks," extending horizontally across one or more columns and separated by short horizontal rules. According to present-day practice, a headline may be made up of one, two, three, four, or even more decks. The headline of more than four decks is rare although formerly headlines often had as many as twenty decks. Each of the decks is built on a specified plan usually indicated in the office by a schedule. Each office ordinarily has laid out a group of headline models designed for special purposes and positions. The individual models are designated by number in the office and the number indicates the style and size of type, as well as the arrangement of decks. In writing a headline to be set up in any given form, the desk man must take into consideration not only the number of parts and the length of each part, as specified in the schedule, but also the number of letters and spaces in each line since the size of type designated regulates the number of letters in the line. The number of letters and spaces allowed is usually indicated in units on the schedule.

Kinds of Decks.—There are at present four varieties of headline decks in common use: (1) the cross-line; (2) the drop-line; (3) the pyramid; and (4) the hanging indention.

1. *The Cross-line.*—The cross-line is, as its name signifies, simply a single line stretching across the space allotted to the headline. In the one-column head, the cross-line may be "flush," so as to fill the entire space from column rule to column rule, or it may be short and centered in the space between the rules. For example:

PACKERS SUED BY ARKANSAS

HE KILLED THREE MEN

2. *The Drop-line.*—The drop-line is a cross-line that has been separated into two or more parts in

succeeding lines. Its first line begins flush with the left-hand column rule and extends to within two or three units of the other rule, leaving white space at the end. Its second line is indented two or three units at the left but extends to the right-hand rule. Its commonest form is in two lines, called the two-part drop-line:

CHRISTMAS FINDS PARIS
BEREFT OF HER YOUTH

STATE TO AID WAR
ON WHITE PLAGUE

In the three-part drop-line, the middle line is of the same length as the others but centered. All three lines are correspondingly shorter than in the two-part drop-line, e.g.:

NO STATESMEN
COME TO FRONT
DURING BIG WAR

The four-part drop-line (and the rare drop-line of more parts) is built on a similar scheme and the lines are correspondingly shorter:

SLAVS FORCE
TEUTONS OVER
BORDER, SAYS
RUSS REPORT

3. *The Pyramid Deck.*—The pyramid deck, commonly used as a subordinate deck, may be made up of any number of lines from two to five. It is distinguished by the fact that each of its lines is correspondingly shorter than the preceding line, and each is centered in the middle of the column. The last line sometimes contains only one word. It has the appearance of an inverted pyramid and appears most often in three-line and four-line form:

High Ocean Rates the Only Present
Emergency

New Milwaukee Sanatorium Has
Capacity for 250 Patients

Legislature Will Be Asked to En-
large Appropriation Made
for Work in 1913

Judges McMurdy and Sadler
Assert Law Would Curb
Powers to Restrict
Licenses

4. *The Hanging Indention.*—This is made up of a series of two or more lines, in which the first line fills the entire space between the column rules and the succeeding lines are indented at the left and flush with the rule at the right. The last line, indented like the others, usually does not fill the full space, although some newspapers require that the last line reach the right-hand rule also:

Mayor Now Disposed to Shift Park De-
partment to Refectory Building in
Franklin Park

Children's Museum to Stay—Mayor Dis-
posed to Shift Park Department to
Refectory Building in Franklin Park

Members of Ministerial Union Adopt
Resolution Opposing His Appearance
Here as a Revivalist and Calling His
Methods Irreverent

ACCEPTS ALTERNATIVE OFFERED
BY UNITED STATES IN CASE OF
THE PRIZE K D3, FORMERLY BRIT-
ISH VESSEL FARN

As variations of these four standard deck forms, several new varieties have appeared recently and have been used to some extent. One is the flush drop-line, consisting of a series of lines that entirely fill the space between the column rules:

**HARESFOOT TROUPE
LEAVES ON ANNUAL
ROAD TRIP MONDAY**

Another is a new treatment of the three-part and four-part drop-line. In it the first and last lines are written according to common practice, but the intermediate lines are full:

**FREIGHT TRAIN
WRECKED; SPREAD
OF RAILS CAUSE**

Combination of Decks. — With the four common kinds of decks as basis, newspaper men have devised various combinations of the various decks with the idea of combining symmetry with display. In so doing they have established certain precedents that are seldom violated. The cross-line and drop-line are the forms ordinarily used in display lines. The cross-line is commonly used for any deck, although most frequently as the first or third deck. Rarely is it seen as second or fourth. The drop-line usually appears as first deck, in two-, three-, or four-part form, and frequently as third deck, in two-part form under a three-part first deck. It is the form most often used in the top deck, but it is rarely seen in the second or fourth decks. The pyramid and hanging indention are ordinarily used as subordinate decks. They appear as intermediate decks—second and fourth—between display decks of cross-lines or drop-lines. Both forms may be used in the same headline, although ordinarily the two intermediate decks are of the same kind. When the two are used together it is customary to place the pyramid above.

Headlines are most commonly built in two, three, or four decks in present-day newspapers. The single-deck head is rare except as a department head or as a "jump" head on an inside page, and few newspapers use headlines of more than four decks. Headlines may be conveniently classified as major heads, for important stories placed at the top of the column, and subordinate heads, for less significant stories occupying space lower on the page.

The major headline usually consists of three or four decks set in the largest headline type used in the paper. If it is a four-deck head, its first deck is usually a two- or three-part drop-line, its third deck is a cross-line or a two-part drop-line, and its intermediate decks are pyramids or hanging indentions. If it is a three-deck headline, the only variation is the omission of the last deck.

The subordinate headline rarely has more than two decks. The first is usually a two-part drop-line or a cross-line. The second is always a pyramid or a hanging indention. The most frequent combinations are a drop-line and a pyramid, or a cross-line and a hanging indention.

Type Used in Headlines.—In the matter of type for

their headlines, newspapers follow precedents as in other respects. Almost without exception, they set the first deck, whether it be a cross-line or a drop-line, in capital letters. The third deck is likewise ordinarily in capitals. The decks in which pyramids and hanging indentions are used are either in capitals or in small letters with the important words capitalized.

The style of type in the top deck is quite uniformly an extra-condensed bold-face letter—usually one of the many varieties of extra-condensed Gothic. The reason for this is that the tall, narrow, very plain Gothic letter combines legibility and display with the greatest number of units per line. Some newspapers use a more extended, rounded letter for the first decks of subordinated headlines where the type is small, and, in some rare cases, use the extended letter in large heads, although the small number of units per line makes it a difficult head to write. In third-deck cross-lines less uniformity is shown; ordinarily a black-face letter is used but it may be of almost any font, even italic. Pyramids and hanging indentions are usually built up of black-face roman type, if they are in capitals and small letters, or of almost any bold-face letter if they are set in capitals. Uniformity of type is strictly followed in some papers, even to the extent of adopting a single style of letter for every kind of headline, while others endeavor to use every kind of type that their composing rooms afford. The increasing use of headlines set up on the linotype machine is, however, enforcing greater uniformity.

Headline type varies in size from 10-point to 36-,

48-, and even 72-point type in the first deck. The average in major heads is about 36-point, while in subordinate heads a smaller type is ordinarily employed. In other decks than the first, the usual size is 8-, 10-, or 12-point, although it may run larger in the third-deck cross-line.

IV. HOW THE HEADLINE IS BUILT

To fulfill its mission as a bulletin and an advertisement of the news, the headline has acquired a more or less stereotyped form which dictates the content and character of each deck's message. Part of this results from the relative display of the various decks and part of it from the demand in the mind of the reader which has been built up by headline practice. The experienced headline writer knows the requirements by instinct, for he has learned it from many mistakes and blunders. But the beginner, to develop the instinct, must go back to the elementary outlining of material necessary in the building of a successful headline. If he does this conscientiously and on paper while he is learning, he will form habits that will later enable him to do the work by instinct—and do it well.

We say that a headline is "built" and not "written," because each deck is put together separately and because the headline builder does not necessarily begin at the top deck and work down to the end. He undertakes each deck as a separate problem and may leave any deck until the last without regard to the order. If he has planned the separate parts carefully, the finished portions will fit together into a complete whole.

The first thing to be noticed in the building of the headline is the manner in which it is to be read. This largely determines the contents of its various parts. The headline is designed, in the first place, to suit the tastes of two very different kinds of readers. One is a rapid reader who scans rather than reads and takes into his mind only the words that his eye chances to fall upon. It is to interest him that the headline writer alternates brief display decks with more extensive decks in smaller type—just as the newspaper writer forcibly crowds his most interesting words into the first lines of paragraphs. Each is striving to catch the hurrying eye and hold it. The other reader is a more leisurely one who, once he has started to read a story, reads it from the top deck of its headline to its last word. Both kinds of readers are included in every newspaper's circulation and both must be pleased. The headline must therefore be clear and interesting to the man who reads only part of it, as well as to the man who reads it all.

Since it is easy enough to write for the man who reads it all, headline writers are more concerned with making a direct appeal to the rapid reader. This appeal is accomplished mainly by making some decks more attractive than others and concentrating the best work on them. And to be attractive to the rapid reader, the decks must be brief. In the four-deck headline common to most newspapers, this appeal is made in the first and third decks. We can be reasonably sure that the first deck will be read, if any is, and by setting the third in a type that makes it stand out beyond the second and fourth, we can count on having that read also. If the rapid reader peruses more than the first and third decks, it is likely to be after he has read the display decks. In the model headline below, for example, we are quite sure that the first deck and the cross-line will be read and we can logically expect that the second deck will be read after the cross-line.

MAY LET WOMEN —14½ Units
BE MUM ON AGE —14 Units

County Judge Scully Seeking Loophole in Law on Matter —9 Words

WOULD BOOM REGISTRY —19½ Units

Says He Will Remove First Ward Officials Living Outside of Precincts —11 Words

In laying out the content of these four decks, we shall therefore work on the supposition that the order of importance of the decks is first, third, second, fourth. To insure the proper emphasis we shall build them in that order. In the first deck we shall aim to summarize the entire story with the most significant part in the first line. Then we shall choose the next most interesting fact, preferably a striking one, for the cross-line. The other two decks we shall devote to explanation and elaboration of the display decks. To illustrate, let us take this story which appeared in a Chicago daily:

> Every known obstacle in the way of a start in building the new Union station is believed to have been removed.
>
> At yesterday's meeting of the city council an ordinance was unanimously passed, giving the Baltimore & Ohio Railroad the right to build a new coach and freight yard in the vicinity of Fifteenth and Lincoln streets. This will move the railroad's property out of the zone of development of the Union station and leave a clear field for the $65,000,000 project.
>
> The work on the new station must be started by March 23. March 15 is the time limit for beginning work on the Baltimore & Ohio's new yard.
>
> The council also passed an order in favor of the Pennsylvania Railroad, giving it the right to erect a temporary freight shed so that the work of wrecking the sheds along Canal street can be started.

The first step in building a headline for this story is to select the facts that should be presented in it. They are in general as follows:

The new Union station *may* now be built.

All known obstacles are out of the way.

This was accomplished by the city council's action yesterday.

The B. & O. Railroad was given the right to build a new coach and freight yard at Fifteenth and Lincoln streets to leave room for the station—must begin by March 15.

It is a $65,000,000 project.

The work must be under way by March 23.

The Pennsylvania Railroad is permitted to build temporary freight sheds to clear Canal street.

The significance of these facts was of course immediately clear to any newspaper desk man in Chicago. The project of building a new Union station had been hanging fire for many years and many obstacles had already been disposed of. The council's action in this case did not mean that it would be built or that the railroads would take advantage of its action. The story meant simply that the council had granted these privileges to remove what seemed to be the last obstacles and declared that the railroads must comply before the date specified to secure the privileges. To the headline writer, the story indicated that the outlook was promising, although he realized that the railroads might reject the proposal. His problem was to point out this significance in the facts so that his headline should not overstate the case.

With the above schedule of facts in mind as possible material for the headline, the next step is to arrange the facts in four groups to correspond with the four decks required. The first group must contain the most significant fact, and for the third group, facts should be selected that will accord with their prominent position and the shortness of the cross-line. The outline might be as follows:

1. The new Union station now seems assured.
2. Action of city council removes last obstacles in way of $65,000,000 project by granting privileges to railroads—one

privilege is to allow the B. & O. to move yards to Franklin and Fifteenth streets.

3. The work must begin by March 23.

4. Pennsylvania Railroad allowed to build temporary sheds to clear Canal street.

All that remains now is to express these groups of facts in words and phrases that will fit the required space. The first deck, we find, calls for two lines of 15 units each. Here are several possibilities that occur at once:

MAY BEGIN UNION
STATION IN MARCH

TO BREAK GROUND
FOR UNION DEPOT

MAY START WORK
ON UNION STATION

All of these are weak in that the first lines contain little of importance, and each is guilty of stretching the facts. The first is especially bad because it splits "Union Station." Let us try to keep within the facts:

LAST OBSTACLE TO
UNION DEPOT GONE

FIELD CLEAR FOR
NEW UNION DEPOT

RIGHT OF WAY OPEN
FOR UNION STATION

TRACK IS CLEARED
FOR UNION DEPOT

These are closer to the facts, but in each the first line is insignificant. Some of them are too "fat" and some have other faults. Evidently, since they are closer to the requirements, we may improve them by reversing the idea and beginning with the subject, thus:

NEW UNION DEPOT
MAY BE BUILT NOW

UNION DEPOT HAS
CLEAR FIELD NOW

NEW UNION DEPOT
HAS CLEAR FIELD

The last two are better, but "field" is not exactly the right word, although the reporter used it in his story. Substitute a synonym, thus:

NEW UNION DEPOT
HAS CLEAR TRACK

This is more effective because "track" has a railroad flavor. It indicates the possibility without assuming too much. The use of "depot" for "station" would probably be permitted in such a case by most newspapers.

Deciding that the above is satisfactory as first deck, we are ready to attack the cross-line and try to express its idea in the 20 units allowed.

WORK MUST BEGIN MARCH 23

This is good but it is five units too long.

WORK BEGINS MARCH 23

It fits the space but is not entirely true.

MARCH 23 IS TIME LIMIT

Space requirements are met but the line is not entirely clear. Noting that our issue is February 19, we may try a different way of expressing the time:

| ONE MONTH TIME LIMIT |

| MUST BEGIN IN A MONTH |

Not so good because the first is not clear and the second may cause difficulty because of the suppressed subject. Perhaps the third is the best.

We next juggle with the content of the second deck which is to contain about nine average words. As we expressed it in the outline, "Action of City Council Removes Last Obstacle in Way of $65,000,000 Project by Permitting B. & O. to Build New Freight Yards," it is twice too long. Try cutting the first expression, "Council Removes Last Obstacle in $65,000,000 Project by Permitting B. & O. to Build New Freight Yards." Still too long. "Council Removes Last Obstacle in $65,000,000 Project by Permitting B. & O. to Move Yards." This is shorter, but it is evident that we must sacrifice some of the content. "Council Removes Last Obstacle by Allowing B. & O. to Move Yards." This is possible but it involves hyphenating "obstacle." More juggling gives us this:

| City Council Opens Way |
| by Allowing B. & O. |
| To Move Yards |

The fourth deck undergoes similar manipulation to condense its content to ten words. "Pennsylvania Road Permitted to Build Temporary Sheds to Clear Canal Street," "Pennsylvania Road May Build Temporary Sheds to Clear Canal Street," "Pennsy Road May Build Temporary Sheds to Clear Canal Street." Our efforts to fit the space and avoid awkward breaks at the ends of the lines evolve this:

Pennsylvania Road May Build
Temporary Sheds to Clear
Canal Street

Selecting the best of the attempts for the various decks, we put the headline together as follows:

NEW UNION DEPOT
HAS CLEAR TRACK

City Council Opens Way
by Allowing B. & O.
to Move Yards

ONE MONTH TIME LIMIT

Pennsylvania Road May Build
Temporary Sheds to Clear
Canal Street

Another headline writer might have arranged the material thus:

1. The way is now clear for the new Union station.
2. City council opens way for $65,000,000 project but railroads must comply by March 23.
3. The last known obstacles are now removed.
4. B. & O. permitted to build new yard and Pennsylvania Railroad given right to build temporary sheds to clear Canal street.

Working on this basis he might have evolved the following headline:

UNION DEPOT HAS CLEAR TRACK NOW

Council Opens Way for $65,000,000 Terminal, Long Promised

LAST OBSTACLES REMOVED

B. & O. and Pennsylvania Roads May Move Yards and Freight Sheds

The average headline writer would hardly work out the material so minutely, but the process shown above illustrates the way in which the headline takes form in his mind. The student of headline writing will find it to his advantage to group his facts and formulate an outline of the various decks, as illustrated above, while he is learning to arrange his material unconsciously as the skilled desk man does.

V. MECHANICAL REQUIREMENTS

The building of this headline has brought out most of the technical details involved in headline writing but they may be summed up to advantage in a series of mechanical requirements which have grown up gradually with the development of the headline. This list can never be complete for any time after the day on which it is compiled, since every time a headline writer meets a new difficulty and solves it in a new and acceptable manner he has added another item to the list. In general, however, the precedents are well established and recognized in all offices.

1. Length of Lines.—It seems almost unnecessary to repeat that the first consideration in headline writing is to suit the length of the matter written to the space allotted to it, but the problem of line-length is the first stumbling block that the beginner meets. Because of the character of the headline and necessity for symmetry, the words must exactly—not almost—fill the space. More headlines are faulty in line-length than in almost any other essential, and, because of this, it is almost necessary to lay down the rule, "When in doubt, consider symmetry first and content afterward." For, no matter how nicely a given series of words may express the ideas, it cannot be used if it is too long or too short for the allotted space. "Type is not made of rubber," as the printers say, and if a line will hold only 19 units of type of a certain size, 19½ is as impossible as 40, for it will bulge the column rule and allow all the other lines to fall out of the form. Too short a line, in the same way, destroys the symmetry and an attempt to space out between the letters is an acknowledgment of failure. Unless the headline writer takes this into consideration he will cause endless trouble in the composing room and will spoil the appearance of his newspaper.

Counting the Letters.—Before attempting to write copy for any headline, the writer's first step is to ascertain the number of units which each line will hold and mark them opposite the lines on the headline model. In counting the units, he must figure each letter and each space (between words) as a unit. This applies to all letters except *M* and *W*, which count as 1½ units each—and *I* and the figure 1, which count as ½ unit each. All punctuation marks, except the dash and the double quotation mark, count as ½ unit each—the latter count as full units.

Latitude Allowed.—After the number of units allowed in the line is ascertained, the writer can then figure out exactly how much latitude he may take. In the drop-line, he may allow himself a margin of one unit each way. That is, if the normal line contains 16 units, he may consider 15 or 17 possible; but he should not go below 15 or above 17, for 18 or 19 will probably fill the entire line from rule to rule. In a cross-line, he should figure the maximum of the line, from rule to rule, and keep within that, allowing himself latitude only in the way of shortening the line. Less care is required in the building of the pyramid and hanging indention, for a certain amount of space may be taken up between words. In these decks it is well to figure the number of average words. Even so, it is necessary to take into consideration the length of the words, for ten polysyllables will take much more space than ten monosyllables. The careful headline writer takes care to estimate the length of the words so as to avoid breaking a word at the end of the line, and in the case of a hanging indention whose last line is full he must be even more careful.

Form of Copy.—To fulfill the space requirements it is best to write the head, line for line, in exactly the same form as it is to appear in type and to count the units in each line. This will also assist the compositor in setting up the headline. And no headline should be considered finished until the number of units in all its major lines corresponds exactly with the number allowed by the schedule. The bad appearance of headlines that are too short or too long is illustrated by these examples:

WELL KNOWN WESTERNER
KILLED BY TRAIN

ABERCROMBIE MAKES FINAL
FIGHT FOR CONTROL OF CARDS

2. Headline Based on Lead.—The mechanical requirements of newspaper make-up establish the necessity of basing the content of the headline on the content of the story's lead. All facts and ideas in the head must be taken from the lead and no facts should appear in the headline that are not included in the lead. This axiom is made necessary by the fact that in the newspaper office there is no surety that any article will retain its original length in print. The make-up man always has the right to cut down any story to suit the space at his command, and the breaking of unexpected news just before press time may require that he cut down any story—even to the lead. The editorial department prepares for this emergency by crowding the important facts in every story into its lead and by making the lead an adequate summary so that the killing of any number of paragraphs at the end will not destroy the story's clearness. The headline writer prepares for the emergency by confining himself to the lead, the only part of the story that he is sure will appear under his headline. If the lead is not an adequate summary and does not contain the facts that he feels must go into his headline, he must rewrite the lead so as to include the necessary additions. If the headline writer violates this rule, the reader is likely to be annoyed in having his attention drawn to a story by an interesting statement in a headline and then finding that the story itself contains no explanation or elaboration of the headline statement. He does not know that the original story contained further explanation that was cut off in the make-up, but he jumps to the conclusion that the headline writer has read something into the story on his own account. Even if the statement appears in the last paragraph, the reader is annoyed by having to read so far to find it. The evil resulting from the ignoring of this requirement is especially noticeable when the entire headline is based on some minor detail mentioned casually near the end of the story.

Headline versus Story.—The relation of the headline to the story should be after this fashion: The headline contains the gist of the story in skeleton form; the lead elaborates this skeleton in an adequate summary of the principal contents of the story; the running story elaborates the various items mentioned in the lead. In following out this scheme, the headline writer must remember that a lead is not always simply a single paragraph—it may fill half a column. And in the story that has no lead—the feature story or narrative human interest story—he need not heed the requirement at all for he is sure that such a story will appear in its entirety.

3. The Interrelation of Decks. — In the common headline of two or more decks, the interrelation of the contents and grammar of the various decks is very important. As was indicated in the model sample headline building above, it is ordinarily necessary to make a schedule of the contents of the story and outline the contents of the various decks before writing any of them. That is the mechanical process involved in solving the problem.

Interrelation of Content.—Each deck should, in

general, be devoted to the presentation of a separate idea, and the ideas in any given deck should not be greatly related to the ideas of other decks. Each should be an independent statement of fact. In relative importance also, the prominent cross-lines and drop-lines interspersed among the longer pyramids and hanging indentions should be considered first. But to what extent may the pyramids be mere elaborations of the prominent display lines? Many headlines, like the following, use the pyramid only as an explanation of the content of the first line—a reiteration of the first statement in more complete form:

VARDAMAN HAS GOOD LEAD

**Former Governor of Mississippi
Seems Sure of Senatorship**

But more common is the headline, like the following, in which the pyramid presents new or additional facts. It is better, too, since many readers do not read the pyramid and therefore miss the support it gives the display line.

**POSTAL SAVINGS BANK
OPENS AT CHICAGO**

**Two Hundred Depositors Stand in
Line to Start Accounts With
the Government**

In headlines of more than two decks, when there is any interrelation of content, each pyramid is usually related to the display line immediately preceding it.

Interlocking of Grammar.—Grammatical interrelation requires more careful study since it is often present when there is no interrelation of content. The brief, skeleton form of the headline makes necessary the suppression of many necessary parts of speech and the use of a part of speech expressed in one deck and understood in the next. The greatest difficulty is caused by the frequent suppression of the grammatical subject. Whether the succeeding decks be an elaboration of, or an addition to, the idea of the first, the limits of space may require that one noun do duty as subject for the verbs of several decks. The subject may be expressed in the first deck and understood in subsequent decks, thus:

BRYAN WILL EXAMINE
INTO HIS AUTHORITIES

Notifies Democratic Leader Underwood That If He Finds Press Report Correct Fur Will Fly

If the predicate is more significant, the subject may be suppressed in the first deck and expressed in a later deck, thus:

MUST SCRUB CITY HALL FLOOR

Melrose Boy Ordered by Court to Remove Stain Caused by Spitting Tobacco

Either practice is seen in the best newspapers, but both are full of dangers. Unless great care is taken, some of the verbs reaching backward or forward into other decks for subjects will be in the wrong tense, number, or voice, as in the following case:

WOMEN OF SOUTH ARE DEMANDING THE BALLOT

Says States Have Right to Define Electorate

This is especially true when the much-worked subject is a collective noun like "assembly," "class," or audience." The noun may be used correctly either as singular or as plural but it should not be used in both forms in the same headline, as in the following:

INVESTIGATE "WET" VICTORY

Texas Senate Passes Resolution to Inquire Into Late Election

In long heads there is danger in suppressing the subject of a later deck after several subjects have been expressed in previous decks. Very often any one of a number of previous nouns may be the subject of the later verb.

Even when the grammatical subject is expressed in each deck, it is well to keep the attention focused on the principal idea of the headline by employing synonyms and references to the principal subject in succeeding decks. Such a headline as the following results in too great scattering of interest:

**JEWELS SPILLED
ON SIDEWALK BY
DARING ROBBER**

**Paving Block is Hurled Through
Gotham Jewelry Store Window
in Broad Daylight**

TRAY OF DIAMONDS SEIZED

**Women Scream While Detectives
Shadowing Thieves Make
Prompt Capture**

One step beyond this is the suggestion that the verb of each deck be in the same voice, so that the tone of the headline may be uniformly active, or uniformly passive. An alternation of active and passive verbs involves an awkward lack of continuity.

When the subject is suppressed in the first deck, care must be taken in the expression of a subject in the second deck, or the result may be like the following:

URGES BUILDING INSPECTOR

**Movement Started After One is Killed
in Collapse of Structure**

Headlines are often seen in which no subject appears at all. This is especially bad when each deck requires a different subject as in this headline:

TO HEAR MILKMEN'S STORIES

Directs Health Board to Investigate Complaints of Favor

The grammatical interrelation of decks is sometimes carried to the extent of splitting a sentence between two decks, so that both are necessary for clearness. Such a practice is frowned upon by many newspapers since it is usually felt that each deck should be a complete sentence in itself. The following is an example of the "continuous" style:

LAUGHS AT THIEF'S ORDER

Not in Derision, but to Throw Policeman off Scent

This idea of breaking a sentence into a number of parts to develop decks is carried to its highest terms in the headlines of the Cincinnati *Enquirer*. As shown by an example at the end of this chapter, the subject constitutes the first deck, and each succeeding deck is merely a continuation of the same sentence.

The common feeling among headline writers is that the headline should be considered a continuous whole made up of a number of independent parts. So far as possible each deck should be independent in thought and grammar, but the several parts should be so constructed as to emphasize and develop one general idea when put together.

4. **Verbs in Headlines.**—It is now a recognized rule in most newspaper offices that every deck should contain a verb. The inclusion of the verb was the real change involved in the step from the label heading

of the old school to the bulletin headline of the present day. As soon as it became desirable to express action in the headline, the verb became necessary and, since action is the chief characteristic of the modern headline, a deck without a verb is rare. Readers have become so accustomed to the presence of the verb that they are unconsciously dissatisfied with the headline without a verb, even if it is excellent in other respects. Besides giving action to the heading, the verb through its tense expresses the time of the story. The following is an example of the ineffectiveness of the headline without a verb:

PROHIBITION IN ICELAND

Parliament Passes Measure Forbidding Sale of Alcoholic Liquors

Very often, however, although no verb is expressed, the heading is worded in such a way as to indicate the verb that is understood:

LIQUOR A MORAL QUESTION

Should Not Be Allowed to Wreck Political Parties, Says Wilson

The use of infinitives and participles in place of verbs is common. The future tense is often expressed by the infinitive because it saves space:

TO PENSION SCHOOL TEACHERS

The usual practice is to write all headlines in the present or future tense. Although the story may be concerned with an event which took place in the near past, the expression of the action in the present tense in the headline increases the vividness and emphasizes the freshness and timeliness of the news. Incidentally the present tense is easier to write because in most verbs it is shorter and requires no auxiliaries. Hence the headline of speech report reads "Hopkins Speaks on War," not "Hopkins Spoke on War." If it is an event to take place in the future, the infinitive saves the space taken by auxiliaries: e.g., "Hopkins to Speak on War."

Amusing and awkward headlines often result from the attempt to introduce the time into the head—whether the tense of the verb should be changed accordingly is a mooted point:

BADGERS VANQUISH
SUCKER GYM TEAM
LAST SATURDAY

In so far as the requirements of emphasis and space will permit, it is desirable to use active verbs rather than passive, because of the greater sense of action and vividness in the active voice; also because no auxiliaries or prepositions are required. "Flood Sweeps Snake Valley" or "Fire Ruins Hill Home" are more effective than "Snake Valley Swept by Flood," or "Hill Home Ruined by Fire." But whatever the voice of the first deck, it is desirable to use the same in succeeding decks. The question of voice is, however, often determined by the demands of emphasis. When the subject is less significant than the predicate, it is best to put the predicate first, in spite of the passive verb. Thus, "Governor Run Down by Tipsy Chauffeur" is more effective than "Tipsy Chauffeur Runs Down Governor," since the interest is in the word "governor."

5. Choice of Words.—The words used in headlines should be, above all, short, concise, and specific. The limits of space absolutely forbid the use of long words, especially in display lines. To this is added the fact that the heavy, black type of the headline is difficult to read when the words are long and the lines are not broken by frequent white spaces. The words must be concise and exact because the brief space permits of no rambling, and the headline, however short, must be clear at a glance. They must be specific and concrete so as to give an exact picture and create a vivid impression. The headline writer usually thinks twice before he uses a word of more than two syllables. He learns to speak concretely and to cast his thoughts into sharp, vivid words that snap. It may be said, in general, that words of Anglo-Saxon parentage are the most suitable for the headline—both in thought and size. Compare the following:

WIND SPREADS DEVASTATION

OR

WIND RUINS CORN CROP

PASS TRAFFIC LEGISLATION

OR

PASS NEW ROAD RULES

Repetition of important words is to be avoided. It is a generally accepted rule that no word shall appear twice in any of the decks of the same headline. The rule does not apply of course to articles and auxiliaries, but does apply to all nouns, verbs, adverbs, and adjectives. Hence a broad vocabulary is needed unless much time is to be wasted on the hunting of synonyms and synonymous expressions. In the same way, the headline writer avoids duplicating the words and expressions used in the first few lines of the lead. Variety has much to do with the interest of his text. The monotony of repetition is illustrated by this heading:

CARTER'S DEATH AVENGED

Friends Avenge Citizen's Death with Double Murder

The use of synonyms to avoid repetition is one of the commonest characteristics of the headline; e.g.:

STEAMSHIP CALLS FOR HELP

Ocean Liner, Centralia, Is Driven on California Shoals

Articles.—The value of space in the headline makes necessary in most cases the omission of articles and auxiliaries. If the headline is to convey a clear idea, there is little room for "a," "an," "the," etc. The thought appears in skeleton form. Although articles and other unimportant words are generally omitted, it is not considered bad form to include them to help out the balance.

Contractions and colloquialisms are treated in different ways by different newspapers. In some offices their use is strictly prohibited; in others much leniency is evident. A contraction is most often permitted when it is strictly in accord with the generally colloquial tone of the story. In such cases it is effective, while with a more serious subject it would be out of place. The colloquialism tends in general to give the headline a homely, whimsical tone and should be used accordingly, for example:

HUSBANDS AREN'T ALL ALIKE

Widow Smith Is Sure of It, for She's Had Four of 'em

Slang also has its place in headline writing in most offices, although headline writers are ordinarily urged to use it moderately. It should never of course be used in the heading of a serious story for it gives a careless, unconventional feeling that the reader unconsciously carries with him as he reads the story. Slang in headline writing may be treated on the same basis as in news writing. It should never be used when the idea may be expressed as vividly and as briefly in good English. The chief objection to slang is that it is constantly changing and is not understood by all the readers of the paper When there is the slightest doubt on this score, the necessity of clearness should bar it absolutely.

Unconventional Synonyms.—Much the same comment is due to the many handy, unconventional, short synonyms that headline writers have invented to suit the needs of their work. Common among them are "probe" and "quiz" for "investigate," "solons" for "legislators," "dope" for "prediction," "clash" for "controversy," "grill" for "cross-examine," "white plague" for "tuberculosis," "haven" for "hospital," "dip" for "pickpocket," "Pennsy" for "Pennsylvania," "grab" for "acquisition," "fake" for "pseudo," "hello girl" for "telephone operator," "finest" for "policemen," etc. Some of these are actual misuses of good English words—such as "suicide" as a verb, "deny" for "refuse to grant," "win" as a noun, etc. The advantage of these words is that they are short and vivid; they express large ideas in limited space, and on that score many newspapers permit their use. But headline writers generally are admonished to use them with care and to be loathe to coin a new word or misuse an old one in headline writing as in other writing.

Reformed or simplified spelling is not permitted in the headlines of most newspapers any more than in their stories. It will be a boon to the headline writer if it is ever generally adopted, but now the newspapers that use it are few and far between.

Rhyme and alliteration are likewise in high disfavor. The jingle of a rhyming drop-line is usually considered objectionable and the stuttering alliteration is frowned upon. Occasionally when the tone of a story demands a humorous, trivial treatment, the headline writer seeks rhyme or alliteration for their effect. But in the average serious story the jingle is bad because it calls attention to itself, at the expense of its content. As in all other newspaper writing, headline words should convey the thought without obtruding themselves. The effect is illustrated by the following:

JACKSON REPLIES
PATTERSON LIES

TEACHING TEACHERS
TO TEACH TRADESMEN

6. Style in Headlines.—The ordinary rules of English and newspaper typographical style are followed in general in matters of punctuation, abbreviation, quotation, figures, etc., although some special uses have developed.

Punctuation is used as little as possible. No periods are used at the ends of decks except, in some offices, at the end of pyramids and hanging indentions. The period is seldom seen at the end of display decks. Commas are almost never used in display decks and are avoided as much as possible in other decks. When the use of two independent clauses, not joined by a conjunction, requires a separating punctuation point, the semicolon or the dash is used. The usual custom is to use the semicolon in display decks because it requires little space—thus:

HORSE STARTS AUTO; CAN'T
STOP IT; GETS RUN OVER

In pyramids and hanging indentions, the dash is uniformly used, thus:

Stones are Thrown, Shots Fired—One of Wounded Men is Dead

Apostrophes are of course used when necessary; question marks and exclamation marks appear in their proper places.

Abbreviation in headlines is usually governed by office rule or practice. Every newspaper, to be sure, permits in its headlines any abbreviations sanctioned by its style sheet—such as "Mr.," "Mrs.," "Dr.," "Co.," etc. How much beyond the style book the matter of abbreviation may be carried depends on the office. Some newspapers permit "U. S.," "Prof.," "U. of W.," initials of railroads, and similar abbreviations; others strictly forbid them. In some cities, such initials and abbreviations as "L" for elevated railroad, "Y. M. C. A.," "S. I. T. & L. Co." for "Southern Iowa Traction and Light Company," "I. R. T." for "Interborough Rapid Transit Company," are permitted. The practice may be carried so far as to allow "S. P. U. G.," for "Society for Prevention of Useless Gifts," "S. P. C. A." for "Society for Prevention of Cruelty to Animals," "I. W. W." for "Independent Workers of the World," "I. R." for "Initiative and Referendum," "J. D. Jr." for the son of the oil magnate, "G. O. P." for "Republican party," etc. It may be said, in general, however, that excessive abbreviation is to be avoided, because it does not look well in type and because the meaning is not always clear.

Quotation marks are not used to any great extent in headlines because they take valuable space. The quoting of a single word is seldom necessary since any word or word usage that is well enough known to appear in the headline is too well known to require quoting. The use of quotation marks around slang words is usually a feeble apology. Occasionally when the headline is a direct quotation of some man's statement, quotation marks are used to emphasize it and to separate it from the authority. Many newspapers however consider quotation marks unnecessary here; a dash is often used instead. Besides taking space, the marks do not look well in type. To illustrate:

"STUDY CLUB" AIDS
MANY NEWCOMERS

"YOU ARE ROBBING POOR,"
DECLARES GENERAL VILLA

THIEVES! YOU ARE ROBBING
THE POOR—GENERAL VILLA

Figures are largely used in headlines of many newspapers because they are striking and saving of space, but their use is frequently regulated by office rules. In some cases the headline writer must follow the rules laid down in the style sheet for all news writing. In other cases he may use more figures than the rules permit. The usual practice is to establish a definite dividing line—such as 10 or 100—and use figures for all numbers above the line and spell out numbers below except in certain specified cases. The commonest custom is to use figures for numbers of two or more digits and spell out one-digit numbers. In the headline, also, it is permissible to begin a sentence or a deck with figures in violation of the copy rule. When a number expressed in figures is longer than the corresponding word—as "1,000,000" or "million"—it is wise to use the word. A common usage is shown here:

75 SWEPT INTO RIVER

Seven Drowned When Ferry Steamer Hits Shoal and Sinks.

Division of words is not considered desirable in headlines, although it is permitted to some extent. In pyramids and hanging indentions, it is usually well to break a word at the end of a line, but in display lines the practice should be avoided. The bad appearance of hyphenated drop-lines is shown here:

MISS ANNA BARGE ENTER-
TAINED AT SOCIAL TEA

In the same way it is bad form to divide an infinitive, a noun and its article or modifiers, a preposition and its object between two lines. The appearance of an unimportant word, such as "an," "and," "but," "to," etc., is a violation of the idea of logical division of lines. Thus:

FARMER IS KICKED TO
DEATH BY HIS HORSE

7. Emphasis in Headlines.—The emphatic sentence beginning plays as important a part in headline writing as in other newspaper writing. The first word or words of every deck are the ones that catch the reader's eye and it is desirable to make them attractive. Headline writers, therefore, make an effort to place the emphasis at the beginning of each deck. This is especially true in two- or three-part drop-lines in the first deck. The first line should contain the most striking words in the deck, even if this requires grammatical transposition. In the following examples the second is a more effective advertisement of the news:

ENDLESS CHAIN TO COVER
STATE FOR BELGIUM RELIEF

BELGIUM AID WORK PUSHED
BY CHAIN OF STATE CLUBS

The last lines, however, must not be neglected. It is decidedly bad practice to pack the gist of the statement in the first line and then trail out the following lines with adverbs and other useless words to fill the space. The following will illustrate:

Y. M. C. A. AIDS SPECIAL MEN
WITH VERY GOOD RESULTS

INDOOR MEET SHOWS WORK
OF EXCEPTIONAL INTEREST

Every word in the headline must count. The display is too valuable to be wasted on words that simply fill space. Too many young headline writers pad out second and third lines with empty words to reach the required number of units. If the thought selected for the deck, when written in its briefest form, does not fill the space, it should be discarded or amplified with concrete details that add to its significance. Seldom is there a thought so bald that an attempt to give it greater concreteness will not fill the deck and improve it at the same time. The following examples show what might have been done with the padded decks above:

Y. M. C. A. AIDS SPECIAL MEN
IN SECURING NEEDED JOBS

INDOOR MEET SCORES TIED
IN THREE MAJOR EVENTS

Meaningless generalities have no place in headline writing. If the reporter has failed to reduce the thought to its most concrete form, the headline writer must analyze his expression to discover the exact meaning or significance. The general head has little defense. Witness the following generality and the concrete language that might have been used in its place:

DEMOCRATS FAIL TO GRAB
HARMONY SCHEME BY TAIL

DEMOCRATS FAIL TO CLOSE
WRANGLE ON STATE TICKET

ACCIDENT IN MILL
HAS FATAL RESULTS

FIVE MEN KILLED
IN MILL ACCIDENT

Exactness and definiteness in headline writing, as in lead writing, requires the use of names and identifications as well as general allusions to the actors, victims, places, etc. This is especially true of the three- and four-deck head which makes possible exact reference. The actor should not be passed over as merely "he" or "she"; somewhere in the several decks his or her name should appear. In accident and crime stories, the exact place should appear somewhere in a lower deck. The headline, in other words, should not only be a skeleton of the story, but a bulletin, an exact, definite summary that would be clear without future explanation. The following lacks concrete information:

USED SHELLS FOUND
AT SCENE OF MURDER

Shot Marks in Trees Show Where
Victim Was Killed

Ambiguity is closely related to the question of emphasis. Ambiguous words often lead to ludicrous and puzzling headline statements. They can be avoided only by great care in the use of words with two meanings and especially words that may be used either as nouns or verbs:

AUSTRIANS CLAIM
WINS OVER RUSS

8. Connotation of Headlines.—Because of the extreme brevity and baldness of headline statements, the writer of them must think of the meaning that the reader finds between the lines as well as in the words themselves. He must remember that since he has room only to suggest a thought, he must word his suggestion in such a way as to direct the reader toward the proper completion of the thought. He must, in other words, consider the connotation of his words and phrases. In newspaper parlance, connotation is called "tone" or "color," and the headline which leaves an opening for the reader to "read something into the story" is said to be "colored."

Impartiality is a headline virtue demanded in almost every newspaper office. The headline writer is given no more liberty in the matter of expressing opinions than is the reporter. There are, of course, a few newspapers that deliberately write headlines that prejudice the reader for or against the story to follow, but these newspapers do not put the policy in the form of an office rule or publish it in the editorial heading. Independent, unbiased newspapers generally insist that their headlines shall do no more than bulletin the news to follow. They forbid any attempt to prejudice the reader or to pass judgment on the facts. If the headline writer has an opinion, he must keep it to himself; to give an inkling of his personal feeling is a fault. He must be as impartial toward the facts he handles as the ideal judge.

Partiality and color usually creep into headlines indirectly by way of the connotations or associations of the words and expressions used. An unobtrusive adjective buried in a long deck may give the thought a twist that will try the case of the story before the reader learns a single fact. A derogatory noun used as a synonym may carry with it a prejudice that precludes open-mindedness. An overvivid verb may qualify its subject to the extent of reading in a final verdict. Each word must receive careful attention to keep out color. The following is an example of a headline that is an editorial upon, as well as a bulletin of, the news.

TWO ROCHESTER BOYS
GOT JUST DESERTS

Humorous Headlines.—The tone of a headline should strictly accord with the tone of its story. If the facts are serious and the story is a straightforward statement, the head should give the same feeling. If, however, the facts are treated lightly or humorously by the reporter, the headline writer may give his bulletin a humorous twist. While summarizing the news, he will also put the reader in the proper state of mind for the humorous article that follows. The following are examples of successful humorous headlines:

EVERYONE ON TRAIN PEEPED

HAS SMITH 5 WIFES? 'SURE'

JACK DILLON NEARLY
SINKS GUNBOAT SMITH

Nigh Sixty Year,
but Knows a 'Dip'
When He Sees One

Questions are often effectively used in headlines to enforce the impression given by the words. The headline may ask a direct question of the reader to interest him in the story—this kind of question is seldom effective. Or the content of the headline may be put in question form to indicate that the facts are problematical or supposititious, or to show that they represent a possibility. On occasion this use of the question is effective, but it may easily be overworked. The presence of several question headlines on the same page gives the reader the impression that the content of the entire newspaper is an uncertainty. The following illustrate the two kinds of question headlines:

WHERE DO COMPLAINTS AGAINST POLICE GO?

EDUCATION WILL END WAR?

Reference to authority is often necessary when the statement quoted in the headline is too striking to pass as the newspaper's own utterance or when the desk man wishes to relieve the newspaper somewhat of the responsibility for the declaration. The verb "says," or a synonym, is often used in such a case in the headline. A more recent method places the authority at the end of the deck, separated from the statement by a dash. Quotation marks may or may not be used in either case, according to office practice.

"DON'T BE TOO GOOD"—CARNEGIE

VI. FAULTS IN HEADLINE WRITING

The faults to be avoided in writing headlines are, in general, the violations of the newspaper precedents noted above. There are, however, certain faults that deserve special comment and repetition.

1. Waste of Space.—A newspaper headline contains no room for generalities, and yet the wasting of headline space is one of the commonest faults seen in newspapers. Unless the headline gives a concrete, definite statement of fact, that is clear in itself without further explanation, it is ordinarily a bad headline. The headline must give not only the nature of the news bulletined, but must include the exact facts that make it news. Many headlines refer to the chief actor in the story as "he" without once divulging his identity; they detail the results and circumstances of an event without mentioning the place or time of its occurrence. The fault may be avoided by testing the headline with the questions that it suggests in the reader's mind. Does it answer all the essential questions that would ordinarily occur to him as he reads it, e.g., when, where, who, how, why? If it does not answer some of them exactly, it is not a good headline.

2. Dishonesty.—Many headlines are faulty in that they are dishonest. They promise more than the story contains. By virtue of their advertising value, they attract the reader through the suggestion that they head stories dealing with certain facts—the stories then fail to contain the facts advertised. The fault is sometimes caused by an overzealous headline writer's attempt to present the story's significance—he reads too much into the facts. It is sometimes simply the result of a cutting down of the story after the headline writer has done his work; he has gone too deeply into the story for his facts.

3. Exaggeration.—Many headlines go beyond the facts in their stories to the extent of making statements that are untrue or libelous. The statement as presented by the reporter, backed up with qualifying words and explanations, may be safe and exact, but stripped of its explanations in the headline it becomes a falsehood or a libelous utterance. The headline writer has simply emphasized part of the statement or has actually gone beyond the facts, and the explanations that follow do not protect his newspaper. The fault sometimes results simply from the selection of too vivid or too strong a word.

4. Misrepresentation.—One step further is the headline that actually colors the news, not by misstatement, but by misrepresentation. The facts as presented are exact and truthful but they are phrased in such a way as to prejudice the reader before he reads the story. As suggested above, the average, reputable newspaper avoids such headlines, preferring to confine its comment and opinion to the editorial page.

VII. SPECIAL KINDS OF HEADS

1. The Jump Head.—This is a name given to the headline written for the second part of a story that is "broken over" from the front page to an inside page. The jump head introduces the continuation. In some cases the jump head is written by the desk man in advance of make-up; in others it is written by the make-up editor as the emergency of breaking the story arises. The usual jump head expresses the same facts as the original headline in less space and with less prominence. Its chief characteristic is in the manner of reducing the size of the first headline.

The jump head may be the original head set in smaller, more extended type, so that the same words fill the desired space. It may be the same headline, in type and wording, with one or more of the later decks omitted. Sometimes it is merely a repetition of the first deck in its original form. Generally, however, the jump head is the original head rewritten in more compact form. If the top deck of the first headline is a three-part drop-line, the jump head may be a two-part drop-line. A two-part drop-line may be changed into a single cross-line. In some cases the original words are used; in others only part of them appear. The jump head usually makes less attempt to summarize the story; its function is that of recalling the original headline. All of these things are regulated by office practice, however, and many headline schedules contain models of the jump heads to be used with various major heads. Here is an example of a headline and its jump head:

HUERTA AND FRIENDS
CONFER, DEFYING VIGIL
OF SECRET SERVICE

HUERTA AND FRIENDS
HOLD CONFERENCES

(Continued from Page One)

2. The Banner, or Streamer, Headline.—This is a name given to the headlines in large type that stretch across the top of an entire page. They are commonly used by American newspapers to emphasize the most important news and to assist newsboys in selling papers on the street or the news-stand. The banner sometimes appears as a single cross-line which serves as the top deck of the headline of the principal news story. In many papers the banner consists of a series of cross-lines, bulletining one or more stories. Usually when more than one cross-line appear, each is concerned with a different piece of news and serves as the top deck of a separate story. The top cross-line is, of course, concerned with the most important news and is given greater display than those that follow it. Its individual members serve as a striking table of contents of the columns below.

In the writing of the banner head, the advertising element predominates since the headline serves the purpose of the contents bill supplied to newsboys by English newspapers to assist them in attracting attention to their wares. Hence the type of the banner must be sufficiently large and clear to be readable at a distance, and its content must be such as to attract the eye and arouse interest or curiosity. With this requirement in mind, the headline writer constructs his banner heads in accordance with the same rules followed in other headlines. He uses a verb and makes the headline a complete statement of fact. He counts his letters and spaces and adjusts the line to the space allowed. When office practice permits or encourages variety in the make-up of succeeding editions, the headline writer often decides the wording of the banner without reference to space and then selects a type that will adjust the wording to the proper space. When his statement is short, he chooses a large extended type; when he needs more room, he selects small or condensed type.

3. Spread Heads, or Layouts.—The ordinary newspaper headline occupies only one column, and when it grows beyond the column rules it is distinguished by the name "spread," or "layout"; the latter word is borrowed from the art department. The spread was invented by a class of newspapers that try to avoid symmetrical and conventional make-up in displaying the news, and it has since been taken over by the majority of American newspapers. In character and content it differs from the usual one-column headline only in that it spreads over a number of columns. There are no rules for its form; originality is its chief characteristic. Its top deck, which is usually a drop-line of several parts, stretches across the top of the entire layout and may head any number of columns. The pyramids and cross-lines below it may stretch across the entire width of the layout, or cover only part of it. Sometimes several small decks, alike or different, occupy places side by side under the top deck. The story beneath may begin in any column under the spread, or up among the decks; its beginning is usually indicated by leaded or black-faced type and always by the omission of the rule that marks the top of the column.

To write a spread heading, great imagination and knowledge of type are necessary. The attempt is to display the news in a striking way and give the page an attractive appearance. The editor ordinarily makes a diagram of the top of the page and lays out the space carefully before he begins to write. After deciding upon the nature of the spread and the kind of type for each deck, he estimates the letters and spaces accommodated in each line. With this diagram as his model, he writes contents to fill it exactly. In the spread, more than in any other kind of headline, the words must fit exactly and fill the lines evenly.

4. Subheads.—Many newspapers break up the reading matter of their columns with small display lines, called subheads, inserted in the columns at specified intervals. Their purpose is to make the paper easier to read. Such display is used as the linotype machine affords—black-face, capitals, or small capitals—and the subheads are usually shorter than a full line. There are no rules governing the frequency of the subheads, but the ordinary practice is to insert a subhead about once in two hundred words. In content they correspond to chapter headings, since they attempt to summarize the paragraphs that follow or suggest their content in a vivid, interesting way. It is to be noted that a subhead is usually a complete statement, with a verb, and that it attempts to express the idea in an original way. In some cases, the subhead is inserted some distance ahead of the discussion that it suggests so that the reader must go almost to the next subhead before he finds its explanation; by that time the next subhead has caught his eye and his interest is carried further. The purpose is of course to keep up his attention and cause him to finish the article. The subheads are written in by the copy editor as he prepares the copy for the printer.

5. Overlines and Captions.—These are names applied to the printed titles and explanations which accompany illustrations. The overline is a title that is placed above the picture and is usually more of the nature of a label, or name, than an explanation. Many newspapers, however, apply the principles of headline writing to their overlines and make them newsy and interesting. Besides giving the name of the person or thing pictured below, the overline usually points out the picture's relation to the news of the day in a more or less striking way. The overline is frequently set in display type. The caption, which occupies a position beneath the illustration, is usually longer and more of the nature of an explanation of the picture. It describes the person or thing illustrated and points out the significance of the cut. Combined with the overline, it is often so complete in idea and detail that no further story is necessary to explain the printing of the picture. Captions and overlines are usually written by the desk men and must fit the more or less irregular space left by the art department in preparing the illustration.

VIII. UNUSUAL HEADLINES

Because of the desire of many newspapers to attain the unusual in make-up, new ideas in headline writing are constantly appearing and many are so good that they will probably be retained as a part of the newspaper's permanent equipment. Some are new kinds of decks; others are new combinations of decks. A few of the most interesting that have appeared recently are shown below:

Pyramid Top Deck:

ONCE FAMOUS
BEACH RUINED
BY FLAMES

One Sentence Heading (Cincinnati *Enquirer*):

HEALTH

Depends on Cleanliness

Is Belief of Ohio Agricultural Commission,

Which Proposes a Code For the Radical Sanitation of All Creameries

Editorial Headline (Los Angeles *Times*):

Clemency.

EXECUTIONS
POSTPONED.

Life of a Countess May be Spared.

Emperor Holds Back Firing Squad Until He Investigates Personally.

Headline with One-word Lines (Pittsburgh *Dispatch*):

Plot
Laid
Bare

Attorney Forney Tells Why
His Father-in-Law Was
Assaulted

CHAPTER IV

PROOFREADING

Proofreading is the purely mechanical process of noting the errors a printer makes in setting type. It is entirely concerned with mechanics and typography; it is not concerned with style or content. Unlike copyreading, it has nothing of the creative in it and implies no license to correct or alter the author's words. The final authority is the writer's copy; the proofreader's office is to make a detailed comparison of this written copy with the printer's mechanical version and to note all deviations from it. The young proofreader must impress this upon his mind at the outset.

Printer's proof is a hastily made impression of type matter devised to make easier the task of checking up the errors in the typography. It is prepared by the printer as soon as the type is set, and the operation is called *pulling a proof*. The printer places the composed type in a long, narrow metal tray, called a *galley*, passes an inked roller over the face of the type, spreads a sheet of thin paper over the galley, and takes the impression on the paper by passing a small roller over it or by hammering the paper into the type with a block of wood. The resulting impression is called a *galley proof.* When the proofreader has noted the errors in the galley proof and the printer has corrected the type accordingly, another proof is taken—a *revised proof* or *revise.* If a reading of the revise shows up many errors, a second revise may be necessary. Still further proofs are required after the type has been taken from the galley and *made up* into page form. These are called *page* and *form* proofs.

Book Proof.—In the magazine or book publishing office, the original galley proof and enough revises to insure mechanical perfection are read by the office force. A final galley proof, pulled after the last corrections have been made, is sent to the author for any small alterations in content he may desire. The type is then *paged,* and a proof of each page is read by the office proofreader and the author. If the page forms are to be electrotyped, a proof of the electro pages is read as a final checking up before the plates are placed on the press for printing. Even after the matter has been *made ready* on the press, the first two or three impressions, *form proofs,* are folded and read to see that the pages are in the right positions and printed properly. If the pages have not been electrotyped and the material is being printed directly from type, a pressman must watch the printed impressions constantly to note any breaking down of the type or sinking of type areas resulting in imperfect impression.

Newspaper Proof.—In the newspaper office, the first galley proof is corrected by professional proofreaders, or by members of the editorial staff if the paper is a small one. After the revise, a proof of each galley is sent to the managing editor, so that he can look over the day's edition before press time; another is sent to the news editor or make-up man to be used in making up the pages. After the final revise of the galleys, no further proofs are taken until the type has been placed in the forms of the printed pages. A form proof is then usually pulled for a survey of the make-up and the catching of any mixing of type or articles in the making-up. The only real proofreading done in the newspaper office is concerned with the galley proofs. But every newspaper worker should know how to correct proof quickly and accurately, for only the largest offices afford professional proofreaders. When they do, the proofreaders are members of the mechanical force, rather than the editorial staff; in fact, they are usually members of the typographical union.

The Copyholder.—Since proofreading is little more or less than a comparison of proof with copy, the proofreader usually needs an assistant, a copyholder, to follow the copy. The proofreader reads aloud—punctuation marks, capitals, paragraphing, type changes, as well as words—and the copyholder, following the copy, notes discrepancies. As the errors are discovered the proofreader marks the proof. This method is necessary to insure the discovery of omissions and additions that would escape notice if the copy were not followed. Quite often the proofreader follows the lines with a card to aid in concentration.

How the Printer Revises.—Before one can correct proof intelligently and accurately, he must know how the printer handles it in revising the type. His methods explain the more or less unusual means employed by the proofreader. The printer does not, in the first place, read through the proof in search of corrections; he simply glances down the margins of the proof and makes the corrections indicated there. He is not likely, therefore, to notice any corrections placed in the body of the proof. To attract his notice it is necessary to place all corrections in the margins opposite the lines containing errors and to mark them large enough so that he cannot miss them. When the proofreading sign in the margin has called his attention to the error and indicated its nature, he looks through the line for another mark indicating the exact location of the error. Both marks are necessary to insure accurate correction.

THE PROOF MARKS

The proofreading marks used in all offices and known to all printers, except in the smallest country offices, are as follows:

Kind of Type

Cap.	Change to capital letter.
s. c.	Change to small capital letter.
l. c.	Change to lower case, or small letter.
Rom.	Change to Roman type.
Ital.	Change to Italic type.
b. f.	Change to bold-face type.
w. f.	Letter marked is from wrong font.
+ ×	Letter marked is broken or imperfect.
9	Letter marked is reversed, or upside-down.

Punctuation

⊙	Insert period.
,/	Insert comma.
;/	Insert semi-colon.
(:)	Insert colon.
∨'	Insert apostrophe.
∨' ∨"	Insert quotation marks, single or double.
1/	Insert one-em dash.
2/	Insert two-em dash.
=/	Insert hyphen.

Position

//	Make lines parallel.
═	Make lines straight.
tr.	Transpose order of elements marked.

[Move to the left.

] Move to the right.

Move up.

Move down.

□ Indent one em.

Spacing

Put in space between words.

Take out space or correct uneven spacing between words.

Take out all space and close up.

Close up but leave some space.

Insert proper ligature.

Push down space that prints.

Insert space between letters.

| Straighten lateral margin.

lead Insert space between lines.

d. lead Reduce space between lines.

Paragraphing

¶ Begin a new paragraph.

No ¶ Do not begin a new paragraph.

Run in Make elements follow on same line.

Abbreviation

Spell out Substitute full form of word or number.

Figures Substitute figures.

Insertion and Omission

^ Caret indicates place where element in margin should be inserted.

Oblique line through letter indicates that it is to be changed or removed in accordance with margin mark.

Take out element indicated.

stet. Don't make change indicated; let it stand.

and Allow word to remain as it is.

Uncertainty

Qu. Is this right or according to copy?

Out. s.c. See copy to find what has been omitted in composition.

I. HOW TO USE THE PROOF MARKS

There are many technical questions which arise in connection with the use of the standard proofreading marks and many of them are settled only by office rules and practice. But the young proofreader will do well to consider them before he attempts to break away from old established customs or establish new precedents.

1. Position of Marks.—All proof marks should be placed in the margin opposite the error. The printer will not see the correction unless it is so indicated. But the margin signal is not enough. The error must also be indicated in the line so that the printer may know exactly to what word or letter the correction refers.

2. Use All the Marks.—The young proofreader often

wonders why it is necessary to use so many different marks when, as it seems to him, half a dozen will do the work as well. With an intelligent printer, he reasons, it is usually hardly necessary to indicate more than the position of errors and the omission and addition of words. In a large number of cases, to be sure, the error is so obvious that the printer needs only to have his attention called to it. But proofreading, like all other processes involving great accuracy, should be done with the greatest accuracy possible, and a sufficient number of marks to cover all possible cases is necessary. Sometimes the printer is not so intelligent as one might wish; often he is lazy and averse to making any corrections that he can avoid. He is full of excuses to save himself the trouble of resetting a word or a line. The proper proof mark, however, settles the matter beyond all dispute and shuts the door on half the excuses a lazy or stupid printer may make. In the case of the intelligent, reliable man, it saves him the time necessary to puzzle out what the proofreader meant. Again, the use of all the marks indicates to the printer that the proofreader knows his business—and that is often a very good impression to create in the composing room. Experience justifies, all in all, the use of all the proof marks and it is best to begin by learning them all at the outset; if any prove superfluous in any given case, it is easy to discard them.

3. Connecting Lines.—Some inexperienced proofreaders use a connecting line between the error in the line and the mark in the margin. That is, they draw a line from the error, through the typed matter, to the margin and place the proof mark on the end of it. This method may work out satisfactorily if there are few errors in the proof, but in general it is bad practice. If the proof is very "dirty" or has more than two errors in the same line, the many connecting lines result in great confusion. The standard practice is better in every case.

4. Neatness.—Every proofreader should take pride in the neatness of his work. Even if he does not consider neatness an evidence of his skill, he must remember that his careless work may result in serious confusion and delay in the composing room. He should use small proof marks, especially when he is reading closely set small type, and should place them exactly opposite the line which contains the error. If the mark is above or below the line, the printer does not know to what line it belongs. He should also use both margins; that is, he should place the correction in the margin nearest the error. The printer is accustomed to working in from one margin to the center of the line and then going to the other margin to work toward the center again. If a mark is placed in the left-hand margin to indicate an error near the right-hand end of the line, the result is confusion. This is especially true when there is more than one error in the same line.

5. Red Ink.—It is usually best to use red ink in correcting proof because the contrast between the red and the black emphasizes the corrections and because

SEVEN WORKMEN BURIED
IN GASOLENE EXPLOSION

Blast and Fires Destroy Experimentt.
Plant—Men in Blazing clothes
Leap from Widdows

Pittsfield, Ill. June 25.—Seven men were probaly fataly burned today by an explosion of gasolene in the works of the atlas Experiment company. All of the fourteen persons on the secondfloor leaped from the windows blazing like torches.

The explosion came at 3/20 p. m. while most of the workmen were in the Laboratory on the second floor. Without warning a 20 gallon retort burs into flame and blazing petrol [illegible] was sees flying about the room.

The cause of the explosion is not known. Experiments on a new procss for manufacturing were being made at the time, and is it thought that a retort made at the tim ebecame overheated.

"The first hiss of flame was followed by a blast of blaxing gasolene," said Charles R. samuels, foreman of the laboratory, this afternoon. "We boys had no times for frescapes—we jumped;

(Note; this example of corrected Proof is the printed version of the newspaper story which was edited on page 28 The first deck of its head-line was set by hand; the rest of the story was composed on a Linotype. machine.

EXAMPLE OF CORRECTED PROOF

it is easier to make small, legible marks with a fine pen than with a pencil.

6. Oblique Lines.—The use of oblique lines beside proof marks is often a cause of confusion and it is well to adopt a uniform practice. A good rule is to use an oblique line, at the right of the letter or word, to indicate that the letter or word is to be inserted. If the oblique line is used only in this case, it will have a definite purpose, besides serving as a separation between marks. For example: *tr.* means transpose, but *tr/* means insert *tr; lead* means more space between lines, but *lead/* means insert the word *lead; cap.* means capital letter, but *cap/* means insert the syllable *cap,* etc.

7. Marks in the Line.—To mark the location in the line of errors indicated in the margin, a similar uniform practice may be adopted. The caret (‸) should be used to indicate places where words, letters, or punctuation points are to be inserted. The oblique line drawn through the letter or point will indicate that the letter or mark is to be taken out or changed. The use of the two marks for the two purposes is a great aid to the printer in finding the errors to which the marginal corrections refer.

8. Inserted Material.—In inserting matter that has been omitted, if the omission consist of more than two or three words, it is best to write the omitted material in the margin near the proper place, put a line around it, run an arrow to the printed line, and indicate the place of insertion with a caret in the line. Material to be inserted should never be written between the lines, and in writing such material the proofreader should take pains to write it legibly. If more than a line has been omitted or the printer has mixed up several lines, it is well to bracket the faulty lines and write "See Copy" in the margin.

9. Follow Copy.—The proofreader should always follow the author's copy. In every case, the author's copy and the editor's corrections on it are his final authority unless office rules prescribe that he shall follow a certain typographical style and certain rules of spelling in spite of the author's practice. In most cases, however, the editor will adapt the copy to office rules and the proofreader may rely on his editing. In no case should a proofreader attempt to correct proof unless he has the copy at hand for comparison.

II. SOME MECHANICAL DETAILS

Space Justification.—In calling for the removal or insertion of letters or words, the proofreader must always bear in mind the mechanical difficulties under which the printer works. The compositor is dealing with one of the most inelastic things in the world—metal type—and one of the most immovable—the column rule. He cannot put into a line one more letter than the line will hold; if he does, the line will bulge the column rule and cause the lines above and below to drop out. He cannot take a word out without putting something in its place; else the line will be too short. When the proofreader calls for corrections that involve the insertion or removal of material in a line, the printer has only one recourse—he must catch up the added or subtracted space by altering the lines immediately above or below the changed line. The only elastic thing in the line is the space between the words and in any given line its limits of elasticity are seldom more than the width of two or three letters. Hence if the proofreader calls for the insertion of an eight-letter word, considerably more than can ordinarily be caught up in one line, the printer must run the last word over into the next line, catch up what he can there, run over into the third, and catch up the rest there. Sometimes one insertion or one removal will require the altering of four or five lines. The experienced proofreader tries, when the character of the copy permits, to minimize this difficulty by taking into consideration the alteration required by a correction. If he is merely substituting new words, he counts the letters and tries to fit them to the space occupied by the old. If he is inserting a number of words, he tries to insert just enough to fill an entire line so that only two lines will be affected.

Linotype Justification.—The problem of catching up space occupied by corrections is even more serious in linotype composition than in hand-set type. Here each alteration requires the resetting of the entire line, and each line that is affected by the catching-up process must be entirely reset. From the proofreader's standpoint this is bad, because, in resetting a line to make a correction, the printer may make an error in some other part of the line.

Irregular Spacing.—The question of space between words must also be considered. The proofreader sometimes objects to seeing large spaces between words in one line and small spaces in the next and is inclined to call for better spacing. Before he makes the marks, however, he should look over the lines carefully to see whether better spacing is possible without much alteration and catching up. Every line of type must "justify"—must come out even—and sometimes the variation in word lengths makes impossible even word-spacing. Sometimes, of course, a printer is careless in this regard and wastes space in justifying; again he may purposely space out material to increase the amount he has set—since he is usually paid on a space rate. Then it is well for the proofreader to catch him up and require proper justification in his work.

III. WHAT ERRORS TO LOOK FOR

In addition to the errors that may be classed as variations from copy—spelling, punctuation, and content—there are certain mechanical errors that the proofreader must watch for carefully.

1. Alignment.—Every line of type should be entirely or reasonably straight; that is, the bottoms of the letters should all be on the same straight line. In the case of material set up on a worn-out typesetting machine, perfect alignment is next to impossible, but in the case of hand-set material, almost all imperfect alignment is due to the printer's carelessness and should be corrected.

2. Broken or Imperfect Type.—This mechanical fault is common in all kinds of set and the strictness which the proofreader uses in correcting it depends upon the character of the work. Very often what appears to be imperfect type is merely imperfect proof, resulting from a hastily taken impression or poor ink. But since the proofreader has no way of knowing what is the real cause—and, if the work is particular—he is wise to mark the doubtful type. His mark will result at any rate in an inspection of the type.

3. Wrong Face.—The presence of type of a different size or face in any printed matter is impossible in machine work but more or less common in hand-set work. It results from what the printer calls "dirty case," a composing case in which the type has been carelessly distributed. Since the printer works more by feeling than by sight, some letters are more likely to be "wrong face" than others. The chief offenders are *i*, *o*, and *s*. In some kinds of work it is necessary to watch carefully to see that the small capitals *i* and *o* do not creep in as lower case.

4. Reversed Letters.—Upside-down characters are very common in hand-set work, especially when certain fonts are used. Those that cause the chief difficulty are the lower case *o, s, u, n, p, d, c, e*. Sometimes a reversed *n* is used for *u*, reversed *p* for *d*, etc. In every case the error can be noted by the fact that the reversed letter is slightly above the line in most fonts.

5. Other Faults.—Other mechanical errors that often get past the sharpest eye are: the insertion of a word that does not materially alter the sense; the repetition of the last word or syllable of one line at the beginning of the next; and the substitution of one word for another of almost the same length and meaning.

IV. HOW TO IDENTIFY VARIOUS KINDS OF COMPOSITION

It is well for the proofreader to be able to identify the various kinds of composition since certain errors common to one are impossible in another and the character of the composition often affects the corrections. There are three kinds in general use at the present time—linotype, monotype, and hand.

Linotype.—Since in linotype composition each line of type is one piece of metal cast integrally, the easiest way to identify it is by the character of its impression on proof or in the press. In the make-up of galley or page, the various line slugs often vary slightly in size or do not stand firmly on the bottom. Hence one line often stands above the others and makes a heavier impression; or one end of the line may be up and the other down, with a resulting variation of impression. In some cases also all the slugs may be slightly tilted so that the bottom or top of the type of each line is slightly heavier. This variation of impression *by lines* is a sure indication of the kind of set. If the work is done on a machine whose matrices are slightly worn, another identification often shows up—hair-lines between the letters resulting from the fact that the matrices have not fitted together closely and shreds of type metal have been forced between them. If the metal shreds rise high enough to touch the paper, they print very fine hair-lines that are hardly noticeable except under close scrutiny. Very imperfect alignment is often an identification of linotype composition.

Monotype.—Monotype work is more difficult to identify because it is done on a machine that casts each letter separately, so that the result is practically the same as hand work. It can often be identified by the spaces or quads that work up between the words and leave rectangular black impressions on the paper. In hand work, the printer usually uses several small spaces between two words; on the monotype machine, whose line justification is automatic, the spaces are a single piece of metal. This serves as an identification as the single piece is more likely to work up and put a black splotch between words and the splotch is plainly the impression of a single piece of metal. This, combined with the lack of errors common in hand-set and the varying line-impression of linotype work, makes identification possible.

Hand-set Type.—Hand composition is readily identified by the presence of wrong face letters and uneven justification in the same line, since these errors are impossible in machine work.

Errors Common to Various Sets.—In linotype composition, wrong face and reversed letters are impossible, but imperfect letters and bad alignment are common, plus the common typographical errors that are possible on the typewriter. In monotype composition, wrong face and reversed letters are impossible, except after corrections have been made, but the proofreader must watch for "weak" type. If much of the type is imperfect or uneven in impression, this is an indication that the type metal was too hot and the type is honeycombed; if the proofreader allows it to go through, much of it may break down in the press. All errors are possible in hand composition and the proofreader must be on the alert for wrong face and reversed type as well as the other errors noted.

CHAPTER V

NEWSPAPER MAKE-UP

After all the stories that make up an edition have been written, edited, provided with suitable headlines and set in type, after all the advertising has been secured, written, and composed, after all the copy for the editorial columns and other special sections has been "set up," there still remains the task of putting together this mass of material into the form of columns and pages ready for the stereotyper and pressman. This task is called make-up. It involves such a combination of mechanics and editorial problems that it can hardly be said to belong either to the composing room or editorial office. In fact, the task is usually performed by a man from each department working together over the same material. The problems involved are so numerous and complicated that it is impossible to point out anything more than general tendencies and common practices.

The importance of make-up, however, cannot be overestimated. Although the reader is less conscious of it, probably, than of any other characteristic of the newspaper, he is undoubtedly greatly influenced by the mere "looks" of the paper he reads. If clothes make the man, even more so does mere outward appearance make or unmake the newspaper. It is possible to cite many a newspaper whose pleasing, inviting make-up has brought popularity in spite of the fact that its contents are empty, trivial, inaccurate news reports, bolstered up with a weak-kneed, shifty editorial policy—and many a sound, reliable, readable paper has not achieved success simply because of uninviting physical appearance. Magazine editors spend much time and money on the physical appearance of their publications and ponder a long time over the slightest change, but many newspaper editors do not give the matter a thought. Absorbed in the reading matter that passes over their desks, they leave half the problem—that of presenting the reading matter—to a journeyman printer whose only interest is to get the forms closed as soon as possible. Then the editor wonders why the painstaking work of his editorial room and the strength of his editorial policy do not increase his circulation.

Evolution of Make-Up. — Average readers, and some newspaper men, think of the form and make-up of our daily news periodicals as a stereotyped, cut-and-dried form that someone started years ago and everyone since has accepted as the best. They forget that newspaper form and make-up, as we know them, are the result of a long, laborious evolution, a constant trying out and adopting of new ideas. The evolution, furthermore, is not yet completed, for each year brings changes that will last for generations to come. And in this evolution, more progress can be credited to the composing room than to the news office. Every step in the development is more or less directly related to the improvement of mechanical processes. The size and number of pages have changed with the development of printing presses. The character of type has changed with the invention of typesetting machinery. Illustrations have come in with the photographic process of engraving and have been violently affected by the general adoption of stereotyping.

Standardization.—The tendency of recent years has been decidedly toward standardization of make-up. Pages, after growing from a pamphlet size to a spread that was dubbed a "blanket sheet," have settled back into a convenient, pleasing size, so uniform that different papers vary but a few inches in height and width. Headlines have changed from the tiny label to the half-column cross-lines, and back again to the short-deck form that gives greater display in one-third the space. Column widths have shifted back and forth until they made the standard 12½ or 13 ems in all papers. Standardized advertising practice and standardized machinery have accomplished this. The number and position of departments have changed until almost every newspaper carries almost the same sections in the same places. The front page has developed under the growth of street sales from an unimportant cover to the position of most important page in the newspaper, and the back page is fast following suit. Every element of the present-day newspaper is the result of a slow growth brought about by altered mechanical, business, and editorial possibilities, and until the student of newspaper making realizes this, he is not ready to discuss the problems of make-up. Nothing is *right* in the newspaper simply because it is so; precedents are constantly changing and new ideas in make-up are as significant as new ideas in reporting and editing.

I. HOW A NEWSPAPER IS MADE UP

Before we can study the problems of make-up, we must investigate the mechanical processes involved. Much of the problem is dependent upon mechanical possibilities and the conditions under which the task must be done.

Who Makes Up the Paper.—Most newspapers are made up by an experienced printer under the personal guidance of a member of the editorial staff. The latter may be the managing editor, the assistant managing editor, or, if the newspaper is large, a special make-up man called the news editor. Department pages are made up by their editors. Part of the task is preliminary planning, because the act of making-up must be done very quickly. Throughout the day, as the various articles are being set in type, the news editor receives galley proofs and checks them over with a view to planning his make-up. He mentally classifies the articles as regards importance, nature, and headlines, and notes the position requirements slugged into the stories by the city or managing editor. He may even make a diagram of the various pages to assist him in visualizing the finished paper. Just before press time he takes the bundle of proofs and his diagram to the composing room and begins the work of making-up. The material is heterogeneously laid out in galleys of type and his problem is to direct the printer in sorting the mass and fitting it into the rectangular steel "chases" that bound the forms, so many columns wide and so many inches high.

The Make-Up Man's Problems.—The task is complicated by the fact that no two stories are of the same length and usually nothing fits into the place in which it is intended to go. Two stories, for example, whose similar heads call for a balanced position, may vary several inches in length; to place on a line the small headlines below them, the make-up man must quickly decide whether to throw away the last part of one story or break it over into another column or page. Another article is just long enough to fill all of the column except an inch at the end; the make-up man must find a filler for the space, "lead" out the story with strips of metal between the lines, or cut it down to leave room for a short story below it. Perhaps the desk man has written too long a banner head for the type designated; the banner must be reset in more condensed type or cut to fit the space. Sometimes the cutting of a story requires the resetting of several lines to bring the cut at the end of a sentence. The number of mechanical difficulties that arise is infinite. At the same time, while wrestling with the problem of making things fit, the make-up man must remember the display and position demanded by the various pieces of news, for his work will receive the most careful scrutiny as soon as the first copy is off the press and he may be called to the managing editor's office to explain why he buried such-and-such a story at the bottom of the fifth page, although its importance required a place at the top of the fourth page.

No Time to Delay.—The time element is even more serious. With plenty of time and thought, almost anyone could solve the puzzle of making up an edition, but the make-up man must work with one eye on the clock. His task is the last step in the editorial department's work, and it is a serious offense if he delays the closing of the forms five minutes. The length of time required by the last mechanical steps involved in stereotyping and putting plates on the press is figured in seconds; with the mechanical force working at top speed to get an important edition on the street, the make-up man is allowed no time to putter over stories that do not fit.

Preparation for Final Make-Up.—Every effort, of course, is made in the modern newspaper plant to reduce the amount of make-up that must be done, before the last few minutes. As many pages as possible are made up and stereotyped long before press time. The editorial page, woman's page, society page, and in general most of the inside pages are made up hours in advance. The advertising is usually set up and placed in the forms long before press time; only the "Too Late to Classify" want-ad section need be left open and that can be placed on one of the news pages that is made up last. It is usually necessary to hold open two pages until the last minute, the front page and an inside page to accommodate break-overs crowded out of the front page by late news. Just before press time the inside page is made up and sent to the stereotypers. The front page is, however, left until the last second. The make-up man has it partly made up and knows fairly certainly what to do with the remainder of it, but he cannot lock the form until the editorial office sends down word that the last piece of news is in. Even after he has closed it up, the telegraph operator or a belated reporter may bring in a front page story that requires a complete remaking of the page.

Successive Editions.—In large offices the process of making up is not done once, but many times, each day. The number of editions put out by the average newspaper may range from two to ten, seldom less than four, and each must be made up anew to accommodate later news and suit the interest of varying circulation. The "all-day" newspaper is common in the cities, whether it be called an "afternoon" or a "morning" paper. In some cities one may buy after the theater at night the first edition of the following day's paper, dated the next day. The average city morning newspaper closes its first mail edition for distant points between nine and ten o'clock of the evening before. Another mail edition goes to press just before midnight, and a third between one and two A. M. The city edition is not closed until almost four in the morning, and it may consist of two editions, one for distribution by carriers and the other for morning street sale. The afternoon newspaper starts printing its first edition just before nine in the morning. Before eleven it is printing its noon edition. An early mail edition goes to press about noon, and the home edition for the carrier boys is on the press by three. After that it may issue a street edition to catch the reader going home from work, a late sporting edition, or a market edition containing closing quotations. There are rare cases of newspapers that issue ten editions a day, one each hour.

Varying Make-Up.—Each successive edition means a new task for the make-up man. The news pages must be remade to present later news. The mail editions must carry news of interest to readers outside the city, and the city editions must emphasize local events. The banner heads must be changed with each successive street edition, whether or not later news has come in. Usually certain pages, i.e., the editorial page, woman's page, advertising pages, and feature pages, remain the same throughout all the editions, but the remainder of the paper is changed throughout. As soon as the stereotypers have made a matrix of the front page, even before the plates are on the press, the make-up man has ripped open the form and begun the make-up of the next edition.

Make-Up Language.—Some of the expressions used in the printing office indicate the progress of the make-up man's work. When all the copy has been sent to the composing room by the editorial staff, the copy is *all in hand,* and when it is in type ready for make-up it is *all set* or *all up.* Each page *form,* consisting of a steel *chase* which forms the frame for the page of type, is made up on the *stone,* a table with a smooth stone or metal top. After the form is made up, it is *planed* down with a block of wood and a mallet to give it an even surface; any type or slugs that are not standing squarely on their bottoms are said to be *off their feet.* Before the form is *locked up* with wedge-shaped metal *quoins,* it is *justified*—all space at the bottoms of columns is taken up with *leads* between the lines so that no type will drop out when the form is taken away from the stone. Unimportant short material used to fill holes in the make-up is called *filler;* longer material of the same kind, especially feature material in early editions, is sometimes known as *bogus.* The form is then said to be *closed* and is *put away,* or turned over to the stereotypers; if any changes are required after it has been closed, it must be *ripped open.* In some offices, the paper is said to have been *put to bed* when the plates have been bolted on the press ready for printing. The expression is borrowed from experience with flat bed presses which print from type rather than from the semi-circular stereotype plates of the rotary presses commonly used today—*making ready* on the bed of the press is a laborious task common in offices which use flat bed presses.

II. THE REAL PROBLEM OF MAKE-UP

The study of newspaper make-up in its broader sense involves more than the mere mechanical process of transferring type from galleys to form and solving the puzzling problem of fitting stories into irregular spaces. It involves the entire study of the external, physical appearance of the finished newspaper—the problems of printing design and appeal. Studied from this point of view, many of the details involved must be decided upon long before the type galleys reach the make-up man's hands, before the stories are written and set up, even before the type and paper are purchased. In the real process of making up the paper, the make-up man is merely the last step. Many of the problems involved have no definite solution; many are merely questions of taste; to most of them there are many answers. But the young man who is just entering the newspaper business and the old newspaper man who has spent his life over the copy desk, too busy to think of the printer's work, will find it to his advantage to investigate the answers given to these questions by other newspaper men and the precedents followed in other newspapers. In no one of the following discussions will an attempt be made to point out the best practice; the intent is merely to open up the various problems to the interested student of the American newspaper and point out the possibilities. Further study must be carried on with the newspapers themselves. It is hoped that the discussion will arouse interest in the question of why one newspaper achieves a pleasing make-up and why another fails to be physically attractive.

The Front Page.—Because the front page is the most important page in the modern newspaper, it must be studied as a separate problem, although many of its questions apply with equal force to other pages. It is obvious that the necessity of uniformity throughout the newspaper requires that the inside pages conform with the front page in appearance, but it is equally apparent that the front page has many individual problems of its own.

1. *Body type* is the first question and it must be studied with relation to other type as well as to paper. The selection of body type—the type used in ordinary reading matter—involves both size and face, with reference to easy legibility and general appearance sought. What is said of front-page body type applies equally to the inside pages. It is obvious also that only type can be considered that is available on the linotype machine, since most newspapers use that machine or something like it.

The average newspaper reader would probably declare that all newspapers used the same size of type in the body of their reading matter. Such is not the case. The common practice among city newspapers is to set their reading matter in minion (7-point), with unimportant stories in nonpareil (6-point) and in some cases the editorials and important stories in brevier (8-point). Country and small city papers commonly use brevier throughout. Occasionally a country newspaper is found that uses bourgeois (9-point) or brevier on a 9-point body. The reason for this is that the city paper desires to crowd as much reading matter as possible into its pages. The country paper, on the other hand, cannot afford to set up so much material, and therefore uses a larger type; the country paper also is usually set by hand and brevier is easier to handle than minion. But now, when type size seems settled for all newspapers on the basis of their importance, the theory is upset by a large city newspaper which appears with the motto "Easy to Read and Worth Reading" and sets its reading matter in the country paper's type, brevier.

The question is, therefore, open to discussion and can be reduced to one or two issues. The large type insures greater ease of reading and a less crowded appearance. The small type saves space and gives more reading matter to the page. The difference is significant since it is possible to get 1.2 more lines of minion than brevier to the inch. This means that the paper using brevier is sacrificing about 20 lines per column, something over 150 words per column, or over 1,000 words per 7-column page, supposing that the reading matter were set solid. On the basis of readability versus space economy, the newspaper must select its type. It is obviously impossible for the newspaper to use a type smaller than minion or larger than brevier.

The face of the body type is even less obtrusive, but it has more to do with the appearance of the finished newspaper. It involves the question of tone and contrast. In choosing between a thin-faced or a blacker type, the editor must consider its relation to the headline type. Some newspapers seem to desire great contrast for they use a thin-faced body type with a very bold headline type and achieve a contrast that causes the headlines to stand out very prominently on a background that is almost white at a distance. Other newspapers seem to prefer to give their pages a uniformly gray tone without contrast, for they use moderately black body type with light-faced headline type, so that the headlines are accentuated only by their large size and the white space about them. Which is better, uniform tone or contrast, is a question of taste. A glance at a news-stand would convince the student that many an editor never gives the matter a thought, although it may mean the difference between an attractive and an unattractive newspaper.

2. *Display in body type* is significant because of its effect on the finished newspaper. Some newspapers set all their reading matter *solid* without emphasizing any individual parts; others try constantly to make the important leads and significant paragraphs stand out from the surrounding matter. The entire question is limited by the possibilities afforded by the linotype machine, since few newspapers will bother to set individual paragraphs by hand for the sake of display. There are in general only two kinds of display possible on the linotype machines in use in most offices—the use of larger, blacker type and the utilization of white space. The first involves setting all the reading matter in capitals, small capitals, or bold-face type; all of these are possible without changing the machine's magazine, for the average linotype has black face instead of italics. The second involves "leading out," placing strips of metal between the lines to

increase their distance apart, or indenting every line so that the type body is separated from the column rules by a line of white space on one or both sides. It is possible, of course, to set some reading matter in boxes (framed with a line on all four sides inside the column rules), or to use larger type or double measure (lines two columns long), but none of these things can be done without adjusting the machine and adding some handwork.

Whatever kind of display is used in the body type, the page is more readable since the important parts are emphasized. But this is done at the expense of uniformity and dignity of appearance. The utilization of white space instead of black letters accomplishes the display with less contrast. Whichever shall be used and how much are matters of taste to be settled with regard to the policy and appeal sought in the individual newspaper.

3. *Headline display* must be considered by itself and in its relation to body type. If contrast is sought a larger, blacker headline type is used and readability is an important factor. In size, headline type has grown from the 10-point and 12-point, formerly used, to 24-, 36-, and even 72-point in one-column heads; the average is probably 24- or 36-point in major heads and something smaller in subordinate heads. In general a condensed or extra-condensed type is used, but the degree of condensation varies. The thickness and blackness of the letter's line is also different in various newspapers. Some form of the plain Gothic letter is most commonly used in first decks, and a more

rounded letter, like the Cheltenham, appears frequently in the lower decks. Italic letters are seen in the headlines of many newspapers, especially in less significant stories. Greater standardization is now apparent since the setting of headlines on the linotype machines has become common. The matter of size and blackness of headline type can be settled only on the basis of desired display and contrast. But it must be remembered that the largest, blackest letters are not always the most legible; in fact many a headline type that is selected for display fails utterly because it is too hard to read.

The number of decks used depends entirely upon the amount of display desired. If originality and variety are desired in the make-up, one of the easiest ways to achieve them is to depart from the standard two- and four-deck forms. The headline of more than four decks is rare because it takes too much space and few readers are likely to read so many decks. Less than two decks is rarely used because it is hard to say enough in a single cross-line or drop-line, and the contrast between head and story is increased by the lack of a less prominent deck to shade from the one to the other. While a variety in decks gives a certain snap and originality to the paper, it also increases the difficulty of make-up because the unusual headline must be written for one position and cannot be used in another. The use of two varieties of major heads and two of subordinate heads greatly facilitates make-up. The matter of headline display must be decided upon the basis of the newspaper's policy. If the newspaper desires to convey the impression of solid, reliable conservatism, it uses small, inconspicuous headlines; if it desires to appear bright, wide-awake, and enterprising, it uses larger headlines of constantly varying appearance. In either case, however, it is possible to choose a type and form that will blend with the body type without appearing to jump off the page.

Banner headlines have undergone a strange evolution. They were invented to assist in street sales by advertising the news. As evening newspapers depend more largely on street sales than do morning papers, evening papers adopted them rather generally and morning papers did not. The question seems to have been decided mainly on the basis of circulation—is it mainly street sale or subscription? That was the status until the outbreak of the European War. Then, because of the bigness of the news, banners were adopted by many morning newspapers, some of which had a decided reputation for conservative make-up. As the war dragged along and began to lose some of its news value, these newspapers, instead of abandoning the banner headline, continued to use it for other news. We then saw them artificially featuring news for the mere purpose of creating a reason for their banner heads. What the outcome will be, time alone will decide. It seems evident, however, that since the streamer's only value is to assist the newsboy, it will gradually be abandoned by those newspapers which do not depend largely on street sales. Whether or not the banner improves the appearance of the paper is a matter of taste; certain it is that it uses much valuable space and is of little use to the paper that sells by monthly and yearly subscription.

Spreads and layouts have undergone the same evolution as banner heads. They have been borrowed from the evening papers, which used them for advertising purposes, by the morning newspapers which have little use for them. Many a newspaper that boasted of never using a spread more than once a year now is using them every day. It may be pointed out, further, that the spread has served a valuable purpose in emphasizing the occasional "big" story that the office must handle. To readers who are accustomed to modest, one-column headlines as a daily diet, the appearance of a two-column spread indicates news of great importance. Newspaper editors reserved the spread for the stories that called for a "big smash." But when the paper contains a "big smash" every day, there is no longer emphasis in it. When the readers become accustomed to spreads and banners every day, we wonder what the editors will do for the occasional "big story" that requires more emphasis. There are limits even to the extent to which display may be carried.

The use of subheads is another questionable point. They undoubtedly make the newspaper more readable, but they also break up its continuity. Many a system of headlines and body type carefully worked out to give the sheet a uniform, pleasing tone has been wrecked by the use of too prominent subheads. Much care must be taken in selecting them. If the editor desires great contrast on his page, he should of course use conspicuous subheads to accord with the conspicuous headlines; black-face type in capitals and lower case will accomplish this. If he desires a uniform tone, his subheads should set back into the paper; light-face capital or small capital subheads will break up his stories without resulting in great contrast. The frequency of the subheads should be decided on the same basis. In wording and content, the subhead must necessarily accord with the tone of the newspaper. The "snappy," colloquial subhead is decidedly out of place in the ponderous, thoughtful journal, and the empty, label subhead is as much at variance with the lively, popular sheet. All the various elements of the newspaper must accord with its policy.

4. *Number of Stories.*—Although many readers are not aware of it, newspapers vary greatly in the number and length of the stories carried in a single edition—especially on the front page. Many editors are convinced that their readers prefer to read a little about many different subjects; other editors are equally sure that their readers prefer to know all about a few subjects. It would appear that the first idea would be more in accord with the policy of the light, popular newspaper, and yet there are papers of this class that follow the definite policy of printing a few long stories. Certain it is that no newspaper has room enough to print all the news and some selection must be made. If many short stories are used, the page contains more headlines and has greater variety; it gives the reader the impression that he is getting a great amount of

news for his money. It is impossible, on the other hand, to treat any given story in an adequate, exhaustive way in the space afforded by this policy; the reader may get the idea that many things have been hinted at, but few have been fully covered. The result is that the many-story paper appears less thoughtful. It also contains less reading matter because much of the space is devoted to headlines. From the make-up man's point of view, it is much simpler to put together a page of many stories since their relative importance is not so marked and more elasticity is afforded. Beyond this, the decision is a matter of taste and policy which must be determined definitely; middle ground in the matter is difficult to maintain, since variation of length has so much to do with relative emphasis that it can hardly be trusted to a changing news staff. The character of the news thus handled is another matter which has little effect on the length of the stories; uniformly long stories may be as guilty of sensationalism as uniformly short stories and vice versa.

5. *The Breaking of Stories From the Front Page to a Later Page.*—There are newspapers that make a practice of uniformly completing front-page stories on that page. There are others that uniformly begin many stories on the front page and break them to inside pages. The latter practice gives the varied effect obtained by the use of many short stories, without sacrificing the feeling of conclusiveness in the handling of the news. There are certain things to be said for each practice. Much breaking over gives much

variety and interest to the front page; it crowds more subjects into that limited space; it gives the newspaper the appearance of carrying more news than it does; it leads the reader into the advertising pages. Break-overs, however, seriously complicate the task of make-up; any change of the front page requires change on an inside page and the making up of succeeding editions involves the remaking of many more forms. Many readers, also, find frequent break-overs very annoying; they object to turning back to page 6 to complete one story and then to page 3 to find the remainder of another.

When all or nearly all of the front-page stories are completed on that page without breaking over, the question arises of breaking long stories from column to column. If a story begins in column 2 and is too long to be completed in that column, where shall the rest of it be placed? Some papers prefer to place it at the top of the next column, thus carrying the reading matter continuously from column to column. Others place it at the bottom of the next column, separated by a cut-off rule at its head. The second practice, which is the commoner, reserves the top of each column for headlines, but it often involves some difficulty for the reader in finding the rest of the story. The former practice is best suited for the reader who peruses his newspaper from beginning to end like a book; the second is best for the reader who scans and reads at random. On this basis, the editor determines his policy.

6. *Illustrations.*—In former days when wood-cuts

were the only illustrations possible, the only question was one of cost. But since the development of the photographic process of engraving and the growth of syndicate cut services, illustrations have been brought within the reach of every newspaper and their use has become a real problem. Rare is the newspaper of today that does not use some illustrations. The question with the individual newspaper is what kind of illustrations, how large and how many, and in what position. On the front page the problem is especially pressing because illustrations of the right kind doubtless aid in the sale of papers. Some newspapers follow the practice of printing one cartoon on the front page each day; others use the space for a single half-tone illustration of some phase of the news; still others use a number of smaller cuts, usually portraits, scattered about the page. When the paper can secure the services of a good cartoonist, the cartoon is probably the best front-page illustration, but good cartoonists are rare and costly. It is much cheaper to hire a photographer or buy photographs from a syndicate; the cost of the engraving is about the same in either case. When no cartoonist is available, the question can usually be reduced to a choice of one large cut or several small ones. The large cut has the advantage in that it can present a more interesting picture than a one-column portrait; on the other hand, it seems to demand a position at the top of the page and occupies the space valuable for featuring important news. The small cuts break up the page, but they can be placed anywhere and occupy relatively unimportant space. The chief difficulty is the position. Unless symmetrically arranged small cuts make impossible any symmetry in typography—this of course is an advantage in some newspapers. If symmetrically arranged, the cuts give the page a stiff, formal appearance. A large cut or layout of small cuts is even more difficult to place. In a seven-column paper, the cut must be three, five, or seven columns wide to center in the page; in an eight-column paper it must be two or four columns wide to center. Two-column cuts are too narrow and four are too wide. Much doubt has been evidenced of late regarding the advisability of centering large cuts. If the cut occupies the center of the top of the page, it is cut in half when folded on the news-stand and loses its effectiveness. If placed on the right side so as to be on top on the news-stand, it occupies the most valuable space in the newspaper, besides giving an ungainly looking page when the paper is opened. If placed on the left or at the bottom it does not show on the news-stand and therefore loses its value as an attraction for buyers. Some editors can see little advantage in front-page cuts since, unless the stereotyping and press work are excellent, half-tone cuts do not print clearly. The entire problem of front-page illustration is a knotty one and is probably usually solved by the answer of the question, Is the cut worth to us the valuable space it fills?

7. *Position of Prominence.*—This is not a problem but a fact. All editors hold the same opinion in regard to the most prominent positions on the front page,

The two outside columns are the most prominent because they are set off by the margins at the side. The top of the last column to the right is the better for two reasons: (1) it is on top as the paper lies flat on the news-stands; (2) its story can be continued in the first column of the second page. The top of the last column to the left is next in prominence because, as the paper is opened, it is the logical beginning of the newspaper. The other columns are almost equal in importance, although those nearer the right are in plain sight on the news-stand and therefore are slightly better for display. When a large cut occupies the top of the page, the columns beginning under the cut are emphasized. In judging the importance of various columns, some editors consider the appearance of the newspaper on the news-stand; others think of it as opened in the reader's hands. Many editors solve the problem by devoting certain columns to certain news, i.e., the last on the right to local news, the last on the left to national news, the second from the left to news digest and other short material, etc. In some cases a special column is devoted each day to a special article. On inside pages the columns toward the left of each page are usually considered of greatest prominence.

8. *Symmetry.*—Balanced and symmetrical arrangement of headlines and other front-page display is a problem that almost every newspaper has wrestled with. Newspapers in America have ranged themselves into two groups in attempting to solve it. One group makes a conscious effort to attain symmetry; the

other group frankly avoids symmetry and seeks a changing and unbalanced front page. Between there are a few newspapers that maintain a semblance of symmetry at the top of the front page, but make no effort to balance the headlines in the lower half.

While the group that avoids symmetry can hardly be discussed in connection with the question of attaining a balanced front page, it is worth while to notice what the newspapers of this class seek to do. Instead of spreading the news out in an orderly way so as to give several stories an equal chance in attracting the reader's eye, these "dissymmetrical" front pages make an attempt to focus the reader's attention on one spot and to center all interest in one story. They do this, not by a disorderly, hit-or-miss arrangement of headlines, but by a carefully worked-out scheme of display that guides the eye to one spot. In this respect they are as orderly as the front pages which seek balance. There are, however, many editors who frankly follow no scheme of arrangement and simply seek variety by scattering headlines in a kaleidoscopically changing mass each day.

The problem of symmetrical arrangement is in the first place decidedly more difficult in the eight-column newspaper than in the seven-column. To display alternate columns and at the same time to emphasize the two outside columns immediately requires an odd number of columns. In the seven-column newspaper, symmetrical arrangement of the top of the page is usually attained by placing long, display headlines in the first, third, fifth, and seventh columns, and by using shorter, less prominent headlines in the second, fourth and sixth. This method emphasizes four stories and gives excellent balance. In some cases, the headlines in the third and fifth columns, while standing out above the smaller heads, are less prominent than the first and seventh headlines. This gives symmetry while emphasizing two stories. The same balance is accomplished in many seven-column pages by the use of two-column spreads in the first and second, and sixth and seventh columns, with a displayed headline in the fourth column. When a cut is used in the seven-column page, it is usually one column wide and in the fourth column, or three columns wide in the center of the page. In the latter case, two long heads can be balanced below it. The arrangement of the lower half of the page is usually determined by the fact that the stories under the prominent heads are the longest. The first and seventh stories frequently extend to the bottom of the column; the third and fifth extend almost to the bottom; the second, fourth and sixth are shorter. This brings small heads high up in the even-numbered columns and low down in the third and fifth columns. The problem then resolves itself into a matter of keeping these subordinate heads on the same horizontal lines.

Symmetry is more difficult to attain in eight columns because it requires that two columns be grouped together as displayed or undisplayed. Some newspapers solve it by breaking up the space with a cartoon or illustration, and almost invariably they place the cut at one side because the best front-page cut, the three-column cut, cannot be centered in eight columns. It matters not whether the cut is placed to the right or the left of the center, but different effects are attained through the choice of columns. If the cut occupies, for example, the fifth, sixth, and seventh columns, the most prominent headlines occupy the first, third, and eighth columns; less prominent heads occupy the second and fourth, and the fifth and seventh (under the cut). The same arrangement is worked out with the cut in the second, third, and fourth columns. If, however, the cut occupies the fourth, fifth, and sixth columns, the display is placed in the first, third, and eighth columns. In both cases, the balance of the lower half of the page works out just as it does in seven columns. When cuts are not available, the same effect is accomplished by a three-column box.

Make-up Problems of the Paper as a Whole.—Many of the questions discussed above apply equally well to the entire newspaper; uniformity requires that the front page set the precedent for all succeeding pages in the matter of type, display, and general form. There are other problems, however, not included above, that are of equal importance in the physical appearance of the newspaper.

1. *Number of Columns per Page.*—Until recently most newspapers have been printed in seven 13-em columns per page. Within the past few years, however, it has been found that a great saving of paper can be effected by the adoption of eight columns per page, without materially enlarging the sheet. The in-

creased cost of white paper has been largely the reason. The addition of an eighth column on each page of an eight-page newspaper gives an additional 160 inches of advertising space or over 10,000 words of reading matter without increasing the paper cost. The space for the extra column is ordinarily gained by reducing the width of the margins and by narrowing the columns from 13 to 12½ ems—that is, from $2\frac{1}{16}$ to $2\frac{1}{12}$ inches. The narrowing of the columns is not noticeable to the reader and ordinarily no corresponding reduction in advertising rates is made. The extra 20 inches of space per page is therefore clear gain, so far as paper cost is concerned. Some newspapers, however, have been slow in making the change because it necessitates a rebuilding of their presses to accommodate the larger plates.

2. *Number of Pages and Sections.*—On small newspapers which employ flat bed presses, the number of pages is definitely determined by the capacity of the press; all additional pages over the standard edition must be handled as insets or extra sections. This problem is therefore determined for them mechanically. To the newspaper which has a rotary press, the number of pages is a question open to discussion. It is usually determined on the basis of the amount of advertising carried; it is thought by many editors that not more than 40 or 45 per cent. of the newspaper's space should be devoted to advertising. If this proportion is exceeded it is thought that the newspaper loses value as a periodical and therefore as an advertising medium. In a seven-column, eight-page

paper, containing in all 56 columns, the amount of advertising space then should not exceed some 22 to 27 columns. If the advertising department secures more than about 25 columns of display for any one issue, the number of pages and amount of reading matter must be increased accordingly. Ordinarily the pages must be increased in multiples of four, since two-page insets are awkward to handle. When the number of pages is increased four or eight pages, the editor must then decide whether to print the additional pages as a second section or fold them in with the main body of the paper. In some offices this matter is settled once for all by the capacity of the press. When the paper has more than one press of large capacity, either plan is feasible, but the use of a second section doubles the speed with which the newspaper may be printed. On the large rotary presses, the increase in the number of pages decreases the output per minute accordingly; if half the pages can be printed as another section on a second press, the entire paper may be printed as quickly as one section. The speed is offset, however, by the inconvenience to the reader and the danger that many a subscriber will not receive the second section. If the second section plan is adopted the editor must also decide what to do with its first page. Shall he make it a second front page, as some newspapers do, or shall he devote it to some department, such as sports? He sometimes decides the matter by crowding as much advertising into the supplement as possible and selling the front page to a department store.

3. *Position of Advertising.*—This is a matter that is difficult to settle because the advertiser has his own ideas about the position of the space he buys and few newspapers can disregard his wishes. With due regard for his influence, certain phases of the question may be settled within the office. Since the front page has become something more valuable than a wrapper, most large papers are agreed that none of its space should be sold to the advertiser. The large papers that carry advertising on the front page are rare. But on the inside pages practices differ. Some papers succeed in crowding their advertisements together on advertising pages so that their reading pages are kept fairly free of advertising. Only the most powerful, however, are able to do this; the others find it necessary to yield to the advertiser's wish to be near reading matter. In the latter case they sell two or more columns of each inside page, endeavoring to keep the advertisements in the last pages. It is in the selection of the columns to sell that practices differ. Some papers confine their advertisements to the last two columns to the right, reserving the more prominent left-hand side of the page for reading matter; others sell the outside columns on either side, saving the space in the center; others crowd all advertisements into the bottom of the page; still others seem to leave the matter to the printer who makes up the advertisements. A common arrangement is the "pyramid page" which is made up with the widest advertisement at the bottom and successively narrower ads above it, each resting against the right-hand margin.

The result is an upright pyramid of ads on the bottom and right of the page and an inverted pyramid of reading matter at the top and left. The one definite statement that can be made in the matter is that, when business reasons compel the paper to listen to the advertiser's demands for position, the laying out of the advertisements should be considered by the editorial department so that an otherwise attractive make-up may not be marred by a careless and heterogeneous placing of ads. The location of advertisements is as much a part of the problem of make-up as the location of news articles.

4. *Advertising Display.*—There is a growing tendency toward limiting the amount of display to be allowed in advertisements. The movement was started by James Gordon Bennett, Sr., when he refused to allow cuts or display type in the advertisements of the New York *Herald.* Some newspapers have now gone so far as to tell their advertisers in advance what type and cuts may or may not be used, or by fixing a cash penalty for undue display. They realize that all attempts to increase the attractiveness and tone of their pages may be thwarted by one overdisplayed advertisement. The chief evidence of the movement is the tendency to limit the size and blackness of type and cuts in advertisements. Some newspapers now refuse to use any black-faced type larger than a certain specified size, requiring that larger type must be of the outline or shaded variety, which gives display without blackness. In the same way they refuse to use cuts of more than a certain blackness and forbid

the use of broad, black rules or other borders. They thus require that their advertisements conform to the same scheme of tone and contrast that they have selected for their news columns. Many advertisers are obstinate, however, and it is frequently necessary to set up their copy and show them a proof to convince them that they can secure as much display by judicious use of white space as by large type and black cuts. The matter of daily or frequent change of advertising copy is a problem rather beyond our discussion, but many editors are thinking about it in their attempt to make their advertisements as much a part of the reading matter of their papers as their news stories.

5. *Departmentizing.*—To what extent a newspaper's contents should be grouped into classified departments is a problem that has caused much discussion. The newspaper of former days was almost completely divided into departments and special columns. Every item was classified and placed in the proper section. The department scheme is still followed to a large extent in the more conservative of American newspapers. The objection to it, however, is that strict classification of the newspaper's news thwarts the proper displaying of the important stories of the day. To bury an important story in a department seems contrary to the newspaper man's instinct. Hence we find that the average newspaper is growing away from the department idea and the more radical editor is abandoning it altogether. When we find that the department scheme is maintained, we

find it modified by the practice of taking out of the department the important items and leaving under the department head only the routine news. That is, as soon as a sporting story becomes universally interesting it is taken out of the sporting page and displayed on the front page. In the same way, the society item of general interest, the unusual market story, the very important obituary, is found on the front page rather than in its proper classification. Certain departments still maintained in most newspapers are sports, society items, personals (in small papers), markets, obituaries, reviews and criticisms, editorials, etc. But the attempt to classify general news as local, state, national, foreign, shipping, railroad, etc., has been largely abandoned, except in the case of the smallest items. The reasons for and against the department idea depend, as do many other things in the newspaper, upon the clientele to which the editor caters. Undoubtedly the thoughtful, systematic reader, who either reads the entire paper or at least makes a point to read all news of certain kinds, likes to find items arranged in classified sections so that he can discover them all with little difficulty. The haphazard, chance reader, who scans at random seeking only the strikingly interesting or important news—the average American reader—is not willing to spend the time to read through the various departments in search of news. He likes to have the day's "specials" displayed at the top of the menu, for he wishes a few titbits rather than a complete, well-rounded meal. The editor decides the department problem on the basis of his circulation. Some of the common departments, however, deserve special study.

6. *The Editorials.*—The old-time American newspaper featured its editorials and gave them at least a page. Now, however, editorials have generally lost much of their prestige and in many newspapers are being maintained largely as an empty custom. Hence as the editorial page has shrunk gradually into a column or two, it has become a problem of make-up. Since it is customary to place the publisher's announcement at the head of the editorial page, that fact, more than the importance of the editorials themselves, determines its place. The average newspaper still uses a left-hand page near the center of the issue for its editorials, but since the page seldom contains more than two or three columns of editorials, the editor wonders what to do with the rest. Even if the editorials are set in larger type and wider columns, there is still half a page to fill. It is obviously no place for news, and we find a variety of practices exemplified. Some newspapers fill the remaining columns with editorials reprinted from other papers; some fill them with book and theatrical reviews; some develop a humor column and other features; some fill a large part of the space with a striking cartoon. The conservative newspaper finds these related subjects of value, but the more "popular" editor doubts their importance. Very often the page deteriorates into a dead-wood section which is devoted to space fillers, and no one is expected to read it. The development of features that make it as interesting as the rest of

the paper is an indication of great enterprise. Certain newspapers, however, have demonstrated that careful make-up and some consideration of content will make their editorial pages very valuable features.

The status and position of the editorial page suffered a marked change when certain so-called sensational newspapers hit upon the idea of using the editorials as circulation-builders. They at once established a precedent by moving the editorials to the back page. Their idea has been taken up by many less sensational newspapers, and now one of the most conservative journals in the country uses the back page regularly as an editorial section. The change in position has also brought a change in make-up. The back-page editorial is usually set in larger type and double-measure and the entire page is put together with great care. Symmetry is obtained by using the four outside columns for double-measure editorials and filling the central portion with cartoons, anecdotes or other features. This use of the back page was the first step toward developing a practical use for this important section of the newspaper and is undoubtedly very valuable to the newspaper which desires to make a feature of its opinions and comments.

7. *Other Special Sections.*—Some of the other departments that involve questions of make-up are the sporting page, the society section, markets, woman's section, obituaries. Even a page devoted to war news must be considered a department while it is maintained.

The sporting department is maintained as a separate page in almost all American newspapers. In some journals it is more than a page. It is in charge of a special editor and is given a fixed position. Some newspapers feature it by giving it the first page of the second section or by devoting to it a special four-page section on pink or green paper. The principal questions involved in its make-up are: to what extent shall important sporting items be lifted out of it, and to what extent shall other news be injected into it? Some newspapers make a practice of extracting important stories from it to be played up on the front page. Again when sports are dull, they use other news to fill up the sporting page. The practices depend entirely upon the importance awarded to the sporting section. When it is maintained as an important department, it is usually thought best to place all sporting news in it and to keep all other news out.

The society section usually varies in importance in inverse proportion with the size of the city in which the newspaper is published. Society news is of great importance in small cities and of less importance in large cities, although with the attempt to cater to women readers, society news has achieved a greater development in certain large cities. The make-up problem raised is whether society news should be maintained as a separate section of standard size and position, or whether it should be used as a convenient filler to utilize odd space. In newspapers that feature society news, the section is usually maintained in the same position each day under a prominent department heading. Certain journals even place the name of the society editor above it. The independence of the section is often accentuated by a different kind of typography. When the society editor prefers to devote the section to a few longer items, a distinguishing style of subhead is often selected for each item. When shorter items are used, they are often separated by asterisks, by classifying subheads, or even by the use of hanging indention in the set-up. Undoubtedly any variety of make-up that will make the section more attractive and different is of value. Society illustrations have been adopted by many newspapers, and when the newspaper cannot afford daily cuts of local social celebrities, it illustrates this page with syndicate pictures of national society lights. The society editor is usually allowed to break away from the newspaper's style sheet in the use of titles and tabooed expressions. It is to be noted, however, that few social sections are so independent that the managing editor hesitates to remove an important wedding notice or other significant social item to the front page.

The woman's section is a newcomer in the American newspaper because it is only recently that an attempt has been made to cater to the women readers. Its contents and make-up are, therefore, not to any great extent standardized. Each newspaper has its own ideas about the appeal to be made or is casting about blindly, keeping sharp watch for any indication of a successful strike. Certain newspapers have concluded that society news is women's news and have placed the two departments near together or have combined them. Almost every woman's section contains material on dress, fashions, and cooking. "Household Hints" is a common heading. After careful study of box-office business, some editors have placed theatrical news and criticism on the woman's page. Other journals, working on the basis that many women desire more thoughtful reading, have gone in for articles on feminism, suffrage, and related subjects. Whether to make the section light or thoughtful is still a question. It is certain in most editors' minds, however, that the page must be typographically artistic and different from the rest of the paper; the use of illustrations, especially portraits and fashion cuts, is common with most of them. The woman's page is still in its infancy, and no precedents or practices have as yet become established.

The market section is a standard feature in many newspapers. In some cases it is merely a column, containing a general story on market conditions and closing quotations. Other newspapers, considering that this is primarily the business man's page, make a feature of it and employ a special editor to take charge of it. In such a case it is ordinarily subdivided into departments, but its articles carry the newspaper's standard headlines. In make-up it offers no problems strictly characteristic.

Obituaries are mentioned here because many newspapers devote a special section to them and make a point of including biographical sketches to correspond with each day's deaths. Typography is the only make-up question involved. The attempt is usually to condense the section into the smallest possible space, and type is chosen with this idea in mind. In some newspapers, the obituaries are printed entirely in smaller type; in others the first paragraph is in ordinary type and the sketch is in finer type. In some cases, the succeeding obituaries are separated by black-face subheads indicating the deceased's full name; in others a rule separates the items and the obituary is distinguished by the surname in light-faced capital letters run in the first line as a side-head.

8. *The Back Page.*—Next to the front page, the back page is causing the greatest discussion at present. Until recently it was considered a wrapper and of small importance. Most newspapers sold as much as possible of it to advertisers and filled the remainder with unimportant material. Its real importance was pointed out by the so-called sensational newspapers that turned it into an editorial page and set a precedent that is being imitated by many papers of all classes. When its real value became apparent, other editors began to devise other uses for it. One of the earliest was the back-page comic section. Neither use seemed to many editors to justify a sacrifice of the large revenue to be obtained from advertisers for this valuable space. But in 1914 a new use was discovered when a Chicago newspaper turned the back page into a second front page devoted to light, interesting local news. The basic idea was not entirely new, for many small town and some smaller city papers had printed some local news on the back page, interspersed with advertisements. But to eliminate all advertisements

from its columns, repeat the journal's name at the top, and give it as much attention as the front page, was a new step. Whether the idea will be imitated elsewhere is not yet certain, but doubtless the near future will see a marked development in the use of the back page.

9. *Length and Number of Stories.*—As suggested in the discussion of the front page, newspapers show a great diversity of opinion in deciding whether to print a large number of short stories or a relatively small number of long articles. The reasons for and against, as discussed above, apply throughout the paper, although it may be added that the adoption of a definite policy in regard to the matter greatly facilitates the work of the make-up man. The one additional consideration is one of editing. Front-page stories, handled as they are with greater care, are ordinarily likely to be worth the space they occupy. Stories on the inside pages are in many cases long simply because they are loosely written and strung out beyond the length warranted by the facts. Many can be found in almost any newspaper that would be greatly improved by a thorough boiling. Except in the case of so-called human interest stories, nothing warrants an increase in length except the addition of more facts and details.

10. *Fillers.*—To what extent should the make-up man be allowed to use "fillers," two- or three-line items, to plug up the holes in his make-up? In the most carefully edited newspaper, fillers are never used, and the make-up must come out even without them.

In smaller offices, the practice is sanctioned to the extent of providing the make-up man with a galley of ready-made fillers. Jokes, anecdotes, axioms, epigrams, statistics, condensed statements of fact, advertising readers, and anything that can be crowded into two or three lines are used. Some editors use personal items as fillers or even slugs reading "Subscribe for the Leader," "Watch Our Want Ads." The use of fillers is of great assistance in make-up, but much objection is offered on the score that frequent fillers give the page a patchy appearance. Certain it is that they must be chosen with care when they are used, so that the reader may not be annoyed by inadvertently plunging into a silly joke at the bottom of a serious discussion. The practice, while not always bad, can easily be overworked. Afternoon papers are forced to use many fillers by the speed required in the office; many of them keep reprinted articles standing in type for emergencies.

11. *Syndicate Material.*—With the development of the syndicate method of supplying varied reading matter and illustrations in plate and matrix form, the newspaper editor has to give much thought to deciding how much of it to use. Certain it is that by patronizing syndicates he can supply more interesting material to his readers than he can afford to pay for if it must originate in his own office. He can give his readers a broader outlook on the news of the world in words and pictures than his staff can provide, and in general his syndicate material is written in better style than his staff articles. On the other

hand, many of his readers who take two newspapers, may find the same material in both and doubt the value of the subscriptions. Every inch of syndicate material, furthermore, crowds out an inch of local material and to all newspapers local news brings popularity and circulation. Many an unwise editor spends so much time and space on syndicate material that he prints little else—part of the money put into a better local staff would improve his business. Since neither a complete exclusion or an excessive use of syndicate material is advisable, it would seem wise to establish a definite office rule specifying what proportion of the news columns shall be devoted to each kind of material.

12. *Illustrations.*—The question of illustrating the inside pages is as important as that of pictorial art on the front page. It is a problem of what kind and how much. Syndicate pictures in matrix form can be purchased more cheaply than cuts can be made, but undoubtedly they do not have the news value of the local picture. An indistinct, bleary half-tone showing the "Ruins After the Broad Street Fire," snapped by the staff photographer, is certainly worth half a dozen excellent cuts of "Vesuvius in Eruption" or "The Miraflores Locks." A smudgy half-tone of "James Jones, Rock Valley Pioneer," draws many more readers than an excellent portrait of "The Duke of Fido in Hunting Attire." But not every editor has a staff photographer, a nearby engraver, and a purse to illustrate his local news. There is also the possibility of the ever-interesting diagrams, maps, and sketches, to illustrate the news, if some one can be

found to draw them. Regarding number of cuts, it must be remembered that illustrations take valuable space and very few newspapers have space to waste.

13. *Comics.*—The great rage at present is to print a large number of so-called "comics," either in regular series of comic strips, or as illustrations to chance jokes. They may be bought from the syndicates at a price that makes their use very desirable. Many editors, however, scorn their use. Others look upon them as a necessary evil like the Sunday comic supplement, detesting them while realizing that they sell papers. It is certain that when a paper runs a series of good comics, many readers will turn to them before reading the front page; it is also certain that the comic back pages of many city newspapers are read in advance of the news. But on the other hand, while granting this, editors dislike to base the popularity and sale of their newspaper on such trivial features. Hence we see all manner of practices and cannot rightfully condemn any of them without thought.

14. *Ease of Reading.*—This has become so important that "Easy to Read" has already appeared as a newspaper motto. All but the most conservative of American journals have accepted the idea that their pages must be easy to read. In making the decision they acknowledge that they are catering to the casual reader rather than to the thoughtful reader. They are admitting that the man who will wade through an unattractive newspaper is fast becoming unknown. Some of them are forgetting this rare creature entirely

and catering entirely to the casual reader; others are trying to reach both. When the latter ideal prevails, it is not a matter of news, but a matter of type and display, a matter of putting the words in the most legible, attractive form. The problem includes many of the questions discussed above. But once the matter of typography is settled, it is as much the problem of reporters and copyreaders as of make-up man. No printer's skill will make news easy to read unless it is written and edited with that idea in mind. This involves the use of short paragraphs, the frequent use of quotation marks, graphical figures, meaty statements, sentence emphasis, and the knack of developing ideas in headlines. If a newspaper is to be easy to read, everyone in the office must coöperate.

15. *What News to Emphasize.*—Many an editor leaves this important question to the hireling who makes up—except in the case of certain front-page stories. He forgets that it may be made a matter of policy so important that newspapers have won or failed by it. Too few are the offices that have a definite aim, that have analyzed their circulation, as the magazine editor analyzes his, and made a conscious effort to supply and display the kind of material desired by that circulation. Too often it is a matter of what comes into the office and is easiest to secure. One phase of the problem involves the relative value of local and telegraph news. Successful city dailies have made a definite study of this question and follow a definite scheme in the handling and placing of city, state, national and foreign news. Few smaller news-

papers have. Hence we find many small city dailies, while fighting a life-and-death battle with city competition, devoting their front pages to condensed telegraph news and neglecting or burying local events. Little thought is required to show that they cannot win, for their meager outside news is overshadowed by the columns of their city rivals. But, of course, the telegraph news, received perhaps in plate form, is cheaper to handle than local news. The matter is one that must be decided on the basis of circulation and competition. In a town near a great city, where the city dailies early in the morning supply the town's citizens with outside news, the only field left open to the small town daily is local news. In a town far away from a city, however, the city competition is not present and the local daily has both fields to cover. But the question is not entirely confined to small towns. Many large city newspapers are more exclusively local than the smallest country weekly. Sometimes the policy is wise; sometimes it is not—at any rate it deserves study in each individual case. No general rules can be followed.

One step beyond this is the question of the quality of news. Shall it be largely confined to crime and accident, or shall it be devoted to broader, more constructive subjects? This discussion is beyond the range of this book.

CHAPTER VI

SYNDICATE AND ASSOCIATION MATERIAL

Only a small proportion of the material printed in the average American newspaper today is prepared and written in the office. The present-day cost of production is so great that few newspapers can afford to hire a local staff large enough to write the newspaper's entire content every day. A large portion of their material is secured from various coöperative and commercial agencies which are able to keep down the cost for any individual newspaper by supplying the same material to a large number of papers in various localities. In some small newspapers nine-tenths of the reading matter, exclusive of advertisements, is syndicated or association material. The proportion is of course smaller in large city dailies, although most of them depend upon press associations for their telegraph news. Rare is the newspaper which does not devote at least ten per cent. of its space to material secured in coöperation with other publishers.

This coöperative material may be divided roughly

into two classes: association and syndicate material. Association material is primarily current news supplied daily by telephone or telegraph to enable newspapers to secure all the news of the world without maintaining an extensive system of correspondents. It includes also local news supplied in several large cities by city press associations. Syndicate material may include almost any kind of reading matter, supplied by wire, mail, or express, in typewritten form, proof form, plate form, or in stereotype mats. This material is made up of condensed telegraph news, features, fillers, editorials, illustrations, special articles, interviews, speech reports, sporting news, biographical material, ready-made advertisements, short stories, comics, ready-made campaigns, and many other varieties. It is supplied by various methods and various companies and enables an editor to fill up at small cost all the many columns of his newspaper which are not occupied by local news, editorials, and advertisements.

The idea behind the syndicates and associations, whatever may be their form and method, is coöperation, cutting down the cost of newspaper making by dividing it among a number of newspapers. By its means, an editor is able to publish a readable newspaper at a fraction of the cost of individual, independent operation. It would be impossible to include in this brief discussion all the various ways in which newspapers coöperate; it will be sufficient to sketch the commonest plans and the methods by which they are carried on.

I. THE PRESS ASSOCIATION

If every newspaper were forced to depend upon its own resources to gather all the news outside its own city, it would need a correspondent in every city, town, and hamlet throughout the entire world. In the early days of American journalism that is what every newspaper tried to do in a more or less extensive way. But no one newspaper was rich enough to cover the entire world with an adequate network of correspondents and the result was that various individual papers were constantly securing exclusive news of great import, to the dismay of their competitors, or being scooped on important news. The system was impossible; no one newspaper could secure all the news of the day through independent action. Beside this, the system led to a costly duplication of effort. If every one of the thousands of American newspapers had an adequate system of correspondents, most of the inhabitants of the globe would be newspaper correspondents. Coöperation in newsgathering and later in newswriting is necessary—a system by which many newspapers may club together in their correspondence and cover the news of the world through a system of correspondents who represent entire associations of publishers rather than single newspapers. The modern newspaper depends upon such an association for the major portion of its outside news and maintains only a few special correspondents in localities in which it is especially interested.

The association system was started in America in 1848 when several New York newspapers organized themselves into an Associated Press for coöperation in gathering the news of the city. The association has since extended its scope to include the news of the entire world and now supplies news to nine hundred newspapers throughout the country. The organization is still known as the Associated Press and is entirely coöperative. Each member assumes the obligation of supplying to the association the major portion of the news of its locality and in turn receives the news supplied by all the other members, rewritten and condensed in accord with the change in news value resulting from distance. The cost of operating the enterprise is divided proportionally among the many members. Certain newspapers, too small to be full members, receive a daily "pony" service—a condensed version of the world's news to the extent of a few hundred or few thousand words—and pay proportionately. The Associated Press members are in the main morning newspapers and the service is primarily a morning news service. Although it supplies to its members all the important news of the day, its principal field is news breaking between noon and midnight, too late for the evening papers. Ordinarily it has only one member in any city and does not supply its service to non-members.

Another great American news association is the United Press, which supplies telegraph news to evening papers. It is not coöperative, but is a private corporation which sells its service to evening papers at a fixed rate. Its relation to its customers is, however, similar to that of the Associated Press to its members, and in extent and operation it is much the same. Its field is news breaking between midnight and noon, too late for the morning papers. Among the other smaller press associations are the International News Association, operated by the Hearst newspapers and supplying news to a few other newspapers, the Laffan Service, operated by the New York *Sun*, and one or two others. There is a great rivalry between the various associations and a newspaper is as proud of a scoop secured by its association as of one made possible by its local staff. These associations take care of all American news and secure foreign news through correspondents in various parts of the world and in coöperation with the great newsgathering agencies of other countries, such as Reuter's, Havas, Fabre, Bullier, Central News, Stephani, and other agencies.

How the Association Works.—The manner in which these press associations gather and distribute news may be illustrated by the organization of the Associated Press. The entire country is divided into several main divisions with headquarters in New York, Chicago, Washington, Atlanta, Kansas City, San Francisco, and other large news centers. The division headquarters are connected by main trunk lines of leased telegraph wires, some using double or triple wire service. The heart of the entire system is New York City, and from there main trunks run to the West via Chicago, the South via Washington and Atlanta, and to various large cities of New England and New York State. The southern division has its headquarters in Atlanta, Georgia, but much of its news is filed at its two ends, Washington and Kansas City, and meets at Memphis. Washington constitutes a separate center in itself. Chicago is the headquarters of the central division and has trunk lines to the Northwest via Milwaukee and St. Paul, to the Southwest via Kansas City, to the Coast via Omaha, Denver, Salt Lake City, and to St. Louis. Located at various points on these main trunk lines and subordinate to the division headquarters are many district, or bureau, offices, which have charge of the newsgathering and distributing in their immediate vicinities. Some bureaus constitute relay points in which main trunk news is repeated, and from some bureaus go out state circuits, such as the New York state wire, the Kansas state wire, and the Michigan state wire. Grouped about the various bureau and division points are the "pony" services for small newspapers. The system is complicated and is not laid out on a strictly geographical basis because it must harmonize with the many elements of distance and interest that bind various sections of the country together.

In organization the division office resembles a newspaper editorial office. Into it run telegraph wires from the other division headquarters, from the district offices of its division, and from various points in its local district. The work of the office consists in receiving news from these various sources, rewriting it to meet the needs of more or less distant newspapers, and sending it out again to other divisions, to its district offices, and to the various papers in its district. For example, suppose that an important story is sent in to the Chicago division office from its correspondent at Springfield, Illinois. If it is of sufficient interest it is sent in full to the eastern and southern division headquarters and to its various district offices, in slightly condensed form to far western offices, and in greatly condensed form to the newspapers of its district that receive only "pony" service. If of less importance it is condensed for transmission to all points, except within the division. If of local interest only it is sent out only to papers within its own district. At the same time stories are coming in from other divisions that require similar treatment for further distribution. Still other stories, while being condensed for local distribution, are "relayed" through the office from east to west or west to east. All that is needed for the work of the office is a number of telegraph operators and a few editors, known as *filing editors,* who have a highly developed sense of news values. The work of district offices is similar although on a smaller basis. Part of their work is to send directly to the newspapers within the district which receive full or "pony" services.

Most of this material is handled by telegraph. Some correspondence and distribution within a small district is done by mail. Long stories, such as complete speeches, which may be secured in advance, are often sent out to the newspapers by mail, in typewritten or proof form, subject to "release" at a certain hour on a certain date or on the receipt of a release notice by wire. In some districts, pony services are distributed by long distance telephone, by a man in the district office reading into an instrument connected with a number of newspaper offices. In each office simultaneously a stenographer, with receivers clamped to his ears by a head-stall, takes down the news on a typewriter. When the service is received by telegraph, each newspaper must have a telegraph operator or secure the dispatches from the telegraph company's local agent. Most of the work is done by means of wires leased from the telegraph companies and the newspaper that has its own operator is reached directly by a "loop" from the local telegraph office. In New York City the Associated Press is transmitting news to its local members by means of the Morkrum Telegraph Printer, which operates a typewriter at the receiving end.

How the Service Comes to the Newspaper.—A newspaper that gets the complete service supplied to its district receives a more or less steady stream of matter from early in the day until after midnight, and its operator takes down the matter in continuous typewritten form on numbered sheets of copy paper. Each story is headed by a separate date line to indicate its source and its end is indicated by the mark "30" used by the operators. The telegraph editor receives it sheet by sheet, edits it to suit the style and policy of his newspaper, cuts it up into stories, and turns it over to the composing room. After it reaches his hands it is handled as if it were local copy written by the reporters, although there is so much more than he needs that much of it must be thrown away.

Although the service comes in a continuous stream,

rarely is a complete story sent at one time. For the benefit of newspapers that have several editions and wish to get an edition on the press soon after the service begins, as much of the important news as possible is crowded toward the beginning. Hence early in the day, about all the paper receives is a series of leads of important stories, each marked "More" at the end. Thus the essentials of the day's news are received first. Later in the day the remaining parts of these stories come in, labeled "Add Cincinnati Fire," "Add Springfield, Mass., Murder," "Follow Jackson Speech." Perhaps if there is much news, each story is broken into three or four takes arriving at various times. Later come "New Lead Cincinnati Fire," "Revised Lead Smith Trial," "Correction for Chicago Wreck." If the news is being supplied as fast as the correspondent gathers it, the same story may have a number of revised leads as the day progresses. Expecting this, the telegraph editor holds each story as long as possible, if he expects later development, or uses the new lead for a later edition. Frequent break-ins are made for corrections of facts and names in previous stories. More important than these are the "Bulletins" and "Flashes," cut in to hasten the service. For example, if the service is bringing an account of a football game, sent play by play from the press box at the field, the telegraph operator is likely to fall far behind in his sending, although he started sending introductory and descriptive matter long before the game started. Hence to aid the papers that are holding up extras waiting for results, the operator cuts in a "flash" at the end of each period, giving the score at that time. By the end of the game, although he is still sending accounts of plays early in the game, he stops long enough to flash the final score. The newspaper may then close its forms and save the rest of the detailed account for a later edition.

The continuous service is thus broken into many small parts, separated and distinguished by suitable guide-lines, and the telegraph editor must follow it closely to keep the news of his various editions up to the minute. The pony service is usually received in two or three "calls" of a few hundred words each. Since it is designed for small one-edition newspapers, it is sent consecutively and may be handled in one mass after it is all in the editor's hands.

II. CITY PRESS ASSOCIATION

In several large cities, notably New York, Chicago, and Pittsburgh, similar press associations are maintained, coöperatively or otherwise, for the gathering of local news. There are so many police courts, fire stations, hospitals, and other sources of news in a city like Chicago that no one newspaper can afford a city staff large enough to cover them all. By combining in a city association or buying from a city service, which maintains a staff of sixty or eighty reporters, they are able to cover the city at small cost. The city press service receives its news mainly by telephone from its reporters, has it written by a few office men, reproduced in many copies on a mimeograph machine (the desk man writes his story directly on the stencil) and sends it out through pneumatic tubes to various city newspaper offices. The newspaper editor depends largely on the city press for all routine news, usually rewriting the stories, and uses his own small staff to gather other news in which he is especially interested. From the point of view of the reporter, the city press affords excellent experience in newsgathering, but little opportunity to show writing ability. It is, however, the first place the inexperienced beginner goes to when he seeks a position in the city, for if he does well there he is sure of consideration from the local city editors.

III. SYNDICATE SERVICES

Syndicate material is supplied to newspapers mainly by commercial houses which sell their service regularly or on occasion, charging on the basis of column, page, or week. The kinds of material supplied include almost every kind of reading matter that the newspaper editor needs. Syndicate services in general may be divided into four different classes: ready-prints, plate or matrix services, copy or proof services, and picture services. The four groups are not distinct; several different kinds of service may be furnished by the same company and may be combined in a weekly service of various kinds.

Ready-Prints.—This name is applied to a kind of service whereby the inside pages of a newspaper are printed in the syndicate's own plant. It is intended especially for small weekly and semi-weekly newspapers and is dubbed "patent insides." In such a service, the syndicate prints the two or four inside pages of the newspaper, one side of the sheet, and the country editor prints the outside. The syndicate's pages are filled with general feature and informational material, set up in accordance with the newspaper's general size and appearance, and the content is changed for each edition. Such ready-prints cost the newspaper little, if any, more than white paper and the editor is saved one run on the press and half the composition of his newspaper. The syndicate makes its profit from the advertising carried in the ready-printed pages.

Plate Service.—The largest syndicate service received by small newspapers is a stereotype plate service sold by the column or the page. The content of the reading matter distributed thus is written and set in type in the syndicate office; it is then reproduced in the form of thin stereotype plates which are sent out to a large number of newspapers. The plates are one column wide, about two feet long and one-fourth inch thick, with grooved bottoms so that they may be fitted upon standard bases, kept by the newspaper, and thus be made type-high. The editor saws up the plates to fit the make-up of his newspaper and after he has used them returns them to the syndicate so that they can be melted up for future use. An editor who uses much of this matter is said to "edit his paper with a saw."

Almost any kind of reading matter can be purchased in plate form. The editor may buy several columns of condensed telegraph news, shipped to him each day early enough for his edition. His telegraph equipment then consists of a hack saw and a boy to meet the morning passenger train and receive the daily package of plates. He may buy all kinds of feature material, long or short, miscellaneous or classified. It may be a page of farm notes or a page on health. He may buy ready-made editorials and pert paragraphs, fillers and other short items, fashion notes, architectural ideas, political résumés, any kind of reading matter he desires. The syndicate will also supply him with plate illustrations of various kinds—cartoons, photographs of prominent persons and places, sketches, maps, humorous drawings, comic strips. One of the latest developments is a page of ready-made advertisements, written and set up in better form than the editor can accomplish, and cut in such a way as to allow him to insert the name of the local advertiser at the bottom. These advertisements may be classified and accompanied by suitable reading matter to attract the advertiser. All of this material is supplied in the form of plates as wide as the standard column, or several columns, if it is illustrative material. In handling it, the editor saws off as large a piece as he wants to use, slips it upon a base of the proper length, and locks it into the page form. Only a person experienced in such matters can distinguish it from material set in his own office.

Matrix Service.—A modification of the plate service is the distribution of reading matter in the form of papier-mâché stereotype mats. The editor receives the mat instead of the plate cast from it. A saving in shipping cost is thus accomplished, for the mats are very light, but the editor must have facilities for casting plates from the mats.

Biographical Syndicates.—There are regular services which supply biographical sketches and photographs of persons in the public eye. The sketch is printed in compact form and the picture is supplied in the form of a cut, a matrix, or a print that may be reproduced. The editor who buys such a service files the material in his "morgue" ready for instant use as soon as an obituary or biographical sketch in the daily paper is needed.

Photo Syndicates.—Illustrative material for the newspaper may be purchased at small cost from photo syndicates which make a business of taking news photographs in all parts of the world and supplying photographic prints to subscribers. The editor does not ordinarily buy a regular service, but receives batches of pictures at regular intervals, from which he may select those which he wishes to use. He pays for as many as he keeps and sends the rest back. Many of the war pictures that have appeared recently in American newspapers and magazines were secured in this way. In smaller newspapers, however, they were purchased in plate form from companies which bought them from photo syndicates.

Story Syndicates.—A large amount of the fiction and other lengthy reading matter carried by newspapers and small magazines is purchased from syndicates which make a specialty of supplying this kind of material. It is sold in typewritten or proof form and the purpose of the syndicate is to divide up the author's price among a number of publishers. The plan was started a few years ago by a New York magazine which made a business of syndicating to Sunday newspapers the excess of good material that came to it from its contributors. A large part of the content of the Sunday supplement is secured in this way. Many authors now sell syndicate rights on their works, as well as the right of publication in one magazine.

Syndicated Sunday Supplements.—With the growth of the special illustrated Sunday supplement, many schemes have been invented to supply newspapers with the large amount of material needed. One of them is the syndicated Sunday magazines which the newspaper uses as a special supplement of its Sunday paper. Some newspapers print these Sunday magazines in their own plants, or buy the exclusive use of them, but the majority of the newspapers buy their Sunday magazines from a syndicate which supplies them ready printed. There are of course several Sunday magazines and only one newspaper in any city buys the same magazine.

Weekly Syndicate Services.—A combination of the other kinds of feature service is the daily service designed especially for city newspapers of fair size. It consists of a daily bundle of printed pages containing enough reading matter to fill several newspapers and the stereotype matrices of a large number of pictures to illustrate it. The service contains news articles, special features, newsy interviews, editorials, jokes, sporting news, special department material, fillers, comics, cartoons, news photographs, national society news, fashion notes, health notes, material for special campaigns, and many other kinds of reading matter. The service is supplied only to one newspaper in any one city and, were it not for the necessity of publishing some local news, the editor could make his entire newspaper out of the syndicate material. Some of it, in fact, is as newsy and interesting as his telegraph news and can hardly be distinguished from the matter which he receives by wire. The entire service, supplied six days a week, costs him about as much as one good reporter. He clips out what he wishes to use and sends it directly to the composing room. Some newspapers use such a service to fill nine-tenths of their reading columns. The only danger is that they will use too much and neglect their city entirely.

CHAPTER VII

REWRITE AND FOLLOW STORIES

Among the various duties assigned to the desk man in the average newspaper office, there is more or less original writing of various kinds. A fair portion of the newspaper's content requires no newsgathering and hence may be written by a copyreader or some other office man. Some large offices hire special writers, called "rewrite" men, to do this office writing, but few staffs have such a minute division of duty. The average copyreader must be as ready to dash off a story from facts telephoned in by a reporter as to edit copy, as skilled at writing an obituary from facts dug out of the morgue as at writing headlines.

One special form of writing, which often falls to the hands of the desk man, consists of preparing the various kinds of rewrite and follow stories that constitute the foundation of each day's issue. This kind of work results from the fact that any newspaper regards as its news field only one-half the time that elapses between issues. The field of the morning newspaper is from about four o'clock the previous evening to four o'clock in the morning. The rest of the twenty-four hours, from four A. M. to four P. M., is the field of the evening paper. Whatever happens in the newspaper's own field of action is considered material for original newsgathering. Whatever happened in the preceding twelve hours was supposedly covered by its predecessor. Yet, since many newspaper readers buy only one paper a day, the morning paper cannot utterly disregard the events recounted in the previous evening paper, and the evening paper must present a summary of the news printed in the morning paper which appeared since its own last edition. This "re-hashing" of slightly old news results in the special kinds of news story known as the rewrite, the "boiled" story, and the follow-up, or follow, story.

The first step in the preparation of each day's issue is the writing of this "rehash." In some offices it is called "laying the foundation," and it is almost always done by some desk man or subordinate editor. In some small offices the city editor does it. The man who lays the foundation for the rehash arrives long before the rest of the staff and devotes himself to reading the newspapers that have appeared since the last edition of his own paper. He scans them carefully and clips out all items that deserve mention in his own paper. Some items he sets aside in a pile to be rewritten; other items he saves for the city editor to follow up; still others he designates for boiling. Sometimes he does the rewriting himself; in other cases he gives the task to another office man. In such case, he indicates by an underscored word or two the new element to be emphasized. The follow items he lists in the city editor's assignment sheet.

The idea behind the writing of all of these various kinds of "rehash" stories—rewrite or follow—is to give the account a new slant or a new twist. The writer has in mind not only the reader to whom the item is news, but also the reader who has seen the previous account. The difference between the two kinds of "rehash" story is that the rewrite contains nothing more than was in the original story, while the follow story presents later developments and additional facts. The rewrite is based on the first story entirely, whereas the follow requires additional newsgathering.

I. THE REWRITE STORY

The rewrite story, as suggested above, is nothing more or less than an old story retold from a new point of view, rejuvenated by a different treatment that makes it appear new. The rewrite man gives it this new twist by looking through it for a new feature, a new beginning. He writes a new lead on the old facts, playing up the new feature that he has decided to emphasize, and rewrites the entire story in accordance with the new point of view. The result contains no new facts but appears new. It is usually shorter, also, since the rehash is not worth as much space as fresh news.

In seeking this new feature, the rewrite man looks through the old story for some fact or element that the original writer failed to elaborate or emphasize.

If the original story played up the cause of the fire, he emphasizes the property loss or some other striking element. Perhaps he finds only a possibility of showing the relation between the story and some other event—it may be the third murder in two days. Perhaps the story gives him an opportunity to begin his rewrite with the next probable development. He shows the firemen searching the ruins, the police scouring for the robber, or the arrested culprit in the magistrate's court. These expedients failing, he may begin his story with some subordinate item expressed in more striking terms. The following are examples of rewrite leads:

FIRST STORY

Reckless driving was the charge made against Samuel Johnson, bartender, 367 N. Mills street, who was arraigned in municipal court this morning. He was severely censured by Judge Malcolm Smith for failing to slow up while passing the Lincoln school and running down a 4-year-old boy.

This is the third time Johnson has appeared before Judge Smith for reckless speeding and the judge said (and so on for several paragraphs including the judge's remarks).

REWRITE

"I advise you to quit driving an auto."

This advice was given to Samuel Johnson, bartender, 367 N. Mills street, who was arraigned in municipal court this morning on the charge of reckless driving.

FIRST STORY

Collision between a jitney bus driven by John Hanson and a private automobile at Mayner avenue and Newhall street at noon yesterday caused severe injuries to one youth and six other high school boys. They were hurled many feet through the air.

REWRITE

George Bandell, age 15, son of the president of the first national bank, was thrown from his seat in a jitney bus yesterday and severely injured. The bus collided with a private automobile at the corner of Mayner avenue and Newhall street and seven high school boys, including Bandell, were hurled through the air.

The newsiest beginning that the clever rewrite man has at his disposal is usually a forecast of a subsequent development. After reading the story clipped from the previous edition he can usually tell without investigation just about what is happening at the time of his writing, twelve hours later. He knows what the police do immediately after a crime, what takes place at the morgue after a disastrous fire, what goes on at the place where the wreck occurred. To begin with, these subsequent events give the story a newsier twist, but he must take care not to overdo the thing or to forecast something that perhaps did not happen.

The remainder of the rewrite story is a retelling of the original story in condensed form. The writer takes care, however, to build it of new and different expressions, to reverse the order, to emphasize the things that the original writer neglected, and to subordinate the things that were treated fully in the first story.

II. BOILED NEWS ITEMS

The writing of what may conveniently be called the "boiled story" takes care of much of the rewrite material in many large offices. To handle all the material of a previous edition in rewrite stories would take up so much valuable space that much fresh news would need to be omitted or condensed. To save space the rewrite man must either throw away many important items or condense a large number of them to the briefest possible terms. The latter practice has long been common in many offices, and its result is a column or two daily of rehashed material in the form of short items. Ordinarily these items are grouped together under a general heading, such as, "City News in Brief," "Do You Know That—," "The City News Ticker," "Tabloids," "Grist from the Day's Grind," etc. The articles may be classified as telegraph or local, state or national. Sometimes a small headline precedes each item; sometimes the items are separated by short rules and distinguished by a few words in capital letters in the first line.

The writing of such items is an art that requires long practice and a highly cultivated sense of news values. To condense a long story to one or two sentences means that only the most significant facts may be included and that every word must count. Decided emphasis must be placed on the feature, and usually the feature played up is not the one emphasized in the first story. Although the items are short and to the point, they always give an identification of the person concerned, address, time and place. The following will illustrate:

> Falling over a fence around a newly laid cement sidewalk, Roger Ostermoor, aged 47, 841 Seventh street, broke his arm and two ribs last night.

Fire damaged the two-story frame carpenter shop of Carl Goodsole, 165 W. Fifth street, yesterday morning. Damage is $4,500.

The Madison police are searching for Mrs. Emma Hasward, who escaped from the Whitehall insane asylum Wednesday night.

Traffic policemen will wear white caps after June 1, according to Redford Bladen, chief of police.

Two persons were slightly injured when an automobile belonging to Small Smith, 736 West avenue, ran into a telephone pole last night.

The man who committed suicide by throwing himself in front of a Central passenger train Monday night has been identified as William Sand, 293 Maquard street.

Dancing in public parks will be the subject of discussion at the regular meeting of the Citizens' club tomorrow.

Sixteen military organizations in the city have petitioned the major to use his influence to keep picnic parties out of Armory grove this summer.

James Lungwith and Fred Naazur were fined $25 in court yesterday for carrying revolvers. They declared that they had $43 and needed protection.

Because he allowed his 13-year-old daughter to sell postcards and gum on the streets, Henry Grover, a peddler, was arrested yesterday on the charge of violating the child labor law.

III. THE FOLLOW STORY

The follow-up, or follow, story is not always written by the desk man. When additional newsgathering is required the story is turned over to the city editor and is handled by a reporter as an assignment. But since the additional material may frequently be secured by one or two telephone calls to the news sources indicated in the story, the rewrite man often handles the follow.

The first step in the writing of a follow story is to look over the clipping upon which it is to be based, to discover what phases of the story may be followed up, what subsequent developments may be expected. If it is an accident story, the rewrite man may look for more complete data in regard to the fatalities or injuries, the present condition of the victims, the fixing of the blame. If it is a robbery story, he looks into the resulting pursuit, capture, or trial, or, in the case of a public institution, its present financial condition. A murder story affords follow possibilities in the pursuit, capture, or trial hearing of the criminal, the present condition of the victim of attempted murder, the unraveling of the various phases of the mystery surrounding the crime. Suicide offers inquiry into the disposition of the body, the present condition of the victim if the attempt was unsuccessful, the disposition of the victim's estate or the action of relatives. Storms, floods, and other disasters offer follow possibilities for special reportorial assignments. Often the best follow-up is an interview with some of the persons concerned or with some of the authorities who have the case in hand. Once the rewrite man has decided what elements in the story offer follow-up possibilities, he must decide whether to turn the matter over to the city editor or try to secure the necessary information over the telephone.

The writing of the follow story involves characteristic problems. It cannot be treated in exactly the same way as a news story because it does not contain strictly fresh news and is written for two different kinds of readers—the man who read the previous story and the man who did not. Hence it involves the presentation of the subsequent developments, plus a synopsis of the original account. The most interesting part of it is its method of recalling the original incident so as to enlighten the new reader without offending the old with reiterations.

The lead of the follow-up story usually begins with the subsequent developments, stated in newsy form. After this it runs into a résumé of the gist of the previous story with an elaboration of the facts in the case. It is to be noted that this involves the use of the definite article and a reference to the matter which suggests that the writer is merely recalling the previous event. Thus, although the first story referred to the accident as "a fire which destroyed," the follow recalls it as "the fire which destroyed." But in spite of this suggestion of recalling the incident, the rewrite man takes care to elaborate the previous facts and identify the case so fully that the new reader does not feel that he has missed anything. For example:

FIRST STORY

Propped against a telephone pole, the body of 6-year-old Arthur Wendzog, 268 Water street, was found apparently strangled to death at 5 A. M. this morning.

FOLLOW STORY

Two stained rags are the only basis on which the police now hold out hope of obtaining a clue to the murder of 6-year-old Arthur Wendzog, 268 Water street, who was found strangled to death in an alley near his home yesterday morning.

FIRST STORY

London, May 2.—The American oil tank steamer, Gulflight, which sailed from Port Arthur, Tex., on April 10, for Rouen, France, was torpedoed at noon on Saturday off the Scilly islands, according to a dispatch received on Sunday by the Central News agency.

FOLLOW STORY

Washington, May 3.—The torpedoing of the American oil steamer, Gulflight, off the Scilly islands on Sunday, has brought the United States to a critical point in its relations to the present world at war.

After the lead, the first two or three paragraphs are devoted to the elaboration of the new developments, for they are of greatest interest to all readers. The rest of the story is then a synopsis or summary of the material in the clipping on which the follow is based. The summary involves a general reversal of all the material in the first story and usually some condensing. The rewrite man takes pains to vary the expressions used and to play up new features and facts. In the end, he succeeds in rejuvenating the old story and bringing it up to date so that it is interesting to the reader who saw it in the morning paper as well as to the man to whom it is entirely new.

PART II

CHAPTER VIII

TYPE

A knowledge of type—its nature, measurement, possibilities, and limitations—is absolutely necessary for success as a newspaper desk man or editor. The close relation between the mechanical department and editorial staff makes this so. Half the work of publishing a newspaper is nothing more or less than a printing job, and the desk man, acting as he does as director of the printers who are doing the work, should be able to talk their language and understand their work almost as thoroughly as they do. It is not necessary to be able to "stick" type or to operate a linotype machine, but it is necessary to know the problems that the typesetter and linotype operator face. Unless the desk man understands type, he cannot successfully edit copy, write headlines, direct make-up, or intelligently suggest changes in design.

To understand the printer's work, the desk man must know the various ways of measuring type matter and their interrelation, the names of the various sizes, the uses of the various sizes, the various styles of type and their uses, the various families of type, the way in which the printer sets type by hand, the operation of the various composing machines, the additional furniture and equipment used in putting together pages, and above all the language of the printing office, so that he can specify type and indicate his wishes with a fair degree of certainty that the printer will understand his specifications. This would appear very complicated, but a study of the principles of the printer's work and a few visits to the composing room will lay a good foundation for the development of a thorough knowledge. No one, however, should hope to learn all there is to know about type; it is one of the largest subjects in the world.

Inelasticity of Type.—The first and hardest thing to learn about type is its absolute inelasticity. "Type is not made of rubber," as the printers remark. The statement sounds reasonable, but the man who is used to working with longhand or typewritten manuscript sometimes fails to grasp it. He has an unconscious feeling that another word can be crowded into this line or another may be extracted from that without making any material difference. He doesn't realize that every individual letter and space is a separate piece of metal of definite size and that they must fit together with microscopic exactness. A page form is made up of thousands of these tiny pieces of metal fitted together so perfectly that, after pressure has been applied to the four edges of the form, the entire page of type may be handled as one piece of metal without a single piece of metal falling out. It is like a complicated puzzle and every part of it must fit within a hair's breadth; one piece too large or too small will break the even pressure and allow part or all of the form to collapse.

The student must grasp this idea at the outset before going further with the study of type. If necessary he must go to the composing room and try to fit together a few lines of type to see the application of the principle. After that he will never again call for a few letters of pica type in a brevier line or try to crowd an extra letter into a "fat" headline.

The Single Piece of Type.—Every piece of type is a piece of metal with three dimensions. It is a rectangular stick with a flat base, four flat sides, and a flat top on which a letter or character is raised in high relief. The names of the various parts of the type are: the raised character is the *face;* the flat top on which the face stands is the *shoulder;* the body of the piece of type of which the shoulder is the top is called the *shank.* On the bottom of the type is a *heel nick* which gives the type two feet to stand on; in the front side of the shank is another nick which tells the printer, by feeling, which is the bottom of the letter; extra nicks are sometimes cut in the front to distinguish certain small capital letters that may easily be confused with small letters. In the form, the type stands firmly on its flat base, held in an upright position by other pieces of type pressed against its four sides. A number of such pieces of type set together in this way form with their tops a flat surface containing raised characters which press ink into the paper when the form is placed on the press. The fact that in each type the shoulder is slightly larger than the face affords white space about the printed letters. If one type projects above the others it cuts through the paper or raises it away from the other types; if too short it does not touch the paper; if one piece of type is too small in its other two dimensions, it falls out of the form; if too large it bulges the line and other types fall out.

How Type is Measured.—Of the three dimensions possessed by every piece of type, only two are considered in type measurement. The third dimension—the height of the shank from base to top—is the same in all type—0.918 inch. That is, it is the same in all American and English type, although it varies in other countries. The two measurements that must be considered are its width and height as one looks at its end—in other words, the height and width of the letter as it appears on the printed page. This is the only height that is considered in subsequent discussion. Furthermore, the width and height that concern the printer are not those of the raised letter, but those of the shoulder itself—the square end of the type which supports the raised letter. This square shoulder is slightly larger than the letter itself, so as to afford white space between letters and lines and to allow for the varying size and shape of different letters. In other words, since some letters are larger than others in the same font and some extend above or below the general line, the printer must consider the dimensions of the shoulder on which the letter rests. Thus, although *h* is taller than *o* and *p* extends below the line, the shoulders of the types which print *h, o,* and *p,* in the same font, are of the same height, and the printer's measurements deal with the size of the shoulder.

Of the two dimensions of the shoulder, furthermore, the height is the more important. If a line of type is to be straight, all the type in it must have the same height, but there need not be any such regularity in width, so long as the lines come out even at the end. Therefore, although in any given font all the type is of the same height, there is great variation in width. In other words, *m* and *i* are the same height, but not the same width. The *m* type is as wide as three *i* types placed side by side but it fits in the same line because its height is the same.

It is therefore evident that type measurement in general is just a measurement of the height of the type as it appears on the printed page. In the modern point system, to be discussed later, the height of the letter is taken to be the distance from the line formed by the bases of all the letters to the top of the shoulder. The difference between two sizes or two fonts is simply a difference in this dimension.

Old Methods of Measuring Type.—Until very recently there was no definite, universal system of type measurement. Various sizes were designated in general by a series of names—type approximating one-sixth of an inch in height was called *pica;* type of about half that size was called *nonparcil,* etc. But the various sizes varied in different type foundaries and there was no uniformity of size. Pica type made by one foundry might be noticeably larger than pica from another; brevier from one foundry could not be used in the same line with brevier from another. Hence there was endless confusion in the printing offices. If an office had two fonts of minion and the "printer's devil" mixed them up, both fonts were useless until sorted again. Printers were continually forced to "bodge" with cards to make types justify and line.

Not until 1886 was this confusion ended by the establishment of a uniform system of type measurement in all American foundries—a system which all printers now know as the point system. French type-founders began work on a uniform system as early as 1737 and had worked out a plan generally adopted throughout Europe before 1800. In America no attempt to correlate the type of various foundries was made until 1822 and the first definite step was taken by a Chicago firm of type founders which lost its plant in the great fire of 1871. Their system, with some modifications, was adopted by the American Type Founders' Association in 1886. It is now universal in America, although it does not correspond with the European point system. The system is somewhat complicated, also, because it is simply a correlation and adjustment of former sizes to a systematic plan of measurement. The old pica type of one foundry which happened to be about $\frac{1}{6}$ inch tall was taken as the basis and called 12-*point* and other sizes were correlated with it. The standard pica of the point system is, to be exact, 0.16604 inch high.

The Point System.—The unit of measurement in the point system is the *point,* or 1/72 inch. All sizes of type are designated in multiples of this point. Eight-point type is thus 8/72 inch high; 10-point type is 10/72 inch high; 72-point type is 72/72, or 1 inch high. As the point system is the measurement of the shoulder of the type, it allows for space normally shown between lines set *solid,* without *lead* between the lines. Thus nine lines of 8-point type approximately fill 1 inch; twelve lines of 6-point occupy the same space; an inch will accommodate 10.2 lines of 7-point type. On this basis, the number of lines of any size to be set in a given space can be determined.

Names of the Various Sizes.—As the adoption of the point system was only a readjustment of old sizes to numerical measurement, many of the old names are still used in connection with the new system. The new 12-point is the same size as the old pica and therefore is now known as 12-point or pica; similarly the old name brevier is applied to the new 8-point. The following is a list of old names now in use and their point sizes; each is set in the size designated:

POINT SIZE	NAME	POINT SIZE	NAME
4	Brilliant	10	Long Primer
4½	Diamond	11	Small Pica
5	Pearl	12	Pica
5½	Agate		
6	Nonpareil	14	English
7	Minion	16	Columbian
8	Brevier		
9	Bourgeois	18	Great Primer

There are two smaller sizes, *excelsior* (3-point), sometimes used in fractions, and *microscopique* (2½-point), which is mainly a curiosity. In larger sizes, 20-point is sometimes called *paragon,* and 48-point is known as *canon.* Multiples of some of the above sizes are sometimes heard of, such as *double-pica* for 24-point and *double-English* for 28-point. The use of these names is, however, fast disappearing in the printing offices because of the greater convenience of the numerical symbols.

Standard Line.—Although the original point system, applied only to the height of the letter, certain type founders are now using it in connection with the width of the letter. That is, instead of allowing the set-width of the letter to be whatever the face happens to make it, they change the set-width enough to give it a point measurement. The advantage of the system is that with all letters cut in widths which are exact multiples of the standard unit, the point, it is easier to justify the lines—to fill them exactly. The position of the face on the shoulder, also, was until recently variable in different fonts and sizes, and types of different fonts, although of the same point height, would not *line* together, that is, some letters were nearer the top of the shoulder. This difficulty has been overcome by the adoption of the *standard line* in most American and some English foundries. In all type cut on the standard line the distance from the bottom of the shoulder to the base of the letter is the same and type from various fonts will line together. It is to be noticed, however, that there are two standard lines, one for body type and another for display type. Type cut on the display line is designated as the *lining series* and cannot be used in the same line with standard line body type.

Uses of Various Sizes.—The sizes commonly used in newspaper work are nonpareil, minion, and brevier. Agate is taken as the standard of measurement in advertisements, but it is seldom actually used; advertising space is sold by the *agate line* and fourteen agate lines equal an inch of advertising space. Bourgeois, long primer, and small pica are the types most commonly used in book work. Larger sizes are most frequently used in display only.

The special uses of the various sizes are as follows: Diamond is the smallest type regularly made and is used only in small Bibles and prayer-books. Pearl is sometimes used for the same purpose and finds some utility in notes and references in small dictionaries. Agate is sometimes used in market reports in newspapers and for similar purposes. Nonpareil is the smallest type that can possibly be used in book work and even then it is used only for footnotes, indices, etc.; some newspapers use it for very unimportant stories. Minion is commonly used as body type in large newspapers and occasionally as a subordinate type in book work. Brevier is the body type most often seen in small newspapers as well as in cheap book editions; it is commonly used in all printing work when a small type is desired. Bourgeois (pronounced bur-jois) is the type commonly used in magazine printing and in double-column books; it is a readable type but is too small for long lines in book work. Long primer is most frequently used in book work; newspapers also use it for important articles and editorials, especially in bold face. Small pica is the type of rich editions in which space is not important. Pica is the standard unit of measurement for column widths and printing furniture, but it is seldom used except as display or in very rich book work. English is now a display type only although it finds some use in Bibles and other church books for pulpit reading. Great primer, except as a display type, is used only in children's books and large quarto volumns.

Column Widths.—In our study of type measurement, we found that the width of individual letters need be taken into consideration only in connection with the length of lines. As the letters vary greatly in width, printers have found it convenient to adopt one letter, the *m*, as the unit of line measurement. The *m* is used in preference to any other letter because in any font the shoulder of the *m* type is exactly square. For example, in 8-point type, which is 8/72 inch high, the *m* is 8/72 inch wide. Column widths and line-lengths are therefore designated in "ems." Ten ems of 8-point type is 80/72, or 1-1/9 inches, long. Typesetters are usually paid space rates and their work is estimated on the basis of one thousand ems of the type they set, regardless of the space it fills. Although one thousand ems of nonpareil fill only about half as much space as one thousand ems of pica, the printer is paid the same for each.

In measuring column widths and book space in general, however, the pica or 12-point em is used as the standard unit. The pica em is a convenient unit because it is 12/72 or $\frac{1}{6}$ inch wide. The $2\frac{1}{6}$-inch column commonly used in newspapers is designated as 13 ems wide, whether it is set in 6-point or 8-point. Other spaces are designated accordingly as 18 ems, 21 ems, 25 ems, or whatever the case may be, and the length of the line can be figured out on the basis of 6 ems to the inch. To avoid confusion, it is customary to specify in "ems pica"; thus, 8-point Roman, 15 ems pica. An easy way to become familiar with the system is to do a few problems in figuring space on the basis of printing measurements; for instance, how many lines can be used and what line-length should be specified to fill a space 4 inches wide and 7 inches high with 9-point type?

Variation in Width of Type Face.—It has probably been noted that there is much variation in the width of the same letters in different styles of type, although the height of the letters is the same. The 30-point letter *O* used in the usual newspaper headline is decidedly narrower than some other 30-point *O* used in an advertisement. This is because the proportion between the width and height of letters is not the same in all type. Every different font and family has its own proportion, and the proportion may vary within the same font. The reason is that every style of type is cast in three or four different widths to suit special purposes. There is no definite system of measuring the various proportions, but special names are applied to various widths. The type in its common form is designated as *standard width,* narrower type of the same size is called *condensed,* wider type is called *extended,* and the narrowest is known as *extra-condensed.*

EXTRA-CONDENSED 10-POINT TYPE

CONDENSED 10-POINT TYPE

STANDARD 10-POINT TYPE

EXTENDED 10-POINT TYPE

Variation in Body Size.—Although the size of type is measured by the size of the body rather than the size of the letter, there is some variation in the relation between the two. The variation results from the fact that it is often desirable to increase the space between lines, and the type founders make up small type on larger bodies to save the printer the trouble of placing strips of metal, or "lead," between the lines of type. In specifying such type, the printer must give two sizes—the size of the type face and the size of the body. When he calls for 8-point type on 9-point body, he is given a type of the usual 8-point face on a body large enough to give an extra 1/72 inch between each pair of lines. Many fonts are regularly made in this way because their design calls for wide spacing between lines. The 8-point on 9-point body size is common in small newspapers, and 10-point on 12-point body is frequently used in magazine work.

Styles of Type.—Certain general kinds and style of type are so commonly used that they deserve mention here. The kind of type ordinarily used in reading matter is called *body type,* as distinguished from *display type* used in headings and prominent lines. The common body type in use in American newspapers and magazines is designated as *Roman.* In its commonest form it is called *thin-faced* Roman; when it is heavier and blacker it is known as *bold* or *black-face* Roman. Any kind of type, in the same way, is called *bold* when it is heavy and black, and most styles are made both in thin-face and bold. Type that slants toward the right is known as *italic;* it may be thin-faced or bold italic and is usually found in every font. Besides the regular capital and small letters, most fonts also contain another style called *small capitals*—they are capitals of the same height as the small letters of the same size.

This line is set in thin-faced Roman

This line is set in black-faced Roman

This line is set in Italics

THIS LINE IS SET IN CAPITALS AND SMALL CAPITALS

Type Families.—One step beyond the standard styles, which are a regular part of every font of type, is the classification of type into great families designed at various times by different type founders. Certain of the designs go back so far into typographical history that they may be classified in general as *old style, antique, modern,* and *fancy* faces. Old style is characterized by short *serif* (cross-marks at the ends of strokes), long connecting fillets between the serifs and main strokes, and small figures. The lines of old style are frequently wavy and broken in imitation of the imperfect work of early type makers. Antique type has bolder serifs and a uniform line with little shading. Modern type has longer serifs, shorter fillets, greater shading, and large figures. One of the great families known in every printing office is the *Gothic* family, which is characterized by extreme plainness and lack of ornamentation; it is the type most like the "block lettering" used by sign painters. It appears in many different varieties and styles and is the type most used in newspaper headlines. The various kinds of *script* type make another great family, designed to imitate handwriting. In American offices, the type of some foreign countries and of older times is designed as *black letter* because it imitates the lettering of the monastery copyists of the Middle Ages. Among the black-letter varieties are *old English, German text, church text, Tudor, missal,* and other very ornamental letters. Further classification of type by families would be difficult and useless. A study of the catalog of any large type foundry will show that the varieties of faces and styles are almost limitless in number. Only years of study will acquaint one with any considerable number of them.

Printer's Furniture.—Other typographic equipment besides type is usually called *furniture.* It includes many kinds of metal and wooden pieces used to fill space or make impressions of various kinds. Most of it is now made in accordance with the point system and is measured in points or ems pica. Thin strips of metal used to increase the space between lines of type are known as *leads* and are 2 points or 2/72 inch thick. When a single lead is placed between each pair of lines, it is said to be *leaded.* If two 2-point strips are used in each case, it is *double-leaded;* wider leads are called *slugs.* Without leads, it is said to be set *solid.* The blank pieces of type used between words are called *spaces.* The space whose top is exactly square is known as a *quad.* A separate set of spaces must be used with each size of type, of course, and the spaces vary greatly in width. It is through the varying width of these spaces between words that the printer is able to take up or let out space so as to make lines the same length—they are the only elastic element in typography. After the printer has set up about as many words as a line will hold, with average spaces between them, he adjusts the length of the line by substituting thinner or fatter spaces in each position; this operation is called *justifying.* Printers sometimes justify by inserting spaces between letters but this is generally not good practice. Any strip of metal that projects far enough to print a line on the paper is called a *rule;* it is made of brass and its thickness is measured in points. The long rules between newspaper columns are called *column rules* and rules between articles are *cut-off rules.* Every office has rules that will print anything from a very fine line to a thick, black line. If a newspaper is printed with the rules upside down so that the flat bases strike the paper, the effect is called *turned rules.* Some rules are cut so as to print only a short line in the center of the column; others, called *double rules,* print fine parallel lines; others, called *perforating rules,* cut a row of small holes through the paper; others print a line of *leaders. Borders* are decorative rules or series of metal pieces, like type, that may be used as a frame about type matter. When a frame made up of simple straight rules is used in the newspaper it is called a *box.* Printing equipment also includes many varieties of small decorations that may be inserted to give an artistic effect. Some of them are really small cuts, cast rather than engraved. All of this furniture is made of brass, type metal, or wood. Wood is used largely in filling up large blank spaces, for every fraction of space must be made snug and tight. Some large letters and cuts are also made of hard wood to save weight, since a square foot of type matter weighs about thirty-seven pounds.

Other Typographical Terms.—Many of the terms which the typesetter uses are derived from the names of his implements. For instance, he measures his work by the *stickful*—the amount of type which may be placed in the *composing stick* which he uses. The stick is a three-sided metal tray, about as large as the palm of the hand, with one side adjustable to match varying line-length. The printer holds it in one hand and sets type in it, one letter at a time. When full, it holds about two inches of type matter—reckoned as one hundred and fifty words of newspaper type. Each stickful is in turn transferred to a long metal tray, with three sides, called a *galley.* As the first *proof,* or impression, is taken of the type while it stands in the galley, this proof is called *galley proof.*

The operation of taking proof is called *pulling proof.* Corrections are made by *revising* the type matter as it stands in the galley. The type with which the hand compositor works is distributed by characters in the various compartments of a *case,* or flat tray. The sections, or *boxes,* vary in size according to the relative number of types stored in them and they are unlabeled for they are arranged in the same way in all cases and the printer learns their position just as a typist learns his keyboard. It is not necessary for the printer to look at the type, for the position of its box tells him what letter it is and the nick in its shank indicates the bottom of the letter. Capitals are laid out in one case and small letters in another; since the first is ordinarily placed above the latter, it is called the *upper case*—hence capitals and small letters are called *upper case* and *lower case* letters respectively. Each case contains a *font* of type, that is, a complete assortment of a certain size and style of type, including some 275 different characters and a definite number of each character. A complete font includes Roman small letters, small capitals, capitals, figures, punctuation points, and accented letters, italic small letters, capitals, figures, points, and accents, fractions, commercial signs, and "peculiars" which include marks of reference, braces, dashes, leaders, spaces, and quads. A *ligature* is a combination of letters on one shank, such as *ff, fi, fl, ffi, ffl, ỻ, æ, œ.* *Logotypes* are entire words cast on one shank—not extensively used at present. The number of types of each character in a font is determined on the basis of a definite *scheme,* corresponding to the relative frequency of various letters in ordinary reading matter. A size of the font may thus be designated by the number of letters *A* in it. When a foundry catalog lists a certain type as "19A $1.20, 36a $1.30, $2.50," the printer knows that the font will contain nineteen *A* types, thirty-six *a* types, and other characters in proportion.

The manuscript which the printer follows in setting type is called *copy,* and each piece of copy as he receives it is a *take.* The copy indicates not only the content but the style and face of type to be used and other specifications. After the pressmen or stereotypers have used the type, the printer must *distribute* it among the proper boxes of the proper cases. Type purchased, cast, or arranged in letter groups ready for the cases is called *sorts.* If at any time in the process of composing or making up the type becomes mixed, the result is called *pi.* Discarded and broken type is thrown into the *hell-box* to be melted up. Offices which have type-casting machines throw all type of 12-point or less into the hell-box to save distributing it. If in distributing the printer mixes the type of various cases so that many *wrong-face* letters appear in proof, the result is called *dirty case.*

HOW TO SPECIFY TYPE

All copy intended for a printer must contain certain marks to indicate the type to be used and the manner in which it is to be set. These marks are usually written on the upper left-hand corner of the first page and inclosed in a circle to indicate that they are not to be set up. As the marks usually refer only to the body of the copy, separate marks must indicate the style of the headings. When all the headings are alike, one mark opposite the first or at the top of the page suffices, but any variation in heading type must be indicated by other marks, in circles, in the margin beside the heading concerned.

Complete type specifications on any manuscript include name, style, and size of type to be used; length of lines; and general arrangement of paragraphs and lines. Thus a piece of copy might be marked: "8-point Bodoni Script, 15 ems, solid, indent paragraphs 2 ems." If the printer has only one style of body type, as is frequently the case, "7-point Roman, 13 ems, leaded, indent paragraph 1 em." If a special 10-point on 12-point body is desired—"10/12 Roman, 21 ems, solid, hanging indention 1 em."

In the newspaper office it is not usually necessary to mark all copy. The standard column width, usually 13 ems, will be used unless otherwise specified. If the newspaper's ordinary body type is 8-point Roman, the compositor will use that unless directed to use something else. Special display is all that the newspaper desk man marks specially but he must mark it in the language of the printer. Thus space between the lines is secured by marking "lead" or "double-lead"; heavier type is secured by marking "bold face," or "Bl. face," or "all caps," or "Sm. caps"; two-column lines are secured by marking "double-measure, 12-pt. bold caps"; other display may be called for by "hanging indention, 1 em," or "center 11 ems";

a frame around the type body is secured by the mark "Box."

More careful specification is required in the marking of heading type. A type might be marked "12-pt. Caslon Bold Condensed, centered," or "14-pt. Light De Vinne Extended, all caps, flush at left." In the newspaper office, the necessity of specifying for headings is saved by the use of numbers for standard headlines. The composing room and editorial office both have a schedule containing models of the newspaper's common headlines, their numbers, and the type and arrangement. When the desk man marks a headline "No. 8," the printer, by referring to his schedule, knows at once the kind and size of type to be used.

The best way to learn type and its specification is to secure the catalog of a large type foundry and study the faces and names applied to them. Printers know their type by the names given by the founders and each type is indexed with the name of the type within it. But, since no office has in stock all the types listed in the catalog, it is useless to specify a special face without first investigating the styles in the printer's cases.

CHAPTER IX

PRINTING PROCESSES

Because newspaper development has been largely made possible by the invention of labor- and time-saving devices for the printer and because no desk man can intelligently direct a printer unless he understands the processes by which written copy is quickly reproduced in thousands of printed papers by the mechanical staff, this chapter is devoted to explaining the machines and processes that are in common use in modern newspaper plants. No attempt will be made to explain the mere mechanical aspects of the machines; that is the concern of the inventor and the repair man. It is the principle behind the various mechanical processes that the desk man needs to know, as well as the possibilities in speed and output. To understand these principles it is more important to know the historical development of any machine, the various steps which led to its invention and the problems involved, than to be able to identify each lever and gear in the latest model. It is one thing to stand bewildered beside a machine and hear the operator explaining that the matrices are no good and the what-you-call-it lever is worn; it is a more valuable thing to know what the machine does and in general how it operates.

Four Branches of Invention.—There are four branches of mechanical invention that make the modern newspaper possible. One is mechanical type composition. Until inventors worked out machines that would do the work of the hand typesetter, all newspapers were greatly limited in size and speed of production. Until a machine was produced that could compose thirty to forty words a minute, every office was kept down to the comparatively slow pace of the hand compositor. Another great branch has been the development of the rotary printing press with its increased speed and size of output. Between these two processes is the invention of stereotyping which made the rotary press possible. An important subsidiary process is that of photographic engraving, a process which has brought illustrations within the reach of every newspaper. Without these four processes, the modern newspaper with its many interesting illustrated pages, its vast circulation, and its multiple editions would be impossible.

I. MECHANICAL TYPE COMPOSITION

To understand the mechanical substitute for the hand compositor, it is necessary to understand the basic principles of type making, for the machine that does the "typesticker's" work is a typemaker, rather than a typesetter. No composing machine in common use at the present time handles or sets ready-made type; every one makes new type for every word it composes. To understand its principle, therefore, it is necessary to know the steps which led to the development of the type-making machine.

There is nothing new in this modern custom of making type in the printing office. All printers made their own type until about the middle of the sixteenth century—but they made it by hand. Not until about 1550 did type founding become a separate trade. One of the first type founders in England was Joseph Moxon, who established a foundry in 1659. Another was William Caslon of the next century. Binney and Ronaldson were among the first type makers in America, for the trade was not introduced on this continent until late in the eighteenth century. All of these type makers, who established the faces and fonts that we know today, made type by hand for it was not until the middle of the past century that machinery was invented to aid their work. The first successful type-making machine and the progenitor of the machines now in use was invented by an American, David Bruce, in 1838.

The Making of Type.—Since the beginning of type making in 1450, the process has been one of casting, of forcing molten metal into a mold. For every individual letter and character the type founder must have a separate mold, and each piece of type must be cast separately. The mold must be small and deep, with the letter cut in bas-relief in one end. That is the basic principle of all type founding, whether by machine or hand, and of the mechanical composing machines.

Since the shanks of various letters are alike in general shape and size, the part of the mold that must be changed for different letters is the bas-relief of the character—the *matrix,* as it is called. Until very recently, the making of this matrix was done by hand. The first operation was to cut a *counter-punch*—a piece of steel with the letter carved in relief on one end. This was done by marking the outlines of the letter on the steel and cutting away the metal around the letter; the counter-punch is an exact steel duplicate of the finished type. The next step was to drive this counter-punch into a piece of soft steel to make a bas-relief of the letter—a *punch,* as the type founders call it. When this bas-relief has been smoothed and finished, it is the matrix of the type mold. Every step in this process must be repeated for each of the 275 letters and characters in the font to provide a matrix for each letter. The first punch-cutting machine was invented about 1885. Much of the matrix making is now done with this machine or by electrolysis, by plating the counter-punch with copper, peeling off the copper film and backing it up with soft metal to form a matrix.

The mold of which the matrix forms one end consists of two blocks of steel with a square groove in the side of each so that the two when put together form a rectangular casting box. As some letters are wider than others, the mold must vary in the direction of the set-width. In the old process of casting type by hand, the workman fitted a matrix in one end of a type mold of proper size and then with a spoon poured it full of molten metal. To drive the metal firmly into the matrix he gave the mold a vigorous upward shake as he poured the metal. Each type required a repetition of this process. The type was then dressed down for the removal of superfluous metal, especially the jet at the open end of the mold, a groove was cut in the base so that it would stand firmly on its feet, and a nick was cut in one side to guide the printer in setting it.

Type-Casting Machines.—The type-making machines of today do only the casting part of the process. Their molds and matrices are previously made by a punch-cutting process as described above. By the use of a plunger in a pot of molten metal, they automatically do the work of the spoon and the shake employed by the hand type caster. Most of them also trim and finish the type. Their advantage is one of speed; they cast type fifteen or twenty times as fast as a hand-workman—from 3,000 to 10,000 types an hour—and turn out a better product. But these machines, while they are the fathers of the composing machine and are used in some newspaper offices to cast "sorts" for the type cases, can do no more than continue casting the same letter over and over again until equipped with a new matrix. To convert them into composing machines, we need to equip them with some means for changing matrices automatically so that they will cast any letter as it is needed, and set it in its proper place in a galley. Then we shall have a type-casting and composing machine that will do the work of the hand compositor.

Type-setting Machines.—Long before any attempt was made to remodel the type caster for use as a composing machine, inventors tried to solve the problem of mechanical composition by designing a machine to set ready-made type by machinery. At first sight, it would not seem difficult to work out a machine with a series of grooves or boxes to hold the various letters and a keyboard with wires or levers arranged to release the proper types and allow them to slide down into a galley in proper sequence. But there were two obstacles to be overcome. One was the justification of the line—the filling in of space between words to make all the lines the same length. The other was the redistribution of type. The typesetting machine was of little value unless it did away with the slow process of redistributing type. On these obstacles the idea of mechanical typesetting broke. As early as 1822 typesetting machines were patented; the first practical one was brought out in 1853 but it required hand justification; another in 1870 solved the distributing problem but did not justify. Although practically abandoned today, these mechanical typesetters did good service in newspaper work during the middle of the past century. Their inability to distribute type printers made up for by melting up the type as fast as it was used and casting new ready-sorted type on a rotary type-casting machine. The highest development of the mechanical typesetter is the unitype which is used to some extent today; it distributes type automatically but requires hand justifying. About 1890 a machine was invented which set, justified, and redistributed type but it was too costly for practical use. It is probably fortunate, however, that these machines failed, for their failure brought the development of the type-casting and composing machine with its perpetually new type and other advantages.

Type-Casting and Composing Machines. The problem involved in remodeling the type-casting machine into a mechanical compositor, as indicated above, consisted in devising some way to fit a different matrix into the casting box as each letter is needed and to set the type in the galley. The problem has been solved in a number of different ways in various machines but only two are used to any great extent in the newspaper office—the linotype and the monotype. An explanation of the principles incorporated in these machines will illustrate the workings of the others. These two machines must not, however, be confused with the type-casting machines which many newspapers have installed to cast "sorts" for the cases. The type casters, which are really the machines of the type foundry, do not change matrices in response to the operation of keys and do not set the type that they cast.

The Linotype Machine.—The linotype machine derives its name from the fact that its inventor solved the problem of casting, setting, and justifying type by casting an entire line in a single piece. The output of the machine is not a series of separate pieces of type, but a slug which has on its edge the faces of the various letters that make up a single line of type. It is as if the printer had set up the various pieces of type in a line and fused them into a single piece of metal. It operates by means of a line of previously assembled and justified matrices.

Its inventor, Ottmar Mergenthaler, began work on the machine about 1876 and put it into commercial use in 1886. Now it is used by thousands of newspapers, many book publishers, and other printing firms. The original machine has been developed and improved by many successive patents, but its basic principle has remained unchanged. The machine is operated by a keyboard, very similar to the keyboard of a typewriter, electric or other power is required to operate it, and a gas flame keeps its pot of type metal in molten condition.

The basic idea of the Mergenthaler machine is to bring a series of type matrices, corresponding to the various letters required by the printer, into line to form a composite matrix for a mold that casts a bar of metal just the size of a line of type. Its operation involves the assembling of the matrices, the pouring of the molten metal, and the redistribution of the matrices for later use. All of this, including the justifying of the line, is done automatically, as the operator presses the keys, and the line-slugs are deposited in a tray in proper order.

The type matrix of the linotype is a flat piece of brass about 1½ inches long and ¾ inch wide. One end is cut away in a triangular notch with grooves and nicks to guide the distributor. The letter mold, or matrix proper, is on one edge of the matrix. The matrices, of which there are a number for each character on the keyboard, are stored in a magazine at the top of the machine. Separate channels are provided for the matrices of the various letters with gates operated by the keyboard, so that when the operator presses a key the corresponding matrix slides out of the magazine, down a channel in front of the machine, and takes its place in a line beside the keyboard. As successive matrices reach the line, they hang side by side with their type molds in a horizontal line on one side. At the end of each line, the operator moves a lever and the machine does the rest; meanwhile the operator is composing the next line.

After the operator throws the lever, the line of matrices which constitute one line are automatically moved away to the left to take their place in front of a horizontal casting box located in a large wheel. The casting box is just the size of a line-slug and open at front and back; it is really just a horizontal slit in the solid wheel. When they reach the casting box, the line of matrices with their separate type molds form its front surface. From a pot behind the wheel, molten metal is forced into the casting box by a plunger, in sufficient quantity to fill the mold. The metal cools and hardens as the wheel containing the casting box slowly revolves and the finished line-slug is pushed out into a galley at the end of a quarter revolution. Meanwhile a long arm reaching over from the back of the machine has carried the line of matrices to the top of the magazine and deposited them in an automatic distributor. They hang on the distributor rod by the fourteen nicks in the V-shaped notch at the end of each matrix and are moved along the rod above the magazine by a slowly revolving screw. Each matrix has a separate combination of nicks fitting in certain grooves in the distributor rod, and when it reaches its place a break in certain grooves allows it to drop from the distributor and slide into the proper compartment in the magazine, ready to be used again in a later line.

Line justification is accomplished by wedges between the matrices. Whenever the operator strikes the space bar in the keyboard, a long, thin wedge moves into the line and hangs loosely between the matrices that compose the words on each side. As the operator throws the lever at the end of the line, the wedges are automatically driven down so as to take up extra space and crowd the matrices closely together. The line is thus filled out with equal spaces between the words before the slug is cast. The justifying wedges are not returned to the magazine but hang in line beside it ready to drop into place.

All operations of the machine are automatic. The operator simply keeps the motor running and the metal hot, presses the proper keys, and throws the lever at the end of each line. A power-driven belt is also used to bring the matrices down from the magazine so that only a slight touch on the key is required. While the operator is setting one line, another is in the casting box and the matrices of another are being distributed in the magazine. If he presses the wrong key or makes any other mistake, he can rectify it by picking out the matrix or rearranging all the matrices of the line as they hang beside the keyboard. Once the line is cast, however, he must reset the line and make a new slug to rectify an error; the old slug he puts back into the melting pot. In the same way, all proof corrections, however slight, must be made by setting new lines to take the place of faulty lines.

Since all the matrices in the machine's magazine are for the same size and face of type, it is quite evident that the machine in its simplest form is limited to one font. Bold-face type of the same font is provided for by the use of matrices with two molds and a device to bring the proper mold into use. But the two faces of the same font are as great a variety as can be secured with one magazine. This inconvenience has been overcome by the development of machines with interchangeable or multiple magazines. Linotypes are now built with two, three, or four magazines and a corresponding range of variety; in others the magazines are interchangeable so that the operator can change from 7-point to 8-point by removing one magazine and slipping another into its place. In this way the machine has been developed until it is now able to set almost any face or size of type in common use; recently machines have been brought out which set type large enough for newspaper headlines or irregular slugs for use in display advertising.

Besides its speed—about 8,000 ems per hour or 35 words per minute—and the fact that only one operator is required to run it, the linotype has certain other advantages and disadvantages. The line-of-type idea is a decided advantage in newspaper work because line-slugs are easier to handle than individual pieces of type and facilitate rapid make-up. On the other hand, the fact that new lines must be cast to rectify errors makes proof revision of linotype work rather difficult and costly. This is offset, however, by the fact that every line is made of absolutely new type and the type is cast only as needed. A few bars of type metal piled in a corner take the place of the extensive type cases of former days. After the slugs have been used for printing, they are thrown back into the melting pot and transformed into new lines. Age and wear in the machine result in bad alignment and hair-lines between letters because the brass matrices, becoming slightly worn, do not fit sufficiently close together to keep molten metal from being forced between them to form ridges that show up as minute lines in print. The most improved linotype machine costs about $3,500, and a new set of matrices costs about $75. The linotype equipment of a large newspaper, including from ten to fifty machines, involves a considerable investment.

The Monotype Machine.—The Lanston monotype is selected for study in this connection because it represents an entirely different principle of mechanical composition and is coming into extensive use in American printing offices. For reasons to be pointed out later, it finds little use in newspaper offices but is used by many magazine and book publishers. It is an American machine and was put into commercial use about 1899.

The characteristic feature of the monotype is that it casts a separate piece of type for each letter and sets up the type in proper sequence, justified ready for use. It is the ultimate development of the basic idea of the casting machine as pointed out above, since it accomplishes the necessary change of matrix in the type mold automatically. Another characteristic feature of the monotype is that it consists of two separate machines —a keyboard and a type caster—which may be operated at different times and in different places. The output of the keyboard is a perforated paper roll, like a player-piano roll, which is later used to guide the operation of the type caster in making and setting type to correspond with the copy.

To set up copy on the monotype, the operator manipulates the keys of a large keyboard, much like the keyboard of a typewriter, but, instead of printing the words on a sheet of paper, the keyboard simply punches holes in a roll of paper about five inches wide. Compressed air supplies the power to revolve the roll and transmit the pressure of the keys. Each letter, as its key is pressed, is represented by two small holes in the paper roll; as will be seen later, the two holes supply motion in two directions to the matrix-grid of the type caster. Each succeeding pair of holes is below the preceding pair on the roll. The keys on the right-hand bottom rows punch only one hole each, but all the others punch two; 225 variations are possible.

Justification is accomplished by another perforation at the end of the line to regulate the size of spaces between words. When the operator nears the end of a line, the fact is indicated by a bell and a cylindrical scale above the keyboard which revolves as the composition progresses. When he has set enough words to fill the line, the scale tells him what justifying keys to strike—it has kept account of the number of spaces between words and the total amount of space left to be divided. The scale is in the form of two numbers and justification requires the pressure of two keys in the two rows of red keys across the top of the keyboard—one key in each row to correspond with the two numbers indicated on the scale. The resulting perforation sets a uniform width for all the spaces cast in that line. The justification holes come after the letter holes of the line, on the roll, but they precede the line in the type caster for the roll runs backward in the second machine.

The monotype keyboard may be placed in a quiet office far from the composing room and operated by a stenographer. Its paper rolls may be stored away for any length of time, may be used as many times as desired, or may be kept by the author as a duplicate of his work to save composition in later editions. One keyboard may supply rolls for several type casters or, as is more often the case, several keyboards may be used to keep one type caster busy.

The type caster is like the type-making machines used by the type founders, except that instead of one letter-matrix, it has many, arranged to be brought into position in the type mold automatically as they are needed. In the type caster there is a separate matrix for each letter and character in the font, all of uniform size and fitted together in one flat matrix-grid. This is a block of metal about four inches square and one inch thick, ruled in 225 small squares like a miniature checkerboard with a letter mold in each square. When the machine is in operation, this matrix-grid shuttles about above a stationary casting box so that now one letter, now another, forms the end of the type mold. As the grid moves about, the mold automatically changes size to provide for the varying set-width of the shanks of different letters. Behind the mold is a pot of molten metal with a plunger that forces a jet of metal into the casting box and fills the mold for each successive letter. Water circulating through holes in the casting box hardens the metal instantly, and the type is pushed out of the mold and into line in a galley. As each line is filled it is pushed down in the galley to make room for the next.

The shuttling of the matrix-grid is guided by the perforated roll made by the keyboard. The grid has motion in two directions—forward and backward, to right and left. One of the pair of holes in the roll regulates the first motion, the other controls the second. The movement in one direction, by the movement of a metal wedge in the side of the casting box changes the size of the mold to suit the letter. The machine is operated by compressed air and guided by air escaping from small tubes through the holes of the paper roll—just as the player piano is guided by air escaping through holes in the music roll. As each pair of holes comes over the mouths of the tubes, springs give the grid a combined motion in two directions and it is stopped by two vertical plungers, actuated by the escaping air, at the proper place to bring the desired letter-matrix under the mold, the size of the mold is changed, molten metal is forced into the mold, and the finished type is pushed into the galley. The entire operation is done so quickly that the machine casts and sets type at the rate of 150 to 180 a minute. At the same time, the justification holes in the roll adjust the set-width of the spaces for each line, so that spaces of the right width are cast and set between the words and each line comes out exactly even. When not in use in setting composition, the type caster may be used to cast "sorts" for the printer's cases.

As the matter composed by the monotype consists of galleys of individual types, rather than line-slugs, errors are corrected and proof is revised just as if the matter had been set by hand. Once cast and set, the type can be removed or changed to any extent desired without recasting, a case of the same type supplying the needed letters. This, added to the fact that each type is new and fresh, is a great advantage in some kinds of printing work. It is not so convenient for newspaper work, on the other hand, as the line-slugs of the linotype, because individual pieces of type must be handled with greater care and are harder to make up in page form. The fact that monotype composition requires two operations and the ribbon runs backward in the second makes it difficult to divide copy into short takes for rapid handling and lessens the usefulness of the machine in the newspaper office.

Greater variety of face and size is possible on the monotype than on the most improved linotype. All that need be changed to alter face or size is the small matrix-grid bearing the type molds. The printer may have in stock as many grids as he desires and the change from one to another requires but a moment. The matrices, also, do not wear and result in disalignment or hair-lines as in the linotype. The ribbons are interchangeable and can be used to set any face desired; this is accomplished by a standardization of set-widths of letters, a change especially evident in Old Style faces. The same ribbon may be used in setting any desired size of type if the line length is changed proportionately. Some of the large machines are arranged to perforate two ribbons at once, one for small type and narrow measure, the other for larger type and long lines. The operator may thus compose type for a de luxe and a popular edition at the same time. The most important mechanical fault that appears in monotype work is honeycombed type which results from overheating the type metal and consequent bubble-holes which may cause the type to break down in the press.

Other Composing Machines.—In addition to the linotype and monotype, there are several other automatic type-casting machines that are used to some extent in the United States. Among them is the junior linotype, a machine which casts lines of type like the linotype by means of long matrices suspended on endless wires encircling the machine. Since the original Mergenthaler patents have expired, another machine, called the intertype, has been brought out on lines similar to the linotype. Both of these machines are much less costly.

Whatever the machine, its possibilities do not go beyond the work of the hand typesetter; its output is type or slugs set up in long galleys, and subsequent hand make-up into page form is necessary just as if the type had been set by hand. If the machine casts and sets individual types, they must be handled with as great care as hand-set matter; if it casts line-slugs they must be arranged and locked up in the form in the same way. No machine has been devised to take the place of hand work in make-up, and every office, no matter how many typesetting machines it has, must also have some practical printers to do this work. Since the most versatile machine, also, is very limited in variety of size and face of type, a large amount of the display in any publication must be set by hand in the old-fashioned way.

II. STEREOTYPING

The process of stereotyping is that of making metal plates to reproduce the pages of a publication after the type has been set, arranged, and locked up in page form. For the rotary press in common use today, these reproductions must be in the form of semi-cylindrical plates that will fit the rollers of the press. That is, the flat-page form with its myriad type faces protruding from the top surface must be reproduced in a curved plate with the same type faces on the outside surface, as if the flat-page form were picked up by its two edges and bent backward over a barrel. As high-speed web presses are used by all large newspapers stereotyping is a necessary part of the newspaper's mechanical work.

The problem of stereotyping is to make an impression of the page form in some plastic material that can later be hardened and used as a mold. Various methods of stereotyping differ largely in the kind of material used as a mold. The first method, which was invented about 1862, employed plaster-of-paris. This or clay was used in all stereotyping for many years, but it was not entirely satisfactory because it could not reproduce engravings and was too slow for newspaper work.

The Papier-Maché Matrix.—The papier-maché process, which is the common process of today, was invented in France in 1829. It receives its name from the fact that the plastic mold used is a sheet of papier-maché made in alternate layers of thick, unsized paper and tissue paper, pasted together. The mold is called a matrix, or *mat* (in England, a *flong*), and looks like a sheet of heavy cardboard with a smooth surface. When it is moistened it becomes soft enough to take a perfect impression of all the individual pieces of type as it is pressed into the surface of the page form. After it has been baked, it may be used as a mold for molten metal. In practical use, the taking of the impression and the baking of the mat are done in one operation. With the wet mat laid on its surface, the page form is run under a heavy roller, then placed in a press and subjected to heat and intense pressure at the same time. In about four minutes the form is taken from the press and the mat is removed, ready baked for use. Every large newspaper office has several stereotyping presses, heated by steam or electricity, and regulated so that the mat may be baked as quickly as possible without melting or crushing the type of the form. The mat will not only reproduce type and line engravings, but coarse half-tones as well. After the baking, any large blank spaces in the mat are backed up with small pieces of cardboard to keep them from yielding under the weight of the molten metal and allowing the spaces to fill so that they "print up" in the press. In most offices the raw stereotype mats are made by hand, built up of heavy paper and tissue paper rolled and pasted together, but recently a rotary fiong machine has been perfected that makes as many mats in an hour as half a dozen men can make in a day.

Casting the Plates.—The work of taking the type impression and baking the mat is only half the process of stereotyping. To make a plate from the mat, the stereotyper must place the mat in a mold and cast molten metal into it. For the curved plates used on web presses, the mat is bent backward and placed in a semicylindrical casting box. The mat forms the outside surface of the plate mold and the casting box supplies the other surfaces. When the molten metal has cooled, the result is a semi-cylindrical plate with the type faces on the outside surface. This plate must then have its edges trimmed and its inside surface milled or shaved to remove superfluous metal and make it fit the press roll. In small offices this process of casting and trimming plates is done by hand. Larger offices have machines which cast, trim, and cool the plates at the rate of three or four a minute. These machines, of which the autoplate is the best known, have a melting pot as large as a bathtub, two, four, or even more plate molds, and automatic shavers and trimmers to cut the plate into finished shape. The autoplate combines the four operations required in hand casting—a slow task because the plate must cool before it can be handled—and accomplishes the same work in three-fourths of a minute. The machine operates as fast as the stereotyper can feed mats into the various molds. Other machines are the autoplate junior and the multiplate. Ordinarily several plates are made from each mat, for if the newspaper has several multiple presses, it makes perhaps as many as twenty stereotype plates for each page, clamps them all on the rolls, and runs all its presses at full capacity on the one edition. In that way it prints its entire edition of many thousand copies in a very short time. Without the process of stereotyping to reproduce pages it would need to set up type and make up each page many times to secure enough duplicates. Lately some page plates have been made in the form of complete cylinder, instead of the usual half-cylinder form, for the small rolls of duplex presses.

Other Uses of Stereotyping.—The production of page plates for rotary presses is not the only use made of stereotyping in modern newspaper work. Since the process provides a cheap way to produce duplicates of type and cuts, it more than anything else has made possible the extensive syndicates that supply a large part of a newspaper's make-up at less cost than that of setting up the material in the office. As a large number of plates may be made from one mat, the process provides a cheap and convenient way of storing and shipping type impression. Through the process, the syndicate becomes really a coöperative enterprise to divide up the cost of setting type and making engravings—the heaviest item in printing. Once the type is set and the mat made in the syndicate office, many stereotype duplicates can be supplied to newspapers at a fraction of the original composition cost, and many newspapers, especially small ones, buy much of their reading matter and many illustrations in this form. There are a number of syndicates that supply not only feature material but news as well so that a small newspaper within a few hours' express distance from a large city may buy its daily telegraph news in this form, thus saving the cost of telegraph tolls, writing and editing, as well as type composition. The editor who prepares his newspaper in this way is said to "edit with a saw," because he receives the plates in long galley strips, known as "boiler plate," and saws them up to fit his make-up. Many small newspapers get all their outside news in this way and set up in their offices only local news and advertisements. To save shipping expense the plates are cast about one-fourth of an inch thick with grooves in the bottom so that they may be locked upon a standard base and made "type high." The newspaper keeps the thick, heavy metal bases in its own office and receives by express only the thin top plates.

Many newspapers cut shipping expense still further by owning a small mold for casting stereotype plates and purchasing only the papier-maché mats from the syndicate. The mat is so light that it may be forwarded by mail and when it arrives in the newspaper office only a few minutes are required to slip it into the mold and cast a plate from it. This is the method ordinarily employed by syndicates that supply feature material with illustrations. If the material is such that the newspaper may wish to use it again at some later time, the mat is filed away in the office. This is especially true of portraits of prominent persons and pictures of places and things that repeatedly come into the public eye. The newspaper files the portrait mats in its "morgue" of biographical material and thus has a portrait ready for instant use. Since certain syndicates now make a specialty of portraits in mat form, many newspapers keep their morgues up to date by purchasing a regular portrait mat service.

Stereotyping has its faults as well as its advantages. Because of the possibility of imperfect work in the making of the mat or the plate, stereotyped material does not give the clear-cut printing impression of type. It is seldom therefore used in high-grade printing, such as book or magazine work. In the reproduction of half-tone engravings, the papier-maché mat is too coarse to reproduce the minute dots of fine-line cuts and therefore requires the use of very coarse half-tones. But withal, stereotyping is a necessary link in the chain of inventions that have made possible the modern newspaper.

III. ELECTROTYPING

Electrotyping is a more costly but finer substitute for stereotyping. It is a method of reproducing type and illustrations by electricity, or rather by electrolysis. It came into use about 1850 and is now extensively used in fine printing. The fundamental idea of the process is the same as that of stereotyping—to take an impression of type matter and use it as a mold for casting plates. But the mold in this case is of copper and is made by electrolysis, much like the process of silver-plating.

The type form or cut to be electrotyped is first reproduced in wax by the simple operation of placing the form upon a sheet of wax and subjecting it to pressure in a steam press. The resulting wax mold with the impression of the form on its surface is then patched up with hot wax and given a coat of graphite to make it an electrical conductor. After the superfluous graphite has been dusted off, the mold is sprinkled with iron filings and a weak solution of copper sulphate. A piece of copper imbedded in its corner makes the electrical connection. The mold is then suspended in a solution of copper sulphate under the action of electric current for an hour or two. By electrolysis a thin film of pure copper is deposited uniformly over its surface. When the copper film is about 0.005 inch thick, the mold is removed from the solution and the copper film is peeled from its surface. Zinc chloride solution is then brushed over the back of the film and sheets of tin foil are laid over it and melted down into the film. The copper sheet is then backed up with molten lead. The finished plate is slightly over one-eighth inch thick and must be mounted on a base to be type-high. It is no more or less than a copper-plated stereotype of the original form. The process produces only one electric plate, but the plate is thinner and lighter than the type form and has a copper printing surface.

Electrotyping is commonly used in book publishing and to some extent in magazine publishing since it results in a very fine printing impression. In book work it is especially valuable because the thin electrotype plates may be stored away between editions more compactly than type forms and save keeping costly type and furniture tied up in idleness. These advantages offset the high cost. Electrotyping is used to a large extent in advertising. To insure good make-up in their advertisements, many concerns prefer to supply ready-made electrotype plates to newspapers and magazines than to trust to the type supply and skill of unknown printers. Advertising plates supplied in this form are commonly known as "electros."

IV. PRINTING PRESSES

All of the mechanical typesetting and stereotyping machines would be of little use to the modern newspaper if the high-speed perfecting press had not been invented. It alone makes possible the tremendous circulation of city newspapers; without it daily circulation would be measured in thousands rather than tens and hundreds of thousands for, whatever the circulation, it must be printed in an hour or two. The huge mass of machinery called a rotary web perfecting press, capable of printing and folding 100,000 or more eight-page newspapers an hour, seems beyond the understanding of any brain except that of a skilled machinist, but its basic principles are easy to grasp if one remembers that it is the climax of a mechanical development toward a single goal, simple enough in itself. The idea of the designer of a multiple rotary press is identical with that of the maker of the first wooden hand press; both were seeking to build a machine to do the same thing at the greatest possible speed. The fundamental idea of press work is to spread ink on a type form, lay a sheet of paper over the form, press the paper firmly upon the type so that it will receive an inked imprint, and remove the printed sheet. This is the simple operation that a printing press must perform and every step in its development has been toward designing a machine that would perform this operation better and at higher speed.

The Hand Press.—The first printing press, such as that used by Gutenberg when he began to print from movable types about 1450, was the simplest possible solution of the problem and continued to be used, with slight modification, for three hundred and fifty years, until after 1800. This first kind of press was built of wood and consisted of a flat bed, on which the type form was placed, and a superimposed platen with wooden screw and wheel to press the paper into the type. The pressman inked the type with leather pelt-balls and laid each sheet of paper on the form by hand, but the press was an improvement over the former practice of taking an impression with a mallet and a block of wood. This first press had little advantage in the way of speed over hand imprint, but it furnished a more even impression with less care on the part of the pressman. The first improvement, which came about 1550, was a metal screw and a movable bed, or *rounce,* arranged to slide on a greased track so that the form could be brought out from under the platen for inking. About this time someone added to the movable bed a hinged *tympan* with a *frisket* hinged to it—

a cloth-covered wooden framework which served as a holder to keep the paper from flying off the form as the bed was pushed into position under the platen. The next step was to add a series of levers to the screw to give greater pressure. This improvement came in the Blaew press, invented in 1620—a wooden press with sliding bed capable of turning out 200 to 350 "pulls" per hour, or about 100 to 150 copies of a four-page paper. This was the kind of press used by Benjamin Franklin, and its use required nine separate hand operations for each impression. The first iron hand press was the Stanhope press which was built in England in 1798 and had a more complicated system of levers to turn the screw. With twelve hand presses of this type, operated by twenty-four men, the London *Times* in 1814 got out its edition of 10,000 copies in about six hours. In 1816 an American brought out the Clymer Columbian press which had no screw, but secured pressure through a series of levers. This was supplanted in 1822 by the Smith press which used a simple toggle-joint in place of the complicated levers. The final development of the hand press came in the Washington press, which had a simplified toggle-joint and a bolted frame to secure greater strength. The press was broadly used and is still used for fine work. It has a windlass to move the bed, an improved tympan and frisket, and automatic ink rolls, but it is little faster than the first wooden press of 1450. Many a famous American newspaper began publication on a Washington hand press, and many offices, especially engraving plants, now use it as a proof press.

The First Power Presses.—When steam power came into use, press designers went to work on power presses, but their first efforts met with the obstacles of securing the continuous motion that power requires. It was necessary to give the press moving parts. Power could be used to draw the bed back and forth, but to adapt it to applying pressure on the platen at the right time and to handle paper was more difficult. The first power press, which was brought out in 1810, was merely a modified hand press with a toggle-joint operated by a cam to drive the platen down upon the paper. In 1814, Koenig's steam press carried the modification further and secured 1,000 impressions per hour. The idea was further developed in the Treadwell and Adams press of the '20's by making possible feeding at both ends. These presses were built mainly of wood with a power-operated platen in the center and two beds that shuttled in from the two ends. With four men to lay on sheets and four more to remove printed sheets, such a press printed 4,000 to 5,000 impressions an hour.

The Cylinder Press.—But these presses were unsatisfactory because too much time was wasted in the raising and lowering of the platen. The next idea developed was the use of a cylindrical platen which rolled over the type form. The idea was worked out in various ways with a stationary bed or a stationary platen. The first press of this kind was the Koenig press of 1813 which had one large cylinder that made three impressions for each revolution, stopping after each impression for the bed to return. It is to be noted, however, that the bed of this press was moved by a rack-and-pinion system so satisfactory that it continued in use until very recently. In 1814, Koenig built a press with a small continuously moving cylinder; by placing two cylinders side by side and transferring the paper from one side to the other by means of tapes he made it a *perfecting* press—that is, it printed both sides of the paper. Napier's press of 1830 brought in smaller cylinders and grippers to assist in feeding paper sheets. Before the middle of the century, Hoe and Co. had developed various types of cylinder presses that are still in use. This is the type of press known in American printing offices today as the *flat bed* press. The *stop cylinder* idea came back in 1852 in lithographic presses.

But even this type of press was too slow. Each sheet of paper must be fed in by hand, limiting the speed to about 2,000 impressions per hour, and the reciprocating motion of the bed made useless any attempt to increase the speed by the development of automatic feeders. Improvements have brought the cylinder press up to the highest speed that can be attained in printing directly from type in a flat-page form, but the flat bed press must be fed by a skilled pressman and is too slow for newspaper work.

Type Revolving Machines.—To attain greater speed it is obviously necessary to eliminate the reciprocal motion of the bed, to substitute a cylinder revolving in one direction for the flat bed. This requires that the type be placed on the circumference of the cylinder—a difficult problem—but the next step in press design was the application of this idea. In 1848, the London *Times* installed a press, called the Applegate Machine, which was arranged so that the type form could be placed on the curved surface of a cylinder. The printing cylinder was 5½ feet in diameter and stood in a vertical position; its surface was not an exact curve, but was made up of a number of flat surfaces each as wide as a column. The type was secured in these flat surfaces by V-shaped column rules. Each column therefore presented a flat surface and "overlays" on the impression cylinder were necessary for perfect imprint. The press had eight impression cylinders, grouped about the printing cylinder, and with eight men feeding in sheets of paper, it printed 10,000 copies an hour. Only one of these presses was constructed because in the meantime there had been built in America, in 1846, the Hoe Type-revolving Machine, which carried out the idea with greater perfection. Its type was held on the surface of the cylinder by V-shaped rules, but the arrangement was such that the flat surfaces were eliminated and the type surface was a perfect curve. The first of these Hoe type-revolving presses was built for the Philadelphia *Public Ledger,* and had four impression cylinders, giving an output of 8,000 sheets an hour printed on one side. Later type-revolving presses with as many as ten impression cylinders were built, increasing the capacity to 20,000 an hour. Several New York dailies used them. But these presses were far from the ultimate goal sought, since they required one man for each impression cylinder to feed in sheets of paper and the highest speed that a feeder can attain is about 2,000 sheets an hour. They also printed only one side of the sheet at a time.

Web Paper and Stereotyping.—The problem to be solved then was one of feeding the press and its solution was difficult as long as individual sheets of paper had to be used. In 1861, however, improved machines in the paper mills made possible the purchase of paper in continuous rolls and the development of stereotyping offered a substitute for the type-revolving idea. Papier-maché stereotyping has been used in book work since 1829, but it was not until 1861 that it was developed sufficiently to reproduce pages of newspaper size. With the curved stereotype plate it was possible to substitute small cylinders for the huge type-revolving cylinders and to increase the output of the press by adding more printing cylinders. As all the motion was continuous, it was also possible to print from a roll of paper, rather than on separate sheets. With the development of impression cylinders that lessened the "offset" on the back of the paper, it was easy to run the sheet continuously from one printing roll to another so as to print it on both sides. Thus the rotary web perfecting press was evolved. *Web* is the name applied to the roll of paper, and *perfecting* means "printing on both sides." The only problems that remained were those of cutting and folding the sheets.

The Rotary Press.—The first web perfecting press in England was the Walter Machine built for the London *Times* in 1862. It had a single long roll to which the paper was returned for impression on the reverse side and used cutting cylinders to separate the sheets. The newspapers were delivered flat and no folding machine was attached to it until about 1870. In America, the Bullock web press was built in 1865 and had an automatic folder; it received its paper from a roll, but cut it into sheets before the paper reached the printing cylinders. Hoe and Company improved the cutting and delivery processes in 1871 and developed the speed of this single roll rotary to 18,000 copies per hour. In 1875, the same company devised a rotating folder of greater speed which prepared the way for future developments; all later rotaries printed the paper before cutting it. The printing press had now reached the stage of operating at high speed with no hand work and its future development was simply one of refining and adding to its mechanism.

The huge web perfecting press of today, reduced to simplest form, consists of a roller with two, four, or eight stereotyped plates on its circumference, a platen roller to press the paper against the printing plates, an ink roller revolving against the plates, and a continuous sheet of paper running between. Such a set of rollers prints, of course, only one side of the paper, but the paper may run on through a similar set a few feet away at the same speed for reverse impression. If each roller carries four page plates, four pages are printed on each side of the paper as it passes through the two sets of rollers, and the result is an eight-page newspaper. If each roller carries eight plates, the two sets print sixteen pages. Just beyond the printing cylinders is a folding machine that automatically cuts and folds the paper into separate newspapers as fast as it comes out. Suppose, however, that the press is built with two pairs of printing rollers receiving paper from two webs and feeding the two streams of paper into the same folder. The result is a multiple press that will print papers twice as large or will print twice as many papers of the same size. Thus the capacity of the press can be increased *ad infinitum* by the addition of more sets of printing rolls. For color supplement work, the paper may be run through several sets of printing rolls, each printing a different color on the same page.

Multiple Rotaries.—The first step in the development of the multiple rotary was the Hoe Double Supplement press built in the early '80's. It had one eight-page and one four-page printing roll and folded and pasted the various sheets together. In 1887, the first quadruple press, a combination of two simple rotaries, appeared; it printed 48,000 eight-page papers per hour. The sextuple was evolved in 1889 by the combination of two double supplement presses in one. It prints 90,000 four-page papers, or 72,000 eight-page papers, or 48,000 twelve-page, or 36,000 sixteen-page, or 24,000 twenty-four-page papers an hour. It has three double rolls, two folders, and uses about twenty-six miles of paper an hour. The next step was the octuple, with four eight-page rolls—just twice the quadruple—and a capacity of 96,000 eight-page, or 60,000 twelve-page papers an hour. Two of these were then built together in the double octuple for color supplement work, with a capacity of 96,000 four-page papers in several colors an hour. The later double sextuple press has twelve eight-plate cylinders and prints 96,000 twelve-page papers in black, or 48,-000 sixteen-page papers in color each hour.

These various combinations are built in special forms to suit the individual purchaser. There is no standard design, but there are three general arrangements of rolls. The two parts of the quadruple or sextuple may be built at right angles to each other with the folder between; the various sets of rollers may be placed in two or three decks, one above the other; or they may be placed in tandem, one behind the other. One form is called the *straightline* because of the direct course of the paper through the press. A more recent form is the *duplex,* which uses smaller rollers and cylindrical page plates. Because of the large size of the newspaper page, the multiple presses are very large affairs, costing many thousands of dollars, but they alone make possible the tremendous circulations of today. A battery of several multiple presses, all printing from duplicate stereotype plates, will print the largest newspaper's entire edition in a very short time.

Other Kinds of Presses.—Modified rotary presses are now used to a large extent for printing magazines and books. The only difference is that each revolution of the printing rollers prints thirty-two or sixty-four magazine pages instead of eight newspaper pages. There are, of course, many variations in the construction of rotary presses and many different models; it is possible here to give only the basic principle. Many steps also have been omitted in the description of the development of the high-speed press. There are many other kinds of presses working on slightly different principles that have not been mentioned although they are in common use. One of them is the well-known job press which is an ingenious machine using a flat form and flat platen.

Offset Printing.—Offset printing is a new kind of press work whereby the impression on the paper is made, not directly from the surface of the type or printing plate, but by means of a transfer of ink from the printing surface to a rubber surface and then to the paper. It was invented about 1884 and further developed by the construction of the rotary offset press in 1906. The process is based on an accident that occurs every day in the printing office—when a printer feeding a high-speed job press misses a sheet and carelessly allows the press to print on its platen. If he does not at once put on a clean platen, the next sheet inserted receives an impression on both sides, one from the inked type and the other an *offset* from the ink deposited on the platen. An English publisher casually noticing that the offset impression was more attractive than the direct impression, received the idea which has since developed into offset printing. The process is a mechanical duplicate of this printing office accident with the direct impression omitted and a rubber platen inserted in place of the paper or composition platen used in direct printing.

In the rotary offset press, the roller which carries

the printing surface prints directly on a roller with a smooth rubber surface. The inky image thus deposited on the rubber roller then becomes the printing surface for a sheet of paper pressed against its surface by a second platen. This results in a richer and smoother print than is ordinarily obtained by direct impression. Further, it furnishes a means of printing from various kinds of printing surfaces at the same time. Formerly relief, intaglio, and lithographic printing required separate presses and different kinds of presswork. But it matters not what kind of plate is used in the offset press, the rubber roller takes ink from one as well as another. In this way various kinds of engravings may be combined in one printing surface and printed in one operation.

"Make-Ready."—As many newspapers are still printed on flat bed presses, many newspaper men confront the old problem of "making ready" which has delayed many an edition. As even the most perfect type does not give an absolutely level surface, it must be brought to a perfect plane after it has been placed on the bed of the press. This involves pasting pieces of paper, or *underlays,* under low areas of type, or *overlays* upon the part of the platen that bears on the low areas. Especially in the making ready of pages containing cuts is the work arduous. Make-ready requires more time than stereotyping, and careless make-ready always results in uneven impression. Some make-ready is required on a rotary press, although most of the unevenness of the type surface is eliminated when the pliable mat is placed in the mold.

"Fudge."—Fudge printing is an interesting phase of web press work used by newspapers that make an effort to print extras containing up-to-the-minute news. As it takes about seven minutes to make a stereotype plate, even after a page form has been remade to include later news, and several more minutes to place the new plate on the press, the newspaper is driven to various mechanical expedients to have a sporting extra with a full account of the game ready for spectators as they leave the field or a market extra containing closing quotations in the street as soon as the stock exchange closes. Fudge is one of these expedients. A fudge plate is a front-page stereotype plate with a blank space about two columns wide and a foot long in the upper right corner—perhaps there is also a blank space where the banner headline should be. As the paper passes over the fudge plate this space on the front page receives no impression. But further on in its course the paper passes over a small roller, called the fudge roll, which contains just enough type to fill the blank space. The fudge roll has no stereotype plate, but has ingenious clamps to hold linotype slugs on its surface. Only a moment is required to stop the press and change these slugs, and the news can thus be brought up to the minute without delay. To facilitate the use of fudge in extras, some newspapers have a linotype machine and a telephone or telegraph operator in the pressroom. Changes in the banner head to accord with the changing news are accomplished in the same way. Because the fudge is on a separate roller, also, it can be printed in red or green ink to emphasize its content. Another expedient is a type-high blank space in the plate in which the final score can be stamped with a steel punch.

Ready-Prints.—In connection with press work, the ready-prints used by many country newspapers may be mentioned. To save composition and press work, many country editors purchase their paper from syndicates with one side of each sheet already filled with feature articles and other general material. All that the editor need do is to print his local news, advertisements, and editorials on the other side of the paper, and fold it so that the ready-printed material is inside. He is saved not only all the composition of the inside pages, but one run on the press as well, and the ready-print costs him little, if any, more than white paper. Because the ready printed pages are always folded inside, they are often dubbed "patent insides."

V. ENGRAVING

Until about thirty years ago the only illustrations available for newspaper use were wood-cuts—pictures laboriously carved by hand in hardwood blocks. Wood cuts were costly because they required skilled workmanship, it took much time to make one, and the resulting print was not highly artistic. Hence few newspaper printed pictures except small stock cuts used mainly in advertising. The situation was entirely changed about 1880, however, when the photographical engraving process came into commercial use.

Cheap, attractive illustrations are now within the reach of any newspaper.

Line Engravings.—The line engraving is the simplest photo engraving and the one that was developed first. By a line engraving is meant an illustration consisting of a white background and black lines with shadings of fine black lines and no tones or smooth masses of shading—a pen and ink drawing is a good example. Such a picture has only two tones, black and white. The making of such a cut is accomplished by a process almost as simple as the making of a photograph. The picture that is to be reproduced is placed in a strong light and photographed on a sensitized glass plate in a large camera. When this plate has been developed it is used as a negative to print the picture on a sheet of zinc or copper whose surface has been covered with a sensitized coating, just as a photographic print is made on sensitized paper. Treatment with ink and rubbing with cotton after a water bath develops the plate and removes parts of the sensitized coating and leaves on the metal plate lines and areas of coating corresponding to the black lines and areas in the original drawing. After the remaining coating has been built up with a coating of dragon's blood, a red substance that clings to the sticky lines, and hardened, the metal plate is immersed in a nitric acid bath which etches, or eats away, the unprotected areas and leaves the coated lines untouched. The plate, after proper cleaning, bears on its surface in relief the original drawing as clean-cut as if engraved by hand. This plate is then a line engraving that may be used to print the picture on paper. But it prints only black lines without tones. Because it is usually made of zinc, it is commonly called a *zinc etching.*

Half-tone Engravings.—The half-tone engraving is a modification of the line engraving whereby the blackness of the impression is broken up into contrasting tones. It is obvious that when only black ink is used in printing, an unbroken area will print nothing but solid black. To produce a gray or a lighter tone with black ink, the printing area must be broken up into small parts of varying size to shade into the white surface of the paper. This is what the half-tone process does—it breaks up black areas into fine points.

In principle the half-tone process is based on photographic methods similar to those of the line engraving; the only difference lies in the use of a screen to break up the solid black areas. When the negative is exposed in the camera, a screen is placed in front of the negative to break up the light. The screen consists of two clear glass plates with fine parallel lines ruled on their surface with a diamond or acid; one plate is ruled horizontally and the other vertically so that together they make a grating of fine crosslines. The result of the exposure is a negative in which the unaffected coating consists of a series of small dots. When this negative is used to print on a sensitized metal plate, the same effect is produced. Etching of this plate produces an engraving whose surface is made up of hundreds of small points varying in size according to the tones of the original picture. There are of course many variations in the practical application of this process, but this is its principle in simplest form. For ordinary work the half-tone plate is made by stripping the film from the negative and laying it on the metal plate instead of printing its form on a sensitized coating.

Using the Cuts.—The line engraving is ordinarily made on a zinc plate and the largest areas between the lines are *routed out* with a cutting tool to make it more clear-cut. It is used for printing cartoons, line drawings, and all illustrations that consist of black lines. The plate is about one-fourth inch thick and is tacked upon a wooden block to make it type-high. Its size is governed by the position of the camera's lens in the production of the negative.

The fineness of the half-tone is regulated by the fineness of the screen. For newspaper work when stereotyping is necessary, a coarse screen is used, a screen with from sixty to one hundred lines per inch. This produces an engraving with relatively large points on its surface, and the black dots that compose its tones are plainly visible on the printed page. Such plates are usually made of zinc. For finer work, a screen with from one hundred to one hundred and sixty lines per inch is used and the points and dots become so small that they can hardly be seen. For such engravings zinc is too coarse-grained and copper plates must be used. Coarse zinc half-tones are used most in newspaper work because they are cheaper and the stereotype mat will not take an accurate impression if the lines are closer together than sixty or eighty lines per inch. The finer copper half-tones are used for printing that is not stereotyped. In some cases a fine half-tone is used in stereotyped work by leaving a hole, or mortise, in the stereotype plate and setting the original engraving into it.

Make-Ready.—When the original type and cuts are used in the press, making ready involves evening up the cuts with overlays or underlays to "bring out" the tones. In very fine work the pressman may spend several days making ready. In stereotyping, an overlay of stiff paper is usually placed on the mat over a cut to press the mat firmly into it. A fine cut when properly made ready will reproduce with black ink the delicate shades of the original photograph; to produce the sepia and other tones, the printer uses brown ink of the shade of the darkest portion of the picture.

Both zinc and copper cuts are mounted and handled in the same way. Their cost varies from five cents a square inch for line engravings to twelve or fifteen cents an inch for fine copper half-tones. In newspaper work their size is specified in column width only for the size of the drawing then determines the vertical dimension; in all work in fact only one dimension need be given and a cut of almost any size may be made from one drawing by relative enlargement. For the best half-tones, clear-cut glossy photographs are required; for the line engraving a drawing with much contrast is necessary.

Color Engravings.—Colored pictures are printed by means of a development of the photo engraving process requiring a separate line engraving or half-tone for each color. Since all colors are but combinations of the three primary colors, red, yellow, and blue, three plates properly shaded and overlapping in mixed areas, will reproduce all the known colors and combinations of colors. There must be a plate that contains all the blue areas, a plate containing the red areas, and another the yellow. To reproduce the picture with these three plates, each must be printed with colored ink successively on the same sheet of paper. Often a fourth, or black, plate is added to bring out the shading and tone.

The production of the three plates requires three successive repetitions of the photographic process through different colored glass filters. The colored picture is first photographed through a filter which excludes all but red rays and the red components of mixed rays and produces a negative of the red areas. This process is carried through to completion and a corresponding "red" plate is made. Then the process is repeated for the "blue" plate, then for the "yellow" plate, and finally without a filter for the "black" plate. The four cuts must then be mounted on separate bases and carefully trimmed so that their separate impressions coincide, or register, in printing. The printer then places his yellow plate in the press and prints with yellow ink; then he substitutes the red plate and runs the same pages through the press again printing with red ink—and so on. The result of the four impressions is a colored reproduction of the original colored picture. It is to be noted, however, that the filter used is not of the same color as the ink to be used but a combination of its complementary colors; the filter used in making the "blue" plate is therefore orange. In making colored half-tones, also, the print is not made by stripping the film from the negative but by direct photographic printing; this is to insure perfect register of the minute dots which constitute the half-tone surface.

The engravings may be either line engravings or half-tones, although the latter are usually used. Newspaper color work, the Sunday supplement, is frequently done with etchings printed on a rotary press; the various color plates are mounted on different cylinders and the web runs through them in succession. For finer work, however, half-tones are used. The finest work requires four color plates, as explained above, but much color printing is done with three, or even two, plates. The absence of one of the primary colors is compensated by the use of simpler color mixtures that approximate the tones of the original picture. Color plates are very costly because of the great skill and care required in the making; the four plates for a picture of magazine page size may cost as much as one hundred and fifty dollars; some three-color work costs one dollar an inch.

The Ben Day Process.—The Ben Day process is a method of imitating half-tone work in the background of line etchings. By means of a special film through which ink is rubbed on the drawings or on the metal plate, before it is etched, a stippled effect of uniform black dots or fine rulings is produced in the shaded areas without the use of a screen in the camera. It finds its commonest use in the making of sketches and detailed drawings for newspaper and other publications and is valuable because it saves the draughtsman the work of shading dark portions of his drawing with a pen. The artist merely draws the outlines of his sketch and specifies Ben Day shading in certain areas. There are many varieties of Ben Day stipple work and the draughtsman orders them by number from the engraver's chart.

Rotogravures.—With the invention of the rotary photogravure press in 1906, intaglio printing of illustrated supplements has come into common use and many American newspapers now have such presses. The photogravure is merely the reverse of a line engraving, made by a similar photographic process with grooves and hollows in place of raised lines. Its press work requires the wiping of the plate after it has been filled with ink. When printed on a rotary press it is called a rotogravure. In such a case the film stripped from the negative is not placed on a flat copper plate, but on the surface of a large copper roller which constitutes the printing surface after it has been etched with acid. One side of the roller passes through an ink bath which fills the impressions in the intaglio engraving, the surplus ink is cleaned away with a sharp knife, and the ink is lifted out by the paper which passes over it. After the picture has been printed, the copper roller is turned down in a lathe to remove the engraving. Although merely a reversed line engraving, the rotogravure is given the tones of a photograph by the varying depth of the engraving. It has been used with greatest success with brown ink which gives varying sepia tones. Renaissance photogravure is a combination of intaglio engraving and offset printing.

Other Kinds of Engravings.—The subject of illustrative printing is a large one, constantly changing and developing. The practical processes of today may be divided into four general groups on the basis of the kind of plate used: relievo, intaglio, lithographic, and collotype.

Relievo, or relief, printing is the name applied to all processes which employ plates whose printing lines and areas are raised so as to receive the ink and press it into the paper. The group includes all printing from type, electrotype plates, stereotype plates, wood engravings, half-tone engravings, and line engravings. In each of these the printing, or inked, surface is in relief. It is the kind of printing in common use in all newspapers, publication, and job work.

Intaglio printing is a designation applied to all processes which employ plates whose printing surfaces are in bas-relief, the lines and surfaces which represent the picture are grooves or hollows cut into the plate. In the process of printing with intaglio plates, the grooves and hollows are filled with ink, the surface of the plate is wiped clean, and when the plate is pressed upon the paper the ink is transferred to the paper by absorption and remains in the form of ridges or raised surfaces. An illustration is the engraved visiting card whose ink may be felt with the finger. This class of printing includes copper and steel-plate engravings, stone engravings, acid etchings, aquatint etchings, mezzotint engravings, music engraving, photogravures, Rembrandt photogravures, Renaissance photogravures, and others. The various names designate the material used in the plate and the process by which it is engraved.

Lithographic printing includes all processes which employ flat surfaces to which ink is applied directly in the form of the design desired and absorbed by the paper when the impression is taken. That is, the picture is drawn in absorbent ink directly on the surface of a flat plate and transferred to paper pressed upon it. The work may be done in black or in colors. The commonest illustration is the colored lithograph for advertising purposes. Stone plates were originally used in the process but now, for finer work, aluminum, zinc, and other kinds of plates are used, and various processes have been developed as substitutes for the hand work necessary in the old-fashioned stone lithograph.

Collotype printing is a development of lithographic printing in that it employs an unetched surface, but its surface is a film of sensatized gelatine which receives ink and transfers it to paper. This is the least common of all methods of reproducing pictures and is used only for very fine work.

The Newspaper Art Department.—The art department is a common part of most large newspaper plants of today. Sometimes it consists of a staff photographer with a dark room in the office; sometimes it includes a number of artists and draughtsmen; some newspapers also have facilities for making their own engravings. The work of the art department consists in making and retouching photographs, drawing decorative borders around photographs, making sketches, diagrams, maps, and other illustrative or decorative material. One kind of work consists in making layouts of pictures—groups of photographs interwoven with decorative borders and sketches. As the photographs must be reproduced in half-tones and etchings must be made of the pen work, a layout usually consists of several cuts. To make such a composite picture, the artist does the pen work, borders and sketches, on a large sheet of paper leaving blank spaces here and there for the photographs. He then numbers the photographs to correspond with the spaces and indicates the size to which the photographs are to be reduced. The engraver then makes the separate cuts and puts the layout together. Color work is done in water color or even oil. Attached to the same department are cartoonists and comic artists who provide the newspaper's pictorial humor.

CHAPTER X

SMALL PUBLICATION WORK

The handling of small publications—local "boosting" monthlies, association quarterlies, house organs, propagandist pamphlets, and other small periodicals—can hardly be considered a regular part of the newspaper desk man's work. But since a newspaper is always associated with a printing office, sometimes a job office, a newspaper man is expected by the general public to know all about printing and publishing work and to be better fitted than anyone else in the community to take charge of small publication work. Whenever any body of people determines to issue a publication, it instinctively turns to a so-called "journalist" for advice or assistance. If there is a school of journalism nearby, the first impulse is to ask advice of the instructor or one of his students. In college circles, most student publications are handled by students of journalism who are studying to be newspaper men. Since there seems to be this close relation in the public mind between newspaper work and the ability to edit any small publication, it is well for the newspaper man or journalism student to know something about it.

This discussion will be by no means a conclusive treatment of publishing work or a handbook for the prospective publisher. It is merely a group of convenient methods and systems, classified for reference, and the readiest answers to some of the problems in small publication work. Some of the methods are new; others are as old as printing. They were gleaned from work in large magazine offices and from bitter experience with small publications. Added to the material in preceding chapters, they may suggest a starting point for the inexperienced "editor and business manager" or supply the busy newspaper man or journalism instructor with some ready-made advice to turn over to the worried secretary who has been appointed to the post.

I. PLANNING THE PUBLICATION

The first step in the work of launching a publication is to design its physical make-up. Before the editor approaches a printer for terms or issues a call for "copy," he must have a definite idea of the size, make-up, general appearance, and reading-matter capacity of his publication. Too many young editors leave the consideration of these matters until they have gone to the printer for terms, and the result is that the printer, in order to get down to brass tacks, designs the publication for them. It is then the printer's publication and after it is issued the editor sees a thousand faults in it. If he will plan it and visualize it in advance, he can make it his own publication, and incidentally he will receive better terms and treatment from the printer because of the knowledge of printing he evidences.

Cost Considerations.—The style and appearance of the publication must in general suit its purpose. It may be modest or bizarre, cheap or rich, small or large. These conditions are to some extent determined by the money at the editor's disposal, but in most cases a handsome publication costs no more than an ugly one if the editor knows how to make the most of his money. Pleasing appearance depends upon paper, type, size, and make-up. Of these, paper affects the cost most, because paper is usually the largest item in the cost. But with proper knowledge, the editor may choose a paper of moderate cost and make it appear rich by his selection of size and typographical make-up. To do this, however, he must know paper sizes and the basis on which paper is judged. Pleasing typography costs no more, in general, than ugly typography if the editor knows how to select type and can adjust his selection to the printer's stock, knowing whether to call for machine or hand composition. Size has little to do with the cost if the editor knows how to utilize paper of standard size with the least waste and how to economize on press work, the second largest item in cost. With a clear understanding of the purpose of his publication, the editor may secure a suitable, pleasing make-up without materially increasing expense.

The Capacity Problem.—The planning of the publication involves also an estimate of the amount of reading matter it is to carry. The editor should have a fairly clear idea of the number of articles and their length before he attempts to design make-up. He must know approximately the space that must be devoted to advertising and the position of the space. That is, he must suit his design to the capacity required. Some of the problems he must face are as indicated in the following discussions:

1. Size of Pages.—*The Usual Sizes.*—The general page size is determined mainly by the purpose of the publication and the manner of its distribution. For some purposes the smaller sizes—5 x 7½ or 6 x 9 inches—may be chosen. These sizes are easy to read, easy to mail, and are the largest sizes in which the type-matter may be set in single columns. Larger sizes—8 x 11, 9 x 12½, etc.—require double columns. The largest practical size, 11 x 14, requires three columns. Magazines are at present tending toward larger pages, about 8½ x 12, to accommodate more decorative page make-up and to enable them to sell advertising space next to reading matter. These considerations rarely affect the small publisher and he usually chooses a smaller size because it is easier to mail and pleasanter to read. In choosing the page size, the editor must consider the weight of his paper, for a larger page requires heavier paper.

Standard Paper Sizes—Exact page size cannot be selected until the paper has been chosen, since a variation of half an inch may involve a serious waste of paper. Book paper is made in standard sizes but it is not always possible to secure every size in the paper chosen. The standard sizes are as follows:

22 x 28 inches	28 x 42 inches
24 x 38 "	32 x 44 "
25 x 38 "	36 x 48 "
26 x 40 "	

After the general page size and kind of paper have been selected, the exact page size may be considered with reference to paper size best suited to give the required number of pages with the least press work. The exact page size is determined by dividing the two dimensions of the white sheet by the number of folds, as will be shown in a later section. In figuring these dimensions, the editor should allow for a trim of about one-fourth inch at the top, bottom, and one side of each page after the paper has been folded. A good appearance will usually be assured if a standard proportion of about 5 to 7½ is followed. Another rule is to make the diagonal of the page twice its width. These details the editor can work out with the printer when he chooses the paper, if he has a general page size in mind, but he should not attempt to decide the size of the type body of the page before he knows exactly how large his pages are to be.

2. Number of Pages.—*How Press Work Affects Size.*—The chief consideration in deciding the number of pages is the number of "runs" on the press. Given the page size and the approximate number of pages desired, it is necessary to figure the exact number of pages on the basis of the size of the printer's press. To explain, a small booklet is not printed page by page on small sheets of paper, but a number of pages are made up into one form and printed all at once on a large sheet of paper. The paper is then folded and trimmed into finished form. For example, a sixteen-page publication would be divided into two eight-page forms. Eight pages would be printed on one side of the sheet and the other eight on the reverse; if properly made up, folded and cut, the finished booklet will have sixteen pages. The operation of printing each form is called a "run on the press." And it is the number of runs on the press that has much to do with the cost of the publication, not because of the time required for actual printing, so much as the time consumed in making up the forms and making ready on the press.

Methods of Folding.—To understand how press runs are reckoned, it is necessary to understand the methods of folding that printers employ. Obviously a single leaf of paper printed on both sides is the simplest form of press work; it carries two pages but cannot be bound into a book. The next step is to print two pages on each side and fold the sheet once; the result is called a *folio*—it has two leaves or four pages. If the sheet is folded twice it is called a *quarto;* four pages are printed on each side and the quarto contains four leaves or eight pages. Three foldings gives the *octavo,* with eight pages on each side; it has eight leaves or sixteen pages. The next step is twelve pages on a side, or *duodecimo,* containing 24 pages; this is rarely used in modern printing. Above duodecimo, the number of pages is indicated thus: 16mo, 32mo, 64mo. Mo or ° means in each case that the prefixed

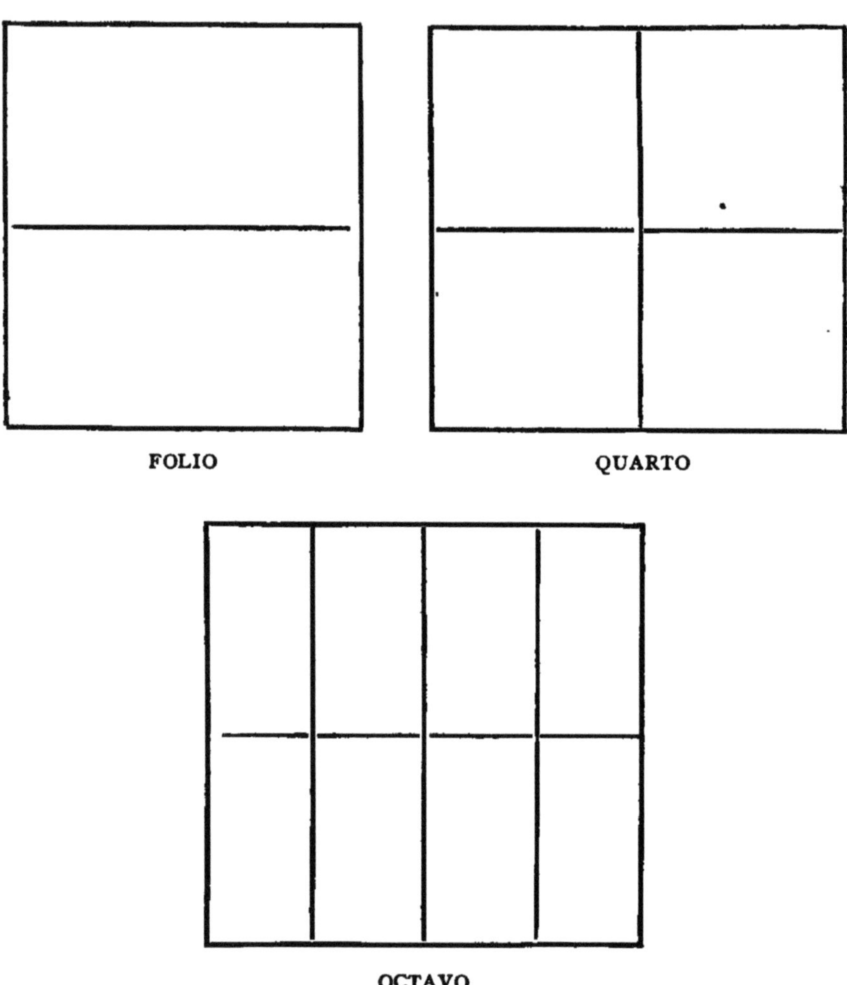

figure indicates the number of *pages* on one side of the sheet or the number of *leaves* in the finished book. A complete table would be as follows:

Unfolded	single sheet......	1 leaf,	2 pages
folio	1 fold...........	2 leaves,	4 pages
quarto	2 folds..........	4 leaves,	8 pages
octavo	3 folds..........	8 leaves,	16 pages
16mo	4 folds..........	16 leaves,	32 pages
32mo	5 folds..........	32 leaves,	64 pages
64mo	6 folds..........	64 leaves,	128 pages

Reckoning Number of Pages.—It will be seen then that the number of pages in the booklet must, in the first place, be a multiple of *four.* An odd number of pages is impossible, and a number not divisible by four means a pasted inset of one sheet. Beyond this, the question is determined by the size of the printer's press. If our pages are so large that the press cannot print more than eight at one time, our publication must be made in octavo form. That means that two runs, the smallest possible number, will give sixteen pages. We would hardly select twelve pages, for that would require four runs—a folio and a quarto, each requiring two runs—and the extra press work would cost more than the composition of the four pages saved. If sixteen are not enough, it is best to enlarge to two octavos, or thirty-two pages, for any enlargement requires two extra runs and we may as well get as many pages as possible out of the press work. Our octavo publication will then economize press work if its number of pages is some multiple of sixteen—16, 32, 48, 64, etc.

Ordinarily however, if the pages are of fairly small size, the printer's press will accommodate a 16-page form and the 16mo is the cheapest size to select. As

16mo carries 32 pages, the publication's number of pages should be some multiple of 32 for greatest economy. When we go beyond octavo, however, the number of pages increases so fast that composition cost goes ahead of press cost and it is economical to increase the number of runs instead of the number of pages. For instance, 48 pages—one 16mo and one octavo—would be cheaper than 64, although four runs are necessary in each case. However 44 pages would not be cheaper because it would require one 16mo, one quarto, and one folio—six runs on the press. Forty pages would require one 16mo and one quarto, but the quarto run would be a costly waste of press work.

It will be seen therefore that some knowledge on the editor's part will go far to save needless press work. In brief, it is usually wise to plan the publication in octavos—multiples of 16 pages—or in 16mo, multiples of 32. Any growth in the publication's size should be in octavos at least, for quartos are wasteful. This figuring is upset sometimes in a printing office that uses duodecimo forms, which lead to the use of multiples of 12 pages. The duodecimo, combined with octavo or 16mo, gives greater elasticity. Printers sometimes handle quartos and octavos by printing the entire eight or sixteen pages on both sides of a large sheet and cutting the sheet in two.

The mechanical working out of this press work can be learned only in the printing office. The arrangement of a 32-page form so that the pages will be in their proper places looks to the editor like a complicated task, but the practical printer works it out from a chart that is a part of his stock in trade. The folding is done by hand or by a folding machine. After folding the booklet is stitched on a wire stapling machine and the pages are cut by trimming off three edges. When the run is more than 16mo, it is customary to cut the sheet in two before folding so that the paper will not bunch along the folded edges. The editor's only part in the proceeding is to insist, occasionally, that the form be made up with care so that the margins of the finished pages will be of equal width.

3. Paper.—*How Paper is Selected.*—Paper must be chosen with reference to these points: weight, strength and body, surface, durability, color, and cost. The weight is usually determined on the basis of the size; the larger the page, the heavier the paper must be. Heavy paper gives the publication a richer appearance but it also increases the mailing cost—sometimes a serious item. In choosing weight, the editor must take care to avoid paper so light and transparent that black type shows through it. Strength and body are almost synonymous with general quality; the stronger and more brittle a paper is, the better its quality—and the greater its cost. Weight has little to do with quality for a heavy paper may be too soft and flimsy to stand press work and folding. It is well to test quality by tearing a corner of the paper or by "rattling" it to see how brittle it is. Surface must be chosen with reference to typography and illustrations. Soft paper prints deeply and hard paper receives only a surface impression. The relation of surface to typography will be discussed under Type, but here the kind of illustrations must be considered. Zinc engravings print well on almost any paper, but half-tones, especially fine copper cuts, require a smooth, hard surface. Durability is of little importance to the small publisher unless he is concerned with a publication that will have future value. Color is more important than is generally supposed because absolutely white paper is rare. Almost all paper is slightly tinted to conceal imperfections. Some papers have a slightly bluish tint; others more of a cream color. The choice between them depends upon the kind of cover chosen and the effect desired. By specifying ink slightly off the black and delicately tinted paper, the editor may secure a pleasing color scheme without additional cost. The cost is determined by the other considerations, and it may be said here that, if the editor has a clear idea of his publication, he can usually find what he wishes in moderately priced papers. It is not wise ordinarily to allow the printer to select the paper; the editor should ask to see the sample booklets sent out by the paper manufacturers and, when unable to choose between two kinds, should ask the printer to send to the paper house for a sample sheet of each to be folded into the form of the finished publication. Paper is retailed by the pound, and the weight given in the sample book is the weight of a ream (500 sheets) of that size. If a sample is marked "25 x 38, 60 pound," the meaning is that 500 sheets of that size weigh 60 pounds. If the same paper is sold in large sheets, however, its weight is listed higher; thus, 25 x 38,

60 pounds may be exactly the same paper as 28 x 42, 70 pounds.

Really to know how to judge paper, however, it is necessary to know something of the manufacture of paper, what it is made of, how it is made, and the various kinds on the market.

Paper Materials.—Paper is made of wood-pulp, wood-fiber, rags, or esparto grass. Rag paper is rarely used for anything except writing paper, and grass paper is mainly used for wrapping and other rough uses. The common printing papers are the wood-pulp and wood-fiber, sometimes called mechanical and chemical pulp. Of these the latter is the better because the wood in it is in long shreds that knit together and give greater strength—it is also more costly because the fibers are separated in the pulp by chemical, rather than mechanical means.

How Paper Is Made.—The general steps in paper making and their effects on the finished product may be described briefly. The ingredients in the paper, rags or wood, are first chopped into small bits, mixed with water or chemicals, beaten, cooked, and reduced to a pulpy semi-fluid mass. In hand-made paper, this pulp is spread out in sheets on wire screens, but hand-made does not concern the small editor. The paper that he will buy is made by machinery. The semi-fluid pulp is poured upon a slowly moving belt of wire cloth that vibrates meanwhile to spread the pulp into an even layer over its surface. If the belt vibrates only in one direction, the paper is not so good because its fibers all lie in one direction. This quality may be discovered by an attempt to tear the paper first one way and then the other. If the top wires in this belt all run one way, with some perhaps higher than others, the paper receives a series of parallel impressions and is called *laid* paper. A belt woven in the form of a grating, however, produces the mesh appearance seen in *wove* paper.

As the wet pulp passes along on the wire belt, it goes under a roller, called the *dandy roll,* which squeezes the water out of the pulp. The dandy roll has a wire cloth surface and the nature of its weave produces the laid or wove effect on the upper side of the paper. It is that dandy roll, also, that puts in the *watermark* by means of raised letters or figures on its surface which make the paper thinner in certain spots. After the paper has left the dandy roll it is dried, either by steam or in a loft where it is allowed to hang for some days.

Judging Paper Surface.—Surfacing is accomplished by means of huge steel rollers, called *calenders,* through which the paper is run. Once through the rollers produces *machine-finished* paper. More rolling produces surfaces ranging through *calendered* to *supercalendered.* Each rolling makes the paper harder and smoother. Some paper is covered with *sizing* to fill the pores and keep ink from spreading. Other paper is filled, or *loaded,* with clay or some similar substance, to give it smoother surface. Other paper is *supercoated,* and still other paper is *enameled* on one or both sides. *Plate* paper is that which has been subjected to great pressure to produce a smooth surface on both sides without filling. Among the unsized papers are *copperplate* and various craft papers. *Antique* paper is a thick, porous paper that has received only light calendering, or none at all. The list of surfaces as they range from rough to smooth is: antique, wove, laid, machine-finished, calendered, supercalendered, coated, enameled, plate, etc. *Deckle-edged* is a name applied to paper that has not been trimmed but bears the natural rough edge produced by the rubber deckles that keep the paper from falling off the wire cloth belt. As half-tone engravings require smooth paper, it is better to choose for them something at least as smooth as calendered paper, on the basis that the finer cuts require smoother paper.

4. Type.—*Size of Type Page.*—The first consideration in the matter of typography is the size of the type page with reference to the size of the paper page, and it is impossible to determine the size of the type page until after the paper has been chosen. Then the type page must be designed with regard to uniform margins on all sides. It is well to allow generous margins, even if this involves sacrifice elsewhere, for broader margins give richer appearance. The smallest margin that can be used with success is $\frac{3}{4}$ or $\frac{7}{8}$ inch; from that the margin may go up to $1\frac{1}{4}$ inches with good effect. Certain unusual effects are produced by unequal margins—wider at the bottom and outside than at other edges—but this treatment requires corresponding richness in typography and paper.

Column Widths.—Shall the publication be set in one, two, or three columns? This is almost automatically decided by the size of body type selected. The extreme column width employed in modern printing is about 40 ems pica, or 6½ inches—and this only with large type—for longer lines are difficult to read. Therefore if the type page is wider than 6 inches it must be divided for any type. With average body type the maximum line length is much shorter. In the case of 7- or 8-point type, the best column widths are from 13 to 18 ems pica, 2⅛ to 3 inches. With 9-point type, the column may safely be 21 ems pica, or 3½ inches, wide. With 10- or 11-point, especially when it is leaded, the width may run to 27 ems, or 4½ inches. On the other hand, the narrowest practicable column for any type is 12 ems, or 2 inches; the narrowest for 9-point is about 18 ems; the narrowest for 10-point is about 21. Columns narrower than these require much running over of words from line to line.

Page Diagram.—The easiest way to figure column widths, etc., is to lay out the page in diagram form. First cut a sheet of paper to the exact size of the finished page. Then with ruler and pencil draw the outlines of the type page, allowing proper margins. Lower the top line enough to allow for the folio head. The result is an exact diagram of the type page and its dimensions can be measured off with a ruler. Its width or line length should be translated into ems pica for the printer—one em equals approximately ⅙ inch. Its height may be translated into number of lines of type by dividing the height by the number of lines per inch of the type selected. For example, if the diagram shows the type body to be 4 inches wide by 6 inches high, the length of lines will be 4 (inches) x 6 (ems per inch) or 24 ems pica. If 12-point type is used, the number of lines will be 6 (inches) x 6 (lines of 12-point per inch) or 36 lines. If more than one column is used, one em should be allowed for column rule between. When small type on larger body is used, the number of lines must be figured on the body size—thus there are only six lines of 10/12 type in an inch although the type face is only 10/72 inch high.

Selection of Body Type.—Body type must be chosen with regard to size, blackness, and style of face. The above discussion will indicate the size of type best suited to given column widths. In general, however, the best sizes for small publication work are 9-, 10-, and rarely 12-point. For fine work, it is better to adopt a small face on a large body, as 9/10 or 10/12, than to use a large face. The same effect may be produced by leading small type. Blackness of type should be chosen with reference to paper selected. Since soft, rough paper receives a deeper impression than hard, smooth paper, it is best to use fine-cut type on hard paper and blacker type on soft paper. Sharp type also goes best with half-tone cuts. As regards face, standard roman type is best suited to most publications and easiest to obtain. Pretty effects may be obtained by the use of antique, old style, or some decorative face, but when an ornamental type is chosen, the design of the entire publication must correspond with it. It is often possible to obtain some modern decorative face, such as

Bodoni, for example, in all sizes from body to display, and the use of the same family throughout gives a neat appearance. The final decision will however probably be based on the printer's stock.

Selection of Other Type.—Display type must be chosen with regard to body type, just as in newspaper make-up; headings and titles should match reading type. The use of very black titles with light-face body type, or the opposite, ordinarily shows bad taste. The tendency of the present day seems to be toward smaller, lighter display type, since white space gives as great display as much ink. The sizes of type ordinarily selected for titles are 12- or 36-point. Whether in capitals and small letters, or all capitals, depends on the length of the title, but it is well to select two or three standard headings to be used for various purposes throughout the publication. Unless the editor has a natural feeling for typographical display, he is wise to select his titles from the same family as his body type or from some family of similar cut and decoration.

With the question of display type, goes that of folio heads and other details. Folio heads are page headings, including page numbers, that are repeated at the top of each page. They may be of ordinary type or, better, of some lighter face. The capital or small capital of the body type makes a good folio head. The editor must also decide the kind of rules to be used under and over the folio head—or the omission of rules. If authors' names are to be set at the head of the articles, it is well to set them in black-face capitals and small letters of the body type. If they are placed at the end of the article, small capitals of the same type are good. All of these details are mentioned because it is well for the editor to decide them, since the average printer is too busy to give them thought and is inclined to reach for the nearest case when he needs a display type.

Kind of Composition.—Whether the publication is to be machine- or hand-set depends largely on the printer's facilities. More faces are available in hand-set work, but delay may accompany this advantage. Ordinarily hand-set work makes proof correction easier than linotype work, for the resetting of line slugs to make revisions requires successive proofs until all errors have been eliminated—but on the other hand a "dirty case," meaning careless type distribution, will cause great trouble. Monotype work does away with both of these difficulties, but few job printers have these machines. Before the final decision on the matter is made, it is well to see a sample of the printer's machine work to judge the age and condition of the machine.

Type Specifications.—When all matters of typography have been settled, it is well to make up a schedule of the various kinds of type and to repeat type specifications in every succeeding piece of copy. Specify in each case, not only the size and face of type, but the column width; in the margin opposite each title, repeat the size and face to be used. Many annoying misunderstandings will be avoided if this course is followed.

5. Illustrations.—The average small publication is limited, in the matter of illustrations, to zinc etchings for line drawings and sketches, and half-tones for reproductions of photographs or wash drawings. It is well to use copper half-tones and specify a screen of about 150 lines per inch. In specifying sizes it is necessary to give only one dimension, for the other is determined by the size of the picture unless part of it is cut. The usual specification is width since the cuts must ordinarily accord with column widths employed. It is well also to work out a page design before ordering cuts. Engravers charge by the square inch for these cuts on a definite schedule that may be secured from the nearest house—about 5 cents for line engravings and 10 to 12 cents for half-tones. To insure the best cuts, drawings should be in black ink on white paper and photographs should be clear-cut, glossy prints. Obviously the size of the drawing or photograph has little to do with the size of the cut since it may be reduced or enlarged at will. When the cuts come from the engraver it is well to examine the engraver's proofs carefully and to insist that the printer use great care in making ready on the press.

6. The Cover.—A cover for the publication more than pays for itself in the improvement of appearance that it gives. When the outside page is printed on the same sheet and folded with the rest of the pages, manifold troubles arise. Unless the folding is absolutely accurate the printed matter is seldom centered perfectly on the page, and unless inking is perfect there is a constant variation in impression. If the cover must be dispensed with, some of these difficulties may be avoided by the use of very little printed matter on it and the elimination of any semblance of a border that may accentuate bad folding. The chief reason for a cover is to supply heavier outside pages to give shape and form to the booklet. To accentuate this, a paper of different color and texture may be chosen. Ordinarily cover paper is inexpensive, but the cover adds extra cost for it requires separate press work. Hence it is well to limit the printing upon it to the two outside pages so that the extra press work may be reduced to one run. The pretty effects produced with a cover that laps over the inside pages is offset by the cost of extra trimming and binding—for with such a cover the two parts of the publication must be trimmed separately before binding and the loose leaves are difficult to handle. As for the printed matter on the cover, it is best to use as little as possible and to set it in relatively small type. If the publication must carry a list of officers, the names of the editors, or the table of contents, it is wise to place them on an inside page. All that is usually needed on the cover is the name of the publication, the date, the volume and series number, and perhaps some special announcement of its contents—perhaps the names of leading articles in a small box. If a very decorative cover is selected, it is well to have an electrotype or cut of it made to avoid any possible typographical errors in succeeding issues; a mortise may be cut in the electro for contents and date or they may be placed at its top or bottom. The question of advertisements on the cover will be discussed later.

7. The Title Page.—The position and content of the title page are rather well established by precedent. If an entire page is devoted to this purpose, it should be the first right-hand page in the book. A great saving of space can be effected, however, by reducing this material to a title heading at the top of the first page of reading matter. When a list of editors, officers, or contents must be included, a good plan is to devote the top of the first right-hand page to title heading and the bottom to this additional material. As this matter is set in display type it is wise to select type to correspond with the title type used throughout and on the cover. Here again white space makes better display than large, black type since heavy type may show through on the next page. In content, the title heading should include the name of the publication, the name of the publishers, the publication office, the number of issues per annum, the price per issue and per year, the volume and series number, and the date of the issue. Unless the names of the editor and business manager appear elsewhere, they should be included here. If the publication is mailed as second class matter, the title heading should carry a notice reading: "Entered as second class matter on—(date of entrance)—at the postoffice at—(city and state)—under the Act of Congress, March 3, 1879." This is also a good place for copyright notice if the publication is copyrighted. Some small editors also include a list of advertising rates and other notices, but these may usually be dispensed with. Large magazines and newspapers usually place this material on the editorial page, but the first page is a better position in a small publication since it rarely has a distinct editorial page.

This material is mentioned here because much of it is required by the postal authorities. In addition, the publication must carry at stated intervals an announcement of ownership sworn before a notary. It is well to consult the local postmaster in regard to the postal laws before venturing upon such an enterprise. Copyright is secured by sending two copies of the publication and a small fee to the Copyright Bureau, Washington, together with proper blanks secured from that office.

8. Advertisements.—*Where to Place Them.*—The position and make-up of advertisements must be determined at the outset. The small editor will find himself almost forced to yield to the advertiser's desire to be near reading matter and should plan make-up accordingly. A good method is to devote the left-hand pages in the back of the publication to advertising, beginning at the back and working forward through the booklet as far as necessary. If all advertisements are kept on left-hand pages back of the book's center, a maximum of 25 per cent of the space will be devoted to advertising—a good ratio—and all advertising space will face reading matter. The question of selling the back page and the two inside pages of the cover to advertisers is a serious one. It is usually possible to charge a higher rate for these positions but little is gained for the extra press work—a second run for inside covers—will destroy the profit. The advertisement on the back page also injures the appearance of the small publication far more than the price can offset—clean covers give distinction.

Uniformity in Appearance.—Matters of typography and make-up should be settled before any advertisements are accepted. More and more publishers are limiting the size and blackness of type in advertising display, especially near reading matter. A good plan is to refuse to use in ads larger or blacker type than is employed in the largest title. The printer should also be urged to confine himself to one style of type throughout, preferably the style used in reading pages, and to secure all display through small type offset with white space. Illustrations allowed in advertisements should strictly accord with the rest of the make-up—no black cuts should be permitted. Many advertisers will call for fancy borders about their ads, but the appearance of the publication will be greatly improved by the use of the same kind of border for every ad—perhaps a single heavy rule. This will secure uniformity and give all advertisers a fair chance in attracting notice. Some editors even reset ads when advertisers supply electros that do not accord with their make-up, since they realize the value of uniformity. It would be foolish, of course, to announce such a policy in advance, for the average advertiser does not give the matter a thought, and the balky advertiser can usually be convinced by a proof of a well-set ad conforming to the editor's policy. The typographical rule is needed mainly to govern the careless printer who has a weakness for large type and for the nearest case.

9. Model of Design.—After the editor has decided on

the make-up, it is well to incorporate it in a *dummy model* to guide the printer and settle misunderstandings. To make such a dummy, the editor should secure from the printer a sheet of the paper chosen, folded, trimmed, and stitched in final form with cover attached. On each paper he should draw the outline of the type matter to show its size and position, the line length and number of lines. At the top of each page he should indicate the content of the folio head, on special pages he should mark the extreme limits of space to be occupied in display, and on various pages the amount of space to be left for headings. A line about the advertising pages will show the standard border size. Throughout he may indicate the kind and sizes of type to be used in various places. When finished, the dummy will be a complete working model of each issue. One copy may be given to the printer and another may be retained by the editor as it will prove of great value in estimating space and paging proof. It will form a part of the printer's contract like the drawings which an architect attaches to his building content and specifications.

Sample of Publication Design.—As an example of design and its problems, the following will illustrate the working out of a small publication for a special purpose. It was a small monthly designed to combine greatest artistic effect with low printing cost. A large page, about 9 x 12, was chosen for its possibilities in illustration and artistic page make-up. Thirty-two pages were selected because the printer's press could handle that size in two octavos. For economy a cover was dispensed with and a heavy paper was chosen to make up for its absence. The paper used was a calendered book paper, slightly cream in color, 36 x 48 inches in size, running 110 pounds to the ream. After folding and trimming the pages were $8\frac{3}{4}$ by $11\frac{1}{2}$ inches, and had uniform margins of $\frac{7}{8}$ inch on all sides. Hand-set body type was chosen because the printer had only a worn-out Junior Linotype and in his cases was a large stock of the Bodoni family. The 10/12-point Bodoni Book was selected as body type with 12-, 18-, 24-, and 36-Bodoni Bold for headings. There were also a few fonts of script and italic of the same family so that the one style of type could be used throughout. Headings were to be set in 24-point capitals and small letters and in 18-point capitals, with an occasional 36-point heading on an important article. Light-face 12-point capitals were to be used in folio headings. No type larger than 24-point was to be used in advertisements and each was to have single-rule border.

The front page outside carries the name in a box, 3 x $6\frac{3}{4}$ inches, near the top; this was drawn up and reproduced in a zinc etching. The volume and serial numbers and the date were in small type below it. The rest of the page was blank save the title of the leading article in 36-point capitals and small letters in the center below the cut. Page 2 carried an advertisement. Page 3 had the board of editors and publisher's announcement in a box at the top and an announcement of the succeeding issue below. Page 4 carried a layout of photographs or a cartoon. Reading matter began on page 5 below a title heading. From this point through page 15, each page was in two columns, set in 10/12 Bodoni Book in 27-em columns with no column rule; each column had 56 lines and each page carried about 1,100 words. Each article heading stretched across the entire page and consisted of a title in 24-point bold capitals and small letters centered, the author's name in 10-point capitals and small letters, and a three-line summary in 10-point italics, indented 4 ems on each side. The first word of each article was a 24-point capital. All articles began at the top of right-hand pages, extended through either two or four pages, and if necessary were broken over to the back. Thus the best article lengths were approximately 2,000 and 4,000 words. Illustrations were ordered in single and double column widths and each page was treated as a separate problem of make-up. Pages 16 and 17 were devoted to editorials, set in 10/12 Bodoni Book, in two 25-em columns, and each page was surrounded by a single-rule border. The editorials were short and separated by three asterisks; each began with a 24-point letter. These pages were the exact center of the book.

Back of page 17, all reading matter was set in three 18-em columns. The headings were of the same design but in smaller type. All advertisements of full-, half-, or quarter-page size were placed on left-hand pages; their make-up was begun at the back and was never to go further forward than page 20. Advertisements sold by the column inch were placed in the last column to the right of the reading pages, as near the back as possible. The pages back of page 16 were used for articles breaking over from the front, for unimportant material, for departments, and miscellaneous reading matter. The design afforded a magazine of great capacity at small cost, and a great flexibility of make-up. The uniformity of typography gave it great richness.

Specifications of a Quarterly.—Ideas for a smaller publication may be suggested by this description of a periodical designed for best appearance at least cost. A small page, 6 x 9, was selected so that it could be mailed in envelopes. The paper inside was a cheap antique since no illustrations were used; it was also cream-colored and as light as could be handled on the press, because the publication was not entered as second class matter and it was desired to keep the mailing cost down to 1 cent per copy—meaning that the copy, cover, and envelope must not weigh more than 2 ounces. The lightness of the paper required a cover—cheap stock of a light-brown color. The size chosen was thirty-two pages because the printer's press handled a 35 x 48 sheet and could print the entire booklet in two 16-page runs. A uniform modern face of type was selected for all reading matter and display as the printer had a fairly complete stock of one family. All reading matter was set in 10-point type, single leaded, 27-em columns and 42 lines per page with side margins slightly less than ¾ inch and broader margins at top and bottom. Less type on the page would have improved the appearance but sacrificed capacity. All headings were set in 12-point black-face capitals and the author's name was in 8-point capitals and small letters. Some unimportant material was set in 8-point type. Folio heads were 10-point light capitals, in single rule above and double rule below.

The outside cover carried simply the name, date, volume and serial number, and a box at the bottom containing a brief list of contents. All other cover pages were blank. The first page inside had the title heading at the top and a box containing officers' names at the bottom. The three inches of space between was devoted to the beginning of the leading editorial. From that point on articles succeeded each other continuously, beginning where they would, although an attempt was made to place headings near the tops of pages. No articles were allowed to end at the bottom of right-hand pages, but a few lines were always carried over to lead the reader to the next title. Beginning with page 18, all left-hand pages were devoted to ads, sold in full, half, and quarter pages, set in uniform type not to exceed 24-point, and boxed in a single-rule border. In the special number each year that carried the convention program, the program was carefully divided into sessions and placed on the right-hand pages in the back—a page to a session. This pleased advertisers and enabled the editor to charge higher rates in this issue.

II. HANDLING THE COPY

Exact Length Important.—As soon as the publication has been designed and the contract let to the printer, the editor is ready to begin turning in copy. The work of designing should have indicated the most suitable article lengths, and the editor should establish certain lengths for certain purposes. Whoever his contributors may be, he will find his work simplified if he asks for a definite number of words when he calls for copy. Instead of asking for "a short article," he should ask for "a 2,000-word article" or "3,000 words on the subject." The length should be determined on the basis of the number of words carried on each page.

Form of Copy.—All copy should be typewritten before it is given to the printer. If the author does not type it, the editor will find that the cost of typewriting will be saved in mistakes avoided. It is much easier also to estimate space that typewritten copy will fill. The copy should be double- or triple-spaced on one side of the paper and should have liberal margins for corrections. Before giving it to the printer, the editor should edit it as carefully as the newspaper desk man edits reporter's copy, since extra charge is made for changes in proof. For the sake of uniformity, he should establish definite rules of typographical style, punctuation, spelling, and grammar. These matters may be treated in accordance with suggestions in Chapter II, although the small editor must exercise greater care in altering the content of articles. Every piece of copy should bear type directions at the head of the first page. These should be indicated in printing office terms, inclosed in a circle, and should include the size and style of body type, the column width, and the size and style of various display lines, also whether underscoring material should be set in bold or italic type. In tabulated material, a diagram or model should indicate the form.

Proof Corrections.—When the material is in type, the printer will supply galley proof, which should be corrected carefully in accordance with the suggestions in the chapter on "Proofreading," and the usual signs should be used. It is well to have someone follow copy so that changes in content may be noted. When a change of content due to the printer's error is noted it should be marked "See Copy" to avoid charge for correction; other extensive changes not in accord with the copy should be recorded so that the correction bill may be checked. After the galley proof has been returned, it is well to read a revise to see if corrections have been made. In linotype material it is necessary to see successive revises until all mistakes have been eliminated, for the new line-slug may have another error. After all errors have disappeared, two proofs should be supplied for use in making a page dummy, which will be described later.

Copy Record.—As all the copy for an issue is rarely turned over to the printer at the same time or handled together, the task of keeping track of it is a complicated one. To simplify this, the editor will find a "copy record," in some such form as the following, of great assistance. A separate record should be kept for each issue and the several columns indicate the progress from copy to finished form, with the dates entered to serve as a check on a dilatory printer.

Name of Article	Estimated Length in Number of Words	Copy Rec'd	Copy Sent to Printer	First Proof Rec'd	Rev. Proof Read	Length in Type Lines
Smith's paper....	3,000	3/14	3/15	3/18	3/20	300
Book reviews.....	1,000	3/15	3/15	3/20	3/22	100
Programs........	1 page	3/12	3/12	3/18	3/20	42

Diagram of Make-up.—As the galley proofs of material pile up on the editor's desk, it is a bewildering task to take account of the space they will fill, and some system must be devised to keep track of them or the editor will find himself on press day with several pages too few or too many. A diagram that expresses the editor's ideas of the finished make-up in graphic form will simplify the problem and make easier the puzzling task of paging. The following diagram is one that works successfully and is simple to draw and fill out. In the outline, each page is represented by an oblong space, with the page number in the corner. The pages in the left-hand column are left-hand pages and those in the other column are the pages that face them. The advantage of this system is that it enables the editor to see opposing pages in proper relation. Pages 1 and 32 stand out alone, because no pages face them.

After the diagram has been drawn, the first step is to indicate on the proper pages the material whose position in the book is fixed, i. e., the title pages, advertisements, etc. Then it is possible to see graph-

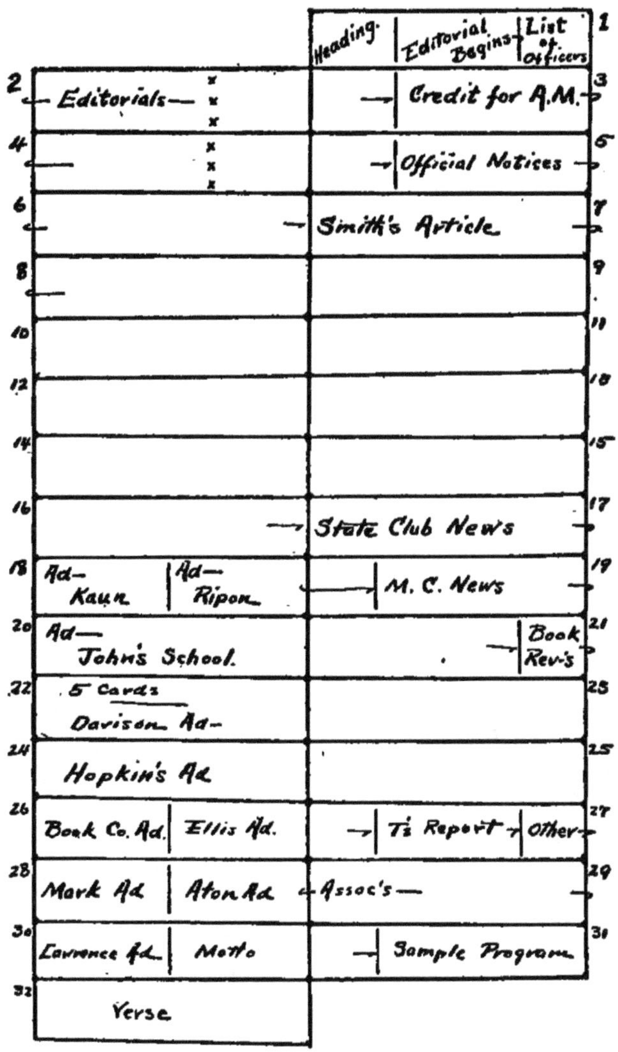

ically how much space there is to fill and to estimate it exactly on the basis of the number of lines of type per page. As each piece of copy reaches the revise proof stage, it may be entered up in the proper place and enough space is left for it on the basis of the number of lines in it, including the heading. Just before press day, when most of the copy has been set up, the diagram indicates exactly how many lines of space remain to be filled. The diagram then serves as a model to be followed in paging and furnishes an easy way to try out various make-up possibilities—easier than cutting and pasting proof.

III. MAKING THE PAGE DUMMY

Paging Proof.—A page dummy is an exact working model of a finished publication to guide the printer in making up galleys of type into page forms. The printer can, of course, page the type without a dummy, if the consecutive order of articles is suggested to him, but it is well for the editor to follow the example of magazine editors and work out make-up themselves. This must be done if any attempt is to be made to secure artistic make-up, which involves treating each page as a separate problem. The dummy is made by cutting the galley proof into page lengths and pasting it on sheets of paper that indicate the finished pages. The easiest method is to bind up enough sheets to give the required number of pages—i. e., 16 leaves give 32 pages—number them in order, write the proper folio head across the top, and paste on each page the proof of the type matter that is to appear on that page. The sheets should be large enough to allow for corrections and directions in the margin. If a diagram has been made up in advance, the task is a simple one; without a diagram, it is a matter of cutting, pasting, and fitting until things come even.

Problems in Paging.—Certain principles must be followed more or less rigidly in making a page dummy. The first of these is to make each page exactly the same length; if the make-up allows 42 lines of type, 41 or 43 lines on a page will cause unattractive unevenness. The printer may make up for it by leading out short pages, but that is not good practice. In counting the number of lines, the editor must make due allowance for inserts in smaller or larger type and for each heading; the proof will indicate how much. When the dummy is complete, he must insist that the printer follow it to the line, for an extra line carried over in one place will mean a line carried over on every page following. All instructions may be indicated in the margins and a chance is offered to catch errors missed in former proofs.

Position of Article Headings.—The problem involved in the placing of article headings is concerned with making each page attractive and at the same time with carrying the reader through from page to page so that, when he reaches the end of one article, the heading of the next is before him to attract his notice. Some editors prefer to place all headings at the tops of pages and to make up for varying article lengths by leaving the bottom of the last page blank when the article does not fill it. In such practice, it is customary to begin all articles on right-hand pages to carry the reader through and to facilitate clipping. This method often involves the use of fillers or break-overs and is ordinarily too wasteful of space for the small publication. The practice followed by most small editors is to place the articles in consecutive order without regard for the position of the headings—at the top of the page or the middle, on the left or right. The reader is carried along by the few lines of the preceding article carried over. This system makes attractive pages and economizes every inch of space. It is harder to make up, however, for some attempt must be made to keep headings above the middle of the page and some juggling of articles is involved.

Page Breaks.—Another question is the typographical one of breaking from one page or column to the next. It is considered bad form to break a word from one page to the next and equally bad to leave a partial line —the first or last line of a paragraph—at the top or bottom of a page. Many printers object to this so seriously that they break away from the page dummy to avoid it. The editor must avoid it either by juggling the articles, or, better, by asking the printer to rejustify a line or two in order to crowd back a word or make an additional line. Many paragraphs, it will be found, end in one-word lines which offer elastic points where a line of space may be saved by a small amount of rejustifying.

Page and Form Proofs.—After the editor has submitted his page dummy and the printer has made up the pages, it is best to ask for a page proof of the entire publication for a final checking up of folio heads, page numbers, and all the work of paging. When this has been revised, the publication is ready for the press.

Even then, careful editors go to the printing office on press day to see a form proof or the first sheet off the press. Besides furnishing the last chance to catch errors, it gives an opportunity to see if all pages are right-side-up and in proper place. If the sheet is folded and trimmed it is possible to examine the uniformity of the margins.

IV. THE BUSINESS MANAGER'S WORK

There is so much variation in the financial conditions behind small publication work, that it is impossible to discuss the business end of the work in great detail. There are, however, certain ideas and methods that will assist the small editor, whatever may be his financial backing.

1. Advertising.—*Dealing with the Advertiser.*—Supposing that the publication is to carry advertising, the matter of handling it involves similar problems in all cases. The questions regarding its position, typographical and other limitations, and make-up, have already been discussed. Its character and amount will be determined by the nature of the publication. The matter of soliciting advertising must be determined by the conditions of the work. Whether it be solicited in person or by letter, however, one or two things are always true. Whatever the character and circulation of the publication may be, the editor will find it wise to analyze the appeal of his publication, the reason why it is a good advertising medium, and formulate this appeal in concrete statements that will attract the advertiser. He then has a "talking point" like the salesman of goods. His publication is more than likely to be a class publication circulating among readers of a certain kind, and will appeal to a limited degree to all advertisers who wish to reach this class. But, more than that, there is usually some reason why this publication will supply a cheap and effective way of interesting and reaching this class. It may be the only publication in a large territory going to this class; it may be the official organ of the class; it may be published as a means by which the class of readers exchanges notes. Some thought on the subject will open up larger advertising possibilities than were at first imagined and will furnish a simple way of attracting the advertiser. And in all cases advertising space should be thought of by the editor as a commodity of value, a kind of goods that he has for sale. In no case should advertisers be asked to buy space as a favor or a duty—they should be offered a definite amount of valuable publicity at a proportionate price. If the editor knows his field, he can often express in figures the cost of circularizing the field by letter as compared with the cost of reaching these customers through his publication. On this basis, his advertising becomes a business proposition. His soliciting letters should carry that feeling and should state the value of his space in brief, concise language. Very often when it is hard to convince an advertiser and point out the appeal, it is worth while to write an advertisement embodying the editor's ideas and even have it set in type to show its value.

Checking Advertising Returns.—After the space is

sold it is wise to follow it up with an idea of discovering what returns it is bringing to the advertiser and of increasing its "pulling power." The use of a "key address" in the ad will enable the advertisers to know exactly what business is resulting from it. In most cases, also, it is wise to request a change of advertising copy with each issue as the constant change gives the advertisement the character of reading matter and increases its value as well as enriches the publication. Nothing is so dismal to advertiser or editor as standing cards, unchanging from issue to issue. The change does not involve extra cost since a printer charges about as much for holding the ad in type as for resetting it.

Size of Advertisements.—The division of advertising space depends upon the publication's make-up. If small pages are used, it is best to sell space by full, half, and quarter pages. With larger pages the space may be sold by the column-inch, meaning an inch high and a column wide. Newspapers sell all their space by the inch at the rate of fourteen agate (5½ point) lines to the inch, but such a practice in small publications results in difficult make-up. The prices charged are usually based on what the editor thinks he can get, or on a fair division of cost between subscriptions and advantages. The foundation is the price of the full page. The standard among national magazines of general circulation is $1 per page per thousand circulation—the page being about 7 x 10 inches and containing about 16 column inches. This means that a magazine of 120,000 circulation may charge $120 per page. With a class circulation, the small editor may charge relatively more because his circulation is intensive—every reader is a possible buyer of the class of goods advertised. He uses his page rate as the basis of his schedule but he does not ordinarily divide his rates exactly in proportion to the division of space. The small ad is not so valuable as the large ad, in that it offers less room for display and discussion, but to a certain extent it attracts almost as much notice. Hence a half-page ad is worth more than half as much as a page ad, and a quarter-page is worth more than half as much as a half-page.

The Rate Card.—A sliding scale of rates is therefore necessary to include all sizes that the editor wishes to sell. A certain discount should also be given for contract ads that are to run more than one time, and an extra rate should be charged for special positions, such as cover pages and the first page after reading matter. All of these should be figured out in advance and embodied in a printed rate card to be inclosed in all letters soliciting advertising. The printed card indicates to the advertiser that the editor is businesslike and is treating all advertisers alike. A suggestive sliding scale of rates for a small class publication is illustrated here:

ADVERTISING RATES

Full Page	$15.00
Half Page	8.00
Quarter Page	4.50
One column	8.00
Inch (single column)	1.50

(Cover pages 20 per cent extra)

Dimensions: Size of page, 6 x 9 inches. Two columns. Column length, 7 inches; column width, 13 picas ($2\frac{1}{8}$ inches.)

Forms close 15th of month previous to publication date.

Terms: Cash with order or satisfactory references. Accounts payable quarterly. Ten per cent discount on annual contracts. All advertising next to, or facing, reading matter.

Rates Subject to Change Without Notice

In the above card the scale is based on the price per page per single insertion, which results in a lower page rate on contracts. It might be figured out more completely on the rate card on the basis of a *minimum* price per page (say $20) on any contract:

	Four Insertion Order	Two Insertion Order	Single Insertion
Full Page	$80.00	$42.00	$22.00
Half Page	44.00	23.10	12.10
Quarter Page	24.00	12.60	6.60
Column Inch	8.00	4.20	2.20

This scale has a minimum rate of $20 per page on the greatest discount—for four insertion order—and gives 5 per cent. increase for two insertions and 10 per cent. increase for one insertion. It illustrates the way in which large magazines figure their advertising rates but is rather too complicated for small publication work. A typographical model for the rate card may be secured from any magazine.

Advertising Contract.—Although an advertiser's letter ordering space is almost as good as a contract, many small editors feel that it is safer to use a contract. An advantage of the system is that the contract forms a convenient record for filing in the office; if it is printed on a card of convenient size it may be filed in a card catalog which serves as a handy record of the ads to be carried in each succeeding issue. If it carries in addition a place for recording the acceptance of proof and of payment, the card file saves much bookkeeping. The following is a suggestive model:

Publisher, Sample Magazine, ...191..
1234 First street, City, State.
Please insert advertisement of the undersigned, to occupy ...., commencing.............
for which .... agree to pay $.........................
....

Proof Submitted	Proof O.K'd	Paid
....	....	....

Saving of printing is accomplished by printing the contract on the back of the rate card, since both must be inclosed in letters soliciting advertising. Some editors prefer to use a system of duplicated contracts, but this is of little value unless the advertiser pays in advance.

Proof to be Submitted.—As indicated in the record spaces on the contract card, the editor must ordinarily submit proof of the advertisement before it is published. He sends a printer's proof to the advertiser, as soon as the ad is in type, and delays publication of the ad until it returns with O. K. or corrections. Much difficulty will be avoided at times if these accepted proofs are filed with the advertiser's correspondence.

Billing the Advertiser.—When the advertiser's bill is sent to him, it is well to send him a marked copy in the same mail so that he may be sure the ad was published. Some advertisers wish two copies for their office files. Because of the large number of bills to be sent out each month, it is wise to have a printed bill-head; it is likely to receive prompter payment. Needless to say, also, no one should try to run a publication, however small, without a printed letter-head carrying the editor's name and office of publication. In fact, the smaller the publication, the more necessary is the letter-head, not because advertisers distrust the editor's honesty, but because they wish to be sure that they are buying space in a bona fide publication.

System and Methods.—All of these suggestions will indicate that the advertising branch of small publication work must be conducted in a businesslike manner. No matter how small the publication, the editor must convince the men with whom he is dealing that he is thoroughly businesslike. Money spent on proper letter-head and other printed matter, as well as on typewritten correspondence, will be more than repaid in added prestige and business. Each magazine has a system of its own for handling these matters and advertising managers are usually glad to supply a beginner with samples of their printed matter and an explanation of their various systems. They are often especially glad because they realize that the slipshod business methods and cringing solicitations of many small, insignificant publications are doing much to retard the development of advertising business on a modern basis—the legitimate sale of space as a commodity of definite value.

2. Circulation.—*Wrappers or Envelopes.*—The most serious problem in connection with small publication circulation is that of wrapping and addressing. If the magazine is of small size, 6 x 9 inches, the best wrapper is a cheap manila envelope, large enough to hold the booklet without folding, and printed with the name and address of the publication in the upper left corner. If it is mailed under the second class rate, it should carry the words—"Entered as second class matter in the postoffice at———." It is also wise to print under the name, "Postmaster:—If not delivered please notify publisher and postage will be sent for return." This aids in eliminating dead addresses on lists. If the publication is too large for envelope mailing, the best substitute is a flat manila wrapper rolled around the magazine and pasted. It may be large or small, printed or blank. The wrapper can be handled more quickly than envelopes, but results in a tightly rolled magazine. A bulky publication may be mailed flat in a wrapper, but there is danger that the wrapper will be torn off in the mail.

Addressing.—There are several ways of disposing of the addressing problem. If the circulation is small, less than 500, the cheapest method is to address the envelopes by hand, with pen or typewriter. A large circulation requires the use of an addressing machine. The simplest kind of mechanical addresser is some form of the "mustang mailer," a contrivance used by many newspapers. It requires a printed list of names and addresses on tough colored paper and operates by cutting and pasting one name each time it is pressed down on a wrapper. For its economical operation, the circulation lists should be set up on the linotype machine and kept in type form in galleys; each month, after corrections have been made, the printer takes a proof of the galley for use in the mailer. The chief objection to this method is that the pasted slip is small and indistinct. The next best mailer is some form of the stencil mailing machine which has pasteboard stencils with cut-out letters. The stencils are cheap if someone nearby has a stencil cutter. There are other kinds of automatic addressing machines but most of them are too costly for the small publisher; he must use the facilities which the printer has or he can borrow. In cities, the printers have mailing machines but in smaller towns the editor must rely on the mustang or hand addressing.

Subscription Lists.—The work of keeping track of subscriptions is greatly facilitated by the use of a date or some other sign on the address slip or stencil to indicate the date on which the subscription expires. Some system must also be adopted for classifying the names on the lists. They may be arranged alphabetically or, better, by states or cities. With such a classification and the expiration date, the editor can easily keep his lists up to date by going over the lists after each issue and throwing out dead names.

Subscription Blank.—Methods of developing circulation and following up expired subscriptions are outside this discussion but, if a subscription blank is used, the following is a good form. It should be printed on a piece of paper that may be slipped into a letter and should carry at the head the name and address of the publication.

> Gentlemen:—I am enclosing one dollar ($1.00) for one year's subscription to the Sample Magazine, beginning ....
> Name .... Street ....
> City .... State ....

Postal Rates.—Mailing rates depend on whether the publication may be entered as a second class periodical. If it is not admitted under this rate, it must be mailed as third class matter at the rate of "1 cent for 2 ounces or fraction thereof," and stamps must be affixed to each copy. This often makes necessary some consideration of paper weight. If the weight of each copy is slightly over two ounces, it is better to reduce its size or the weight of the paper than to pay 2 cents on each copy. The weight may be determined in advance by having the printer make up a dummy of the paper selected, of the exact size and with cover attached. If the weight is slightly over the mark, lighter paper or cover or greater trim may reduce it—sometimes an extra 1/8 inch trimmed off one edge will save 1 cent per copy in mailing. The envelope must of course be considered in the experiment and, if the weight is close to the mark, it is well to have the postmaster weigh a copy and give his official sanction. When the circulation is large enough to warrant it, the postmaster may save the editor the work of affixing stamps by allowing him to print "1 cent paid" on the envelope and pay in a lump sum.

The Second Class Rate.—Permission to mail under the second class periodical rate is secured by application to the postal department through the local postmaster. He will require the editor to fill out under oath an application blank containing a long list of questions concerning the nature and business of the publication. If the postmaster thinks, after reading the blank and examining the editor's books, that the postal authorities are likely to honor the application, he forwards it with two copies of a current number of the magazine to Washington. While negotiations are pending, he may if he wishes allow the editor to deposit a sum of money equivalent to the third class rate and to mail an issue or two carrying the note, "Application for entry as second class matter at the postoffice at ——— pending." If the entry is allowed, the amount in excess of the second class rate is then refunded. This rate is granted only to a publication that fulfills the following conditions: It must be issued regularly at stated intervals, as frequently as four times a year, bear a date of issue, and be numbered consecutively. It must be issued from a known office of publication. It must be formed of printed paper sheets, without board, cloth, leather, or other substantial binding, such as distinguish printed books for preservation from periodical publications. "It must be originated and published for the dissemination of information of a public character, or devoted to literature, the sciences, arts, or some special industry, and having a legitimate list of subscribers: Provided, however, that nothing herein contained shall be so construed as to admit to the second class rate regular publications designed primarily for advertising purposes, or for free circulation, or for circulation at nominal rates."

In brief, the second class rate is intended for bona fide periodicals and every attempt is made to close it to advertising publications. To this end, the editor is questioned concerning the amount of advertising he carries, whether his space is open to all advertisers, the relation of his paid circulation to his total circulation, and the intent of the publication. Some leniency is occasionally shown to publications with small circulations and much advertising, on the basis of their intent. All small editors make an attempt to secure this rate not only because of its cheapness—1 pound for 1 cent—but because second class matter is mailed by the pound without stamps and the extra expense involved in the "or fraction thereof" phrase in the third class rate is eliminated. The editor simply delivers his edition, wrapped and addressed, at the postoffice; it is weighed in one mass, and he pays by the pound in monthly or quarterly payments. The admission to the rate gives a certain amount of prestige in the eyes of advertisers, since it indicates that it is a bona fide periodical with a paid circulation.

3. The Printer.—No small publisher should attempt to do business with a printer without a written contract specifying not only the price but the character of the work. The contract should give the kind and weight of paper, the size and number of pages, the kind of cover and binding, the kind of typography, and the character of work in general. It is well also to specify the rate on extra work, such as proof correction and repaging. The contract should be in duplicate, signed by both parties, and sufficiently definite to stand the test of the law court.

Many printers prefer to set a lump price for the publication of a certain number of copies of certain size and make-up. This is especially true when they are bidding low; they hope to make up the difference on extras and additions. When the bid is attractively low, it is sometimes well to accept such a contract, but usually the small editor will find it best to sign a contract more favorable to himself and elastic enough to allow for growth. Such a contract needs to be divided into parts to correspond with the various operations involved. It should specify the rate per page for composition, the charge for additional runs on the press caused by increased number of pages, and the charge for folding and binding per 100 or 1,000 copies. In some cases the specifications cover the cost of composition per page (including additional press work) and the cost of "manufacturing" per 1,000 copies. Either arrangement allows for expansion in size or circulation at a proportionate rate.

In the selection of a printer, it is customary to lay the specifications before several printers and accept the lowest bid. Even so, the editor is likely to place the contract with the printer who has the best mechanical facilities and does the best work, and the bidding is simply a means to ascertain the justness of the best printer's price.

APPENDIX I

LIST OF SIGNIFICANT DATES IN THE HISTORY OF THE ART OF PRINTING AND THE DEVELOPMENT OF THE NEWSPAPER

Dates in History of Printing are in Italics

1418 *Disputed date of earliest piece of printing—Brussels wood-cut of the Blessed Virgin.*

1450 *First book printed from movable types—by Gutenberg in Germany.*

1454 *Small type first used—in Pope Nicholas V. Indulgence.*

1457 First newspaper—*Nuremberg Gazzette*—in Germany.

1465 *Roman type appeared—cast at Subiaco, Italy, by two German printers.*

1475 *Approximate date of first English book—by William Caxton.*

1480 *Printing was well established throughout Europe.*

1501 *Italic type invented by Aldus Manutius, Venice.*

1534 First regular newspaper—*Neue Zeitung aus Hispanien und Italien*—Nuremberg.

1550 *Typefounding established as a separate business.*

1550 *Metal screw introduced in hand press by Danner of Nuremberg.*

1588 First English newsletter—*English Mercurie.*

LIST OF SIGNIFICANT DATES

1615 First daily newspaper—*Die Frankfurter Oberpostants Zeitung*—by Egenolf Eurmel—Father of Newspapers.

1620 First real improvement in the hand press, by W. J. Blaew, Amsterdam—he devised a spring to raise the platen.

1622 First newspaper in England—*The Weekly Newes*—told of German wars—was beginning of "news-books" or "relations."

1622 First advertisement in English periodical—a book advertisement in Thomas Archer's *Corantos.*

1626 First newspaper with a name—Archer's *Mercurius Brittanicus.*

1631 First regular French newspaper—*Gazette de France*—by Theophraste Renandot.

1637 Decree of Star Chamber limiting number of English printers.

1638 First printer in America—Stephen Daye of Cambridge, Mass.

1641 First English journal of domestic news—Thomas' *Diurnall Occurrences in Parliament,* later called *Perfect Diurnall*—its writer, Samuel Peck, is called Father of the English Newspaper.

1650 First official journal—Marchamont Nedham's *Mercurius Publicus,* issued for Cromwell.

1657 M. Nedham published a newspaper entirely composed of advertisements—*Publick Adviser*—rate not based on space.

1659 Joseph Moxon, first English typefounder, began letter cutting.

1660 *Leipsic Gazette* published.

1660 The word "advertisement" began to be used by English editors.

1665 First official organ, in form of newspaper, to reprint laws and proclamations—*Oxford Gazette*—later called *London Gazette*—it appeared after suppression of licensed "newsbooks" and marked end of age of pamphlets.

1681 Beginning of lists of prices and reports—*Merchants' Remembrancer*—English.

1690 First newspaper in America—Benjamin Harris' *Publick Occurrences,* printed in Boston—to be monthly—suppressed after one number. Harris was exiled English editor.

1692 First magazine—*Gentlemen's Journal,* London—monthly.

1693 First woman's newspaper—*Ladies' Mercury,* London.

1695 Beginning of free press in England—ban on parliamentary report removed—licensing of books and newspapers stopped—*Post-Man, Post-Boy, Flying Post,* then appeared.

1695—Appearance of "editors," rather than "authors," of newspapers.

1700 First comic newspaper, *Merrie Mercury,* London.

1700 Approximate date of end of "news-letters" in England.

1702 First (?) daily in England—*Daily Courant*—morning.

1704 First regular newspaper in America—*Boston News-Letter,* by Nicholas Boone—it lived 72 years.

1704 First example of real reporting—in *Boston News-Letter*—a hanging.

1704 Appearance of Daniel Defoe's *Mercure Scandale*—or *Weekly Review of the Affairs of France Purg'd from the Errors and Partiality of Newswriters and Petty Statesmen.*

1706 First penny paper—*The Orange Postman*—half-penny or 1 cent.

1706 First evening paper—*The London Evening Post.*

1706 First provincial paper in England—*Crossgrove's Gazette* at Norwich.

1709 Steele's *Tatler* appeared.

1712 Establishment of Stamp Act—half-penny per half-sheet in red stamps—a shilling for each advertisement—tax of a shilling on every copy or more than one sheet killed magazines.

1719 *Boston Gazette* appeared—a postmaster's newspaper.

1719 *American Weekly Mercury* appeared in Philadelphia, edited by Andrew Bradford, postmaster—contained "Busy Body" articles by Benjamin Franklin.

1721 *New England Courant* started in Boston by James Franklin, later edited by Benjamin Franklin—first rebel newspaper.

1725 *New York Gazette,* weekly, started by William Bradford—later called the *Post-Boy*—was a government organ.

1725 Plaster-of-paris stereotyping developed by William Ged of Edinburgh.

1727 *Annapolis Gazette* appeared.

1728 *Pennsylvania Gazette* appeared in Philadelphia—later edited by B. Franklin—merged with *North American* in 1845.

1728 London coffeehouse men proposed a scheme of syndicating news and advertisements.

1731 *Charleston Gazette* appeared.

1731 *Boston Weekly Rehearsal* started by Jeremy Gridley—very literary—later became *Boston Evening Post.*

1733 *Rhode Island Gazette* started at Newport by James Franklin.

1733 *New York Weekly Journal* started by John P. Zenger—lived until 1752.

1734 Diagrams of Battle of Phillipsburg printed by *American Mercury.*

1734 First newspaper libel suit in America—against Zenger of *New York Journal*—Andres Hamilton, defending editor, secured acquittal by demanding that jury find on fact.

1736 *Virginia Gazette* started at Williamsburg.

1737 First point system of type measurement worked out by Pierre S. Fournier, French typefounder.

1742 *Pennsylvania Journal and Weekly Advertiser* started war on Stamp Act.

1748 *Independent Advertiser* started by Samuel Adams, one of first rebel newspapers.

1752 *New York Mercury* started by Hugh Gaine—ran until 1783.

1753 *Boston Gazette and Country Gentleman* started as real organ of revolutionary party.

1755 *Connecticut Gazette* started at New Haven.

1756 Founding of oldest living continuous newspaper in America—*The Portsmouth* (N. H.) *Gazette.*

1758 *Poor Richard's Almanac* published by Benjamin Franklin.

1762 *New York Royal Gazetteer* founded to combat revolutionary ideas.

1764 *Connecticut Courant* started at Hartford—still published under same name.

1765 "Join or Die" motto, with device of snake divided into eight parts, first used by *Constitutional Courant* (Burlington, N. J.)—editor was William Goddard.

1767 *New York Journal & General Advertiser* started by John Holt as revolutionary organ.

1767 *Connecticut Journal & New Haven Post-Boy* started —now known as *New Haven Journal-Courier.*

1768 First typefounding in America.

1770 *Massachusetts Spy,* tri-weekly revolutionary paper, started—carried "Join or Die" motto in 1774—still published as *Worcester Spy.*

1771 There were twenty-five newspapers in America.

1775 There were thirty-seven newspapers in America.

1776 First paper to print the Declaration of Independence was the *Virginia Gazette*—carried a synopsis on July 19 and the entire document on July 26.

1777 First daily in Paris—*Journal de Paris ou Poste au Soir.*

LIST OF SIGNIFICANT DATES

1767 *Boston Chronicle* founded as Tory organ—ran until 1770.

1784 First daily paper in America—*American Daily Advertiser* of Philadelphia—later merged with *North American.*

1785 Second daily paper in America—*New York Daily Advertiser.*

1785 *London Times* founded by John Walter of logotype fame—known as *The Daily Universal Register. Printed Logographically*—name changed to *The Times or Daily Universal Register* in 1788—became *The Times* three months later.

1786 First newspaper west of the Alleghenies—*The Pittsburg Gazette.*

1787 First real reporter was Joseph Gales who covered first meeting of Congress at Philadelphia.

1791 *National Gazette* started in Philadelphia as Democratic organ.

1792 *State Gazette* started in Trenton, N. J.—still is published.

1793 First paper in Tennessee—*Knoxville Gazette.*

1793 Oldest paper in New York City started—*The Minerva,* founded by Noah Webster, attacked slavery in one of its first numbers—later became *Commercial Advertiser & New York Spectator.*

1798 First iron hand press, built by the Earl of Stanhope, England.

1799 *Sciota Gazette,* Chillicothe, O., started by Nathaniel Willis, "Father of the press of the Northwest."

1799 Fourdinier papermaking machine invented by Robert Louis, Paris.

1800 First official government paper in America—*National Intelligence & Washington Advertiser*—dubbed the *Court Paper*—printed debates of Congress as reported by Gales and Seaton.

1801 *New York Evening Post* started by William Coleman—

oldest paper in city that has continued under same name.

1803 First paper in New Orleans—*The Moniteur.*

1804 First papermaking machine in England erected at Frogmoor Mill, called the Fourdinier machine.

1804 Plaster stereotyping developed by Earl of Stanhope.

1806 First paper in New Orleans after Louisiana Purchase —*Louisiana Courier*—part French and part English.

1806 First American market reports—*Prices Current* in *United States Gazette* of Philadelphia.

1807 Patent granted on plunger idea on which modern typecaster is based.

1808 First paper in Indiana started at Vincennes.

1810 First power press, built by Frederick Koenig—modified hand press.

1811 Expression "Gerrymandering" invented by *Columbia Centinel,* Boston.

1812 First cylinder press, built by F. Koenig in England.

1813 *National Advocate* started in New York by Tammany Hall—James Gordon Bennett became its editor in 1825.

1813 First stereotyped book in America—by John Watts, New York.

1814 First newspaper in Illinois—*The Intelligencer* at Kaskaskia.

1814 Steam press used for first time to print London Times —it was a Koenig cylinder press.

1815 English Stamp duty raised to four pence per copy on newspapers.

1816 *St. Louis Enquirer* founded.

1816 Largest newspaper in New York, *Mercantile Advertiser,* had 2,250 circulation—there were then six dailies and two weeklies in the city.

1816 First steam papermaking machine in America, erected at Pittsburg.

LIST OF SIGNIFICANT DATES

1816 *Clymer-Columbian hand press with lever instead of screw invented.*

1817 *First cylinder papermaking machine—built by Thomas Gilpin at Brandywine, U. S. A.*

1817 *Detroit Gazette* founded—suspended 1830.

1820 *Lithographic printing developed—approximate date.*

1820 *Machine-made paper supplanted hand-made paper about this time.*

1821 *Date of first attempt to set type by machinery.*

1822 *Papier-maché stereotyping invented in France.*

1822 *Hand press with toggle-joint instead of lever brought out by Peter Smith in America.*

1822 *Daniel Treadwell built power press in Boston—modified hand press.*

1822 *Type-casting and composing machine patented in England by Dr. William Church of U. S.*

1822 *First attempt at uniform system of type measurement in America—by George Bruce, N. Y.*

1825 First Sunday paper in America—*New York Sunday Courier*—published on Sunday only.

1826 *Philadelphia Public Ledger* started—as a penny paper.

1826 *Youth's Companion* started in Boston—as a religious paper.

1826—First printing in Wisconsin—1,000 lottery tickets at Green Bay.

1826 William Cullen Bryant became editor of *New York Evening Post.*

1827 First woman's magazine in America, *The Ladies' Magazine,* Boston, by Mrs. Sarah J. Hale.

1827 The Wall street "Blanket Sheets" appeared in New York—*Courier & Enquirer* and *Journal of Commerce*—6 cents per copy—the latter was founded as an abolition paper.

1827 *Applegate & Cowper perfecting cylinder press adopted by London Times.*

1827 *Washington hand press perfected by Samuel Rust, N. Y.*

1828 *Grippers to handle paper on cylinder press invented by Napier.*

1828 *First attempt to cast type by machinery—by W. M. Johnson, U. S.*

1829 First American sporting paper—Porter's *Spirit of the Times,* N. Y.

1830 *Washington Globe* started—part of "Kitchen Cabinet."

1830 *Boston Transcript* founded.

1831 Humor column originated in *Boston Daily Morning Post.*

1831 First railway passenger train—Mohawk & Hudson Railroad.

1831 *Louisville* (Ky.) *Journal* started—merged with *Courier* in 1868.

1831 New York papers established news schooners to meet incoming vessels.

1831 *Boston Liberator,* abolition paper, started by William Lloyd Garrison—published for 34 years.

1831 *Democratic Free Press & Michigan Intelligencer* founded—later *Detroit Free Press.*

1832 First independent penny paper, *New York Globe,* started by James Gordon Bennett in opposition to "Blanket Sheets"—failed at once.

1832 *First cylinder press in America—built by Robert Hoe.*

1832 *Papier-maché stereotyping introduced into England.*

1832 First illustrated journal in England—*Penny Magazine.*

1833 Second attempt to publish penny paper in New York—*Morning Post*—lasted twenty-one days—by Shepard.

1833 First newspaper in Chicago—*The Democrat*—merged with *The Tribune* in 1861.

1833 First successful penny paper in New York—*The Sun*—started by Benjamin Day—small size, much local news, no editorials.

LIST OF SIGNIFICANT DATES

1833 First newspaper in Wisconsin—*Green Bay Intelligencer.*

1834 Fifteen daily papers in New York at this time—population 270,000—largest had 6,000 circulation.

1834 First steam press in Northwest—Cincinnati Commercial Register.

1835 Date of the famous Moon Hoax.

1835 There were then about 1,258 newspapers in United States—none had more than 6,000 circulation.

1835 Wood engraving developed in America about this time.

1835 First steam press in New York—installed by The Sun.

1835 *New York Herald* founded by James Gordon Bennett on $500 capital, penny paper, marks beginning of Independent Press.

1835 Famous money articles begun by *New York Herald.*

1835 First regular stock quotations, published by *New York Herald.*

1835 Idea of news companies to distribute papers, by *New York Herald.*

1835 Cash system in advertisements and subscriptions, by *New York Herald.*

1835 New York papers had pony expresses to Washington and Philadelphia.

1835 Second paper in Chicago—*The American*—later became *The Express* in 1842.

1836 Regular news summaries begun by *New York Weekly Herald.*

1837 First real reporters employed by New York papers.

1837 *New Orleans Picayune* started—built on George W. Kendall's jokes.

1838 Express companies started—began to distribute newspapers.

1838 First steamship line between New York and Europe.

1838 System of foreign correspondence started by *New York Herald.*

1838 *First successful typecasting machine patented by David Brüce, New York.*

1839 *Philadelphia North American started*—eleven papers merged in one.

1839 *Papier-maché stereotyping patented in America by Moses Poole.*

1840 Newspaper war against *New York Herald* because of its independent position—waged by *Courier & Enquirer* and the "Holy Allies." *Herald* had 51,000 circulation, *C. & E.* had 4,200.

1840 *First electrotyped engraving, published by London Journal.*

1840 *First American patent for typesetting machine—Frederick Rosenberg.*

1841 *New York Tribune* started by Horace Greeley as penny political organ.

1841 *Tribune Almanac* started by Greeley—first newspaper almanac.

1841 *Young & Decambre typesetting machine patented (American).*

1842 *London Illustrated News* started—began illustrative journalism.

1843 *Old style type revived in England and America.*

1844 *First newspaper on Pacific Coast—Flumgudgeon Gazette or Bumble Bee Budget, edited by the Long-Tailed Coon—California.*

1844 Electric telegraph perfected—taken up by New York papers at once. First line between Washington and Baltimore, built by Congress.

1844 *Reporting of Sunday sermons begun by New York Herald.*

1844 Famous Roorback Hoax, concerning branded slaves, published by *Albany Evening Journal.*

1844 *Chicago Journal* founded.

1844 *Kronheim's improvement on papier-maché stereotyping patented.*

1844 First daily in Wisconsin founded—*The Milwaukee Sentinel.*

1845 Overland expresses to New Orleans run by *New York Herald* to cover Mexican war—beat mails one to four days.

1845 First war correspondents were engaged in covering Mexican war.

1846 *Alta California & San Francisco Herald* appeared—published by men from *New York Herald.*

1846 Washington and Baltimore telegraph line extended to New York.

1846 Stock company idea of newspaper ownership started by *New York Tribune*—the idea came from France.

1846 First Hoe type-revolving press erected.

1847 *New York Herald* had Henry Clay's speech sent from Cincinnati to New York.

1847 Last of the pony expresses—established jointly by several New York papers.

1847 *Springfield* (Mass.) *Republican* founded by Samuel Bowles.

1847 *New York Herald* eliminated illustrations and other display from its advertisements. Length of insertion limited to two weeks—later to one day. Editorial notice of ad stopped. Every ad reset each day.

1847 *Chicago Tribune* founded.

1848 Associated Press founded—first known as New York Associated Press. Harbor News Association combined with it—its growth into country-wide association came during the '60's.

1848 Applegate's type-revolving press built for London Times.

1849 First paper in Minnesota, *Minnesota Pioneer* (now *St. Paul Pioneer Press*).

1850 Idea of printing from curved stereotyped plates patented.

1851 *New York Times* started by Henry J. Raymond.

1851 There were then 3,000 periodicals in America—2,000 of them newspapers.

1852 First paper in Washington Territory—*Olympia Pioneer & Democrat.*

1853 English tax on advertisements removed.

1853 First successful American typesetting machine—William H. Mitchell.

1854 *Chicago Times* founded—merged with *Herald* as *Chicago Times-Herald* in 1895—merged with *Record* as *Chicago Record-Herald* in 1901—merged with *Inter-Ocean* as *Chicago Herald* in 1914.

1855 Wood-pulp paper began to supplant rag paper.

1857 *Harper's Weekly* founded.

1857 Hoe type-revolving press installed in New York Times office—two ten-cylinder machines were erected.

1859 First verbatim interview—with Gerrit Smith at time of John Brown raid on Harper's Ferry—by *New York Herald.*

1860 End of war between newspapers and telegraph lines which resulted from establishment of the Associated Press.

1860 *New York World* started as a religious and moral daily paper—carried news, but no evil news.

1860 Paper made of esparto introduced.

1860 End of "Blanket Sheets"—*Courier & Enquirer* merged with *World.*

1861 Tax on paper removed.

1864 Famous Lincoln Proclamation Hoax printed by *New York Journal.*

1865 First web press with stereotyped plates, built by William Bullock of Philadelphia.

1865 *Chicago Republican* founded—Charles A. Dana first editor.

1865 *San Francisco Chronicle* founded.

1866 *Chicago Weekly News,* now *The Daily News,* was founded.

1867 *Harper's Bazaar,* fashion paper, started under woman editor.

1867 Steam news yachts used by *New York Herald* to meet vessels.

1867 Cropper treadle platen job press introduced.

1868 *New York Sun* purchased by Charles A. Dana for $175,000—introduced literary ideal in newspaper work—had 65,000 circulation.

1868 Stanley expedition into Anglo-Abyssinia sent by *New York Herald* to find Livingston.

1868 Club subscription idea started by *New York Tribune* —with premium engravings.

1868 Walter rotary web perfecting press built for London Times.

1868 *Atlanta* (Ga.) *Constitution* founded.

1870 About 1,508,548,250 periodicals issued in America.

1870 American Press Association organized.

1870 First automatic folder for web press invented.

1870 Burr-Kastenbein typesetter built—required hand justification.

1871 Directory of advertisers begun by *New York Herald.*

1872 J. G. Bennett refused to sell *New York Herald* for $2,200,000.

1872 *Chicago Inter-Ocean* founded—merged with *Record-Herald,* 1914.

1873 Associated Press had 200 members.

1873 Charge for marriage announcements begun by *New York Herald.*

1873 *Frank Leslie's Illustrated Newspaper* appeared with 70 wood engravings.

1873 First illustrated daily paper in America—*New York Daily Graphic.*

1875 Tucker's rotating folding machine invented—15,000 an hour.

1876 Experiments on Mergenthaler linotype machine begun.

1877 *Washington Post* founded.

1878 *Minneapolis Journal* founded.
1878 *Chicago typefoundry began making type on point system after being burned out in great fire—Marder, Luse & Co.*
1880 *Photo-engraving came into use about this time.*
1880 *Thorn typesetter invented—required hand justification.*
1881 *Los Angeles Times* founded.
1882 *New York Journal* founded—purchased by W. R. Hearst in 1895.
1883 Joseph Pulitzer bought *New York World*—beginning of sensational journalism.
1884 *Offset printing developed.*
1885 *First punch-cutting machine for typefounders.*
1885 *London Times installed its first folding machine.*
1886 *Point system of type measurement adopted by American Type Founders' Association.*
1886 *Mergenthaler linotype machine placed on the market.*
1887 *First quadruple press built—for New York World.*
1888 *Automatic typecasting and trimming machine patented by Henry Barth—100 to 140 per minute.*
1888 *Hoe built first three-page-wide rotary press.*
1890 *First successful machine to set, justify, and distribute type—Paige machine.*
1890 *Photo-engraving becoming established commercially.*
1890 *Chicago Evening Post* founded.
1891 *First sextuple press built—for New York Herald.*
1892 *Three-color engraving process becoming established commercially.*
1892 *Chicago Record* founded as morning edition of *Daily News*—merged with *Times-Herald* as *Record-Herald,* 1901—merged with *Inter-Ocean* as *Chicago Herald,* 1914.
1895 *Rembrandt photogravure process introduced.*
1895 *New York Journal* purchased by W. R. Hearst—beginning of ultra-sensational journalism.
1899 *Lanston monotype placed on market.*

APPENDIX II

STYLE SHEET

(Note. This Style Sheet is one that was prepared by the Department of Journalism of the University of Wisconsin. It is in general a "down" style and is representative of the tendencies of the average American newspaper of today. While it is not ideal in many ways, it is inserted here as a means of emphasizing *accuracy in details*. Accuracy is the great cry of the modern newspaper—accuracy in details as well as facts—and typographical style furnishes one of the most tangible ways of developing accuracy among students of newspaper writing and editing. In the same way, strict attention to typographical style assists the independent student and young newspaper man in developing habits of accuracy.)

CAPITALIZATION.

Capitalize:

All proper nouns, months, days of the week, but not the seasons.

Principal words in the titles of books, plays, lectures, pictures, toasts, etc., including the initial "A" or "The": "The Man from Home."

Titles denoting official position, rank, or occupation, when they precede a proper noun: President Wilson, Judge John R. Holt (but John R. Holt, judge of the circuit court). Avoid long, awkward titles before a name.

Distinguishing parts of names of associations, societies, leagues, companies, roads, lines, and incorporated bodies: Louisiana State university, First National bank, Union Trust company, Northwestern line, Epworth Methodist church, First Wisconsin volunteers.

Common nouns when they precede the distinguishing parts in names of associations, societies, companies, etc.: University of Wisconsin, Association of Collegiate Alumnæ, Bank of Wisconsin.

Only proper noun in geographical names, except when the common noun precedes: Rock river, Fox lake; but Lake Michigan, Gulf of Mexico.

Only the distinguishing parts of names of streets, avenues, boulevards, buildings, houses, hotels, theatres, stations, wards, districts, counties, etc.: Pinckney street, Northwestern station, Grand hotel, Third ward, Second district.

Names of religious denominations, and nouns and pronouns of the Deity.
Names of all political parties: Republican, Bull Moose, Socialist.
Sections of the country: the North, the Middle West.
Abbreviations of college degrees: M. A., LL. D., Ph. D.
Distinguishing parts of nicknames of states and cities: the Buckeye state, the Windy city.
Names of sections of a city: the East side.
Distinguishing parts of names of holidays: Fourth of July, New Year's day.
Names of all races and nationalities except negro: Indians, Caucasian.
Nicknames of athletic clubs and teams: the White Sox, the Gophers.
Names of automobiles: a Ford.

Avoid all capitalization not absolutely necessary.

Do Not Capitalize:

Names of national, state, and city bodies, buildings, officers, boards, etc.: senate, assembly, department of justice, tax commission, budget committee, postoffice, city hall, common council, capitol.
Points of the compass: east, northwest.
Names of national legislative bodies: congress, parliament, landtag, duma.
Common religious terms: bible, scripture, gospels, heathen.
Names of school or college studies, except names of languages: biology, French.
Scientific names of plants, animals, and birds.
Titles when they follow the name: Henry Wilson, professor of Greek.
Abbreviations of time of day: a. m., p. m.; but 12 M.
Names of college classes: sophomore, senior.
College degrees when spelled out: bachelor of arts: but B. A., Ph. D.
Seasons of the year: spring, autumn.
Name of office in list of officers, as in election of officers: The new officers are: president, John C. Walter; etc.
Certain common nouns that were originally proper nouns: street arab, prussian blue, paris green, india rubber, morocco binding, plaster of paris, brussels carpet, etc.
The following nouns after a proper noun: street, avenue, boulevard, place, building, depot, hotel, station, theatre, ward, county, district, etc.

PUNCTUATION.

Omit period after "per cent" and after nicknames (Tom, Sam, Will).
Use a comma before "and" in a list: red, white, and blue.
Punctuate lists of names with cities or states thus: Messrs. Arnold Woll, Racine; R. G. Davitt, Beloit; etc. Punctuate list of names with offices thus: J. S. Hall, president; Henry Stoltz, vice-president.
Use a colon after a statement introducing a direct quotation of one or more paragraphs, and begin a new paragraph for the quotation. Use a colon after "as follows." Make separate paragraph of "He said in part:", etc.
Never use a colon after viz., to wit, namely, e. g., i. e., except when they end a paragraph. Use colon, dash, or semicolon before them and comma after them, thus: This is the man; to wit, the victim.
Use a comma before "such as," but have no point after it.
Do not use a comma between a man's name and "Jr." or "Sr."
Use the apostrophe to mark omission: I've, 'tis, don't, can't, won't, it's (for it is), '87.

STYLE SHEET

Use apostrophes for possessives except in pronouns: the boy's clothes, boys' clothing, Burns' poems, Fox's Martyrs; but ours, yours, its.
Use no apostrophe in making plurals of figures and letters: early '90s, three Rs.
Use no apostrophe in such abbreviations as Frisco, varsity, phone, bus.
Punctuate votes in balloting thus: yeas, 2; nays, 3.
Use an em dash after a man's name placed at the beginning in series of interviews: Henry Keith—I have nothing to say. (Use no quotation marks with this form.)
Use an em dash after Q. and A. in verbatim testimony: Q.—What is your name? A.—Oscar Brown.
Use no commas in "6 feet 3 inches tall", "3 years 6 months old", etc.
In sporting news punctuate thus: Score: Wisconsin 8, Chicago 3. 100-yard dash—Smith, first; Hanks, second. Time, 6:10 1-5. Peters ran thirty yards to the 10-yard line.

QUOTATION.

Quote:

All verbatim quotations when they are to be set in the same type and measure as the context, but not when they are to be in smaller type or narrower measure.
All testimony, conversation, and interviews given in direct form, except when name of speaker, or Q. and A., with a dash, precedes, as: John Keith—I have nothing to say; Q.—What is your name? A.—Oscar Brown.
Names of books, dramas, paintings, statuary, operas, songs, subjects of lectures, sermons, toasts, magazine articles, including the initial "A" or "The": "A Man Without a Country."
Nicknames used before surnames: "Al" Harris, "Bob" Hall.
Use single quotation marks for quotations within a quotation.
Use quotation marks at the beginning of each paragraph of a continuous quotation of several paragraphs, but at the end of the last paragraph only.

Do Not Quote:

Names of characters in plays: Shylock in "The Merchant of Venice."
Names of newspapers or periodicals: the Springfield Republican.
Names of vessels, cattle, dogs, sleeping and parlor cars.

FIGURES.

Use Figures For:

Numbers of 100 or over, except in the case of round numbers, as "a hundred men."
Numbers under 100 when used in close connection with numbers over 100: 133 boys and 56 girls.
Hours of the day: 7 p. m., at 8:30 this morning.
Days of the month, omitting d, th, st: April 29, 1913; July 1.
Ages; he was 12 years old; 2-year-old James.
All dimensions, prices, degrees of temperature, per cents, dates, votes, times in races, scores, etc.: 3 feet long, $3 a yard, 78 degrees, 95 per cent.
All sums of money (with dollar mark or cents): $24, $5.06, 75 cents.
Street and room numbers: 1324 Grand avenue, 69 University hall.
In statistical and tabular matter, never use ditto marks.
In texts from the bible set thus: Matt. xii. 37-40; I. John v. 1-15.
Do not begin a sentence with figures; supply a word or spell out.

ABBREVIATIONS.

Abbreviate:

The following titles and no others, when they precede a name: Rev., Dr., Mr., Mrs., M., Mme., Mlle., Prof. (before a full name

only: Prof. E. G. Hunt, but Professor Hunt), and military titles, except sergeant, corporal, and chaplain.
Names of states, only when they follow names of cities: Madison, Wis. (but never "a citizen of N. Y.").
Names of months that contain more than five letters, but only in dates and date lines: Oct. 10 (not early in Oct.).
"Number" before figures: No. 24.
Saint and Mount in proper names, but not Fort: St. John, but Fort Wayne.

Do Not Abbreviate:

Railway, company, street, avenue, district, etc.: Chicago and Northwestern railway, State street, A. B. Hall company. (Railway and railroad may be abbreviated when initials are used: C. M. & St. P. Ry.).
Christian names like William, Charles, Thomas, John, Alexander.
The titles, congressman, senator, representative, president, secretary, treasurer, etc., preceding a name.
Years ('97 for 1897), except in referring to college classes, etc.
Christmas in the form Xmas.
Per cent: 15 per cent (not 15%).
Cents: 75 cents (not 75 cts. or 75 c.).

DATES AND DATE LINES.

In dates, write Jan. 12, 1914 (not the 12th of January, or 12 January).
Punctuate date lines thus:
MADISON, Wis., Feb. 11.—Fire destroyed the, etc.
Omit state after names of prominent cities. Abbreviate months of more than five letters. Omit year and d, st, th (after figures). Begin the story immediately after dash on same line.

ADDRESSES.

Write addresses thus:
Frank D. Miles, 136 Gilman street. Hiram Swenk, Cuba City, Wis.
Omit "at" and "of" before address. Do not abbreviate or capitalize street, avenue, etc. Spell out numbered streets up to 100th.

TITLES.

Always give initials or first names of persons the first time they appear in a story. Never use only one initial; use both or first name: J. H. Ward, John H. Ward, or John Ward (not J. Ward).
Never use Mr. when initials or first name is given: Mr. Ward (not Mr. John H. Ward).
Give first name of unmarried woman, not initials only: Miss Mary R. Snow (not Miss M. R. Snow).
Always use the title Miss before unmarried women's names and Mrs. before married women's.
Supply "the" before Rev.; supply Mr. if first name is omitted: the Rev. S. R. Hart, or the Rev. Mr. Hart (not Rev. S. R. Hart, the Rev. Hart, or Rev. Hart).
Write Mr. and Mrs. Arthur S. Miles (not Arthur S. Miles and wife).
Write Professor and Mrs. Henry Wilton (not Mr. and Mrs. Professor Henry Wilton).
Avoid long titles, such as Superintendent of Public Instruction Moore.
Never use the title "Honorable" or "Hon."

STYLE SHEET

GENERAL DIRECTIONS

PREPARATION OF COPY.

1. Write legibly; use a typewriter whenever possible.
2. Never write on both sides of the sheet.
3. Double space your typewritten and longhand copy.
4. Use 8½ x 11 soft white copy paper for all your work.
5. Begin your story about the middle of the first page.
6. Number sheets at the top of the page and enclose the numbers in a circle.
7. Put the end mark (#) at the close of every complete story.
8. Enclose all quotation marks in half circles.
9. Underscore "u's" and overscore "n's" in longhand copy.

PARAGRAPHS.

1. Indent each paragraph about two inches.
2. Remember that the length of paragraphs in newspapers does not normally exceed 100 words, and generally ranges from 25 to 70 words.
3. Put an important idea at the beginning of the first sentence of each paragraph.
4. Avoid beginning successive paragraphs with the same word, phrase, or construction.
5. Don't put important details in the last paragraph where they may be cut off in make-up.
6. Make separate paragraphs of introductory statements like "He said in part," "The report is as follows," and end them with colon.
7. Set off as a separate paragraph a direct quotation of more than one sentence without explanatory material, at the beginning of a story.

SENTENCES.

1. Make evident the construction of every sentence so that it may be read rapidly.
2. Avoid choppy, disconnected short sentences.
3. Don't overload the first sentence of a summary lead, by crowding in unessential details.
4. Put an important idea at the beginning of every sentence.

WORDS.

1. Avoid words that are likely to be unfamilar to the average reader, unless you explain them in your story.
2. Don't use trite phrases.
3. Use superlatives sparingly.
4. Use slang only when circumstances demand it.
5. Find the one noun to express the idea, the one adjective, if necessary, to qualify it, and the one verb to give it life.

ACCURACY.

1. Remember that the truth and nothing but the truth, interestingly presented, makes the best news story.
2. Don't try to make cleverness a substitute for truth.
3. Don't forget that faking is lying.
4. Realize that every mistake you make hurts someone.
5. Remember that what you write for newspaper publication is read by thousands and helps to influence public opinion.
6. Be especially careful about names, initials, and addresses.
7. Get all the news; don't stop with half of it.
8. Don't give rumors as facts.
9. Be fair and unbiased; give both sides of the case.
10. Don't misrepresent by playing up a statement that, taken from its context, is misleading.
11. Don't make the necessity for speed an excuse for carelessness and inaccuracy.

INDEX

INDEX

INDEX

www.ingramcontent.com/pod-product-compliance
Ingram Content Group UK Ltd.
Pitfield, Milton Keynes, MK11 3LW, UK
UKHW021933200726
13853UKWH00010B/492